Gries/Suhl (Eds.)
Economic Aspects of Digital Information Technologies

W0245788

GABLER EDITION WISSENSCHAFT

Thomas Gries / Leena Suhl (Eds.)

Economic Aspects of Digital Information Technologies

DeutscherUniversitätsVerlag

Die Deutsche Bibliothek - CIP-Einheitsaufnahme

Economic aspects of digital information technologies
/ Thomas Gries/Leena Suhl (Eds.).
- Wiesbaden : Dt. Univ.-Verl. ; Wiesbaden : Gabler, 1999
(Gabler Edition Wissenschaft)

Softcover reprint of the hardcover 1st edition 1999

Lektorat: Ute Wrasmann / Michael Gließner

Der Gabler Verlag und der Deutsche Universitäts-Verlag sind Unternehmen der
Bertelsmann Fachinformation GmbH.

http://www.gabler-online.de
http://www.duv.de

Höchste inhaltliche und technische Qualität unserer Werke ist unser Ziel. Bei der Produktion und
Verbreitung unserer Werke wollen wir die Umwelt schonen. Dieses Buch ist deshalb auf säure-
freiem und chlorfrei gebleichtem Papier gedruckt. Die Einschweißfolie besteht aus Polyäthylen
und damit aus organischen Grundstoffen, die weder bei der Herstellung noch bei der
Verbrennung Schadstoffe freisetzen.

Druck und Buchbinder: Rosch-Buch, Scheßlitz

ISBN-13: 978-3-8244-6848-5   e-ISBN-13: 978-3-322-85190-1
DOI: 10.1007/978-3-322-85190-1

Foreword

The rapid development of information and communication technologies has been one of the major issues in the world economy of the last decade. Especially, the fast growth of the Internet has introduced completely new economic and related issues, like world-wide Electronic Commerce and its taxing, telework activities, distance learning, and so on. It has become possible to split organizations into small units which may form an electronically connected network taking new shapes in a flexible way. Since the growth of the Internet has been fast and fairly uncontrolled, a strong need for new laws, sometimes called Cyberlaw, has emerged. On the other hand, the individual skills of information technologies may be of critical importance to the success of a person in his or her professional career.

This book discusses several new aspects and economic impacts of digital information technologies. A primer on Internet economics provides an introduction to the structure of the Internet and its economic issues. Further related subjects are taxing of the world-wide Electronic Commerce, Cyberlaw, learning with hypermedia, and distance learning over the network. We also discuss the general impact of information technologies on innovation dynamics, labor demand, and human capital depreciation. Results of a recent survey on European telework activities give insight into rapid organizational changes due to the digitalization of economies. General information technology related aspects, like the need of a rapid transfer of new economic knowledge and semantic integration of online information, are provided.

All authors are members of the Department of Business Administration, Business Computing, and Economics at the University of Paderborn, Germany. We wish to thank Dipl.Wirt.-Inf. Claus Biederbick for the enormous amount of work in editing the book and bringing the individual articles into a consistent form.

Thomas Gries   Leena Suhl

Table of Contents

Collected Abstracts

1. A Primer on Internet Economics
Bernard Michael Gilroy

One of the major developments in the world economy of the last decade has been the complementary globalization of production and the rapid development of information and communication technology as exhibited through the emergence of the Internet. Although the Internet has received a great deal of publicity, there still remains areas of vacuum with regard to research on the economics of the Internet and a more wide-spread understanding of the prime issues involved. After a brief history of the evolution of the Internet industry, a segmentation map of the Internet industry is presented in order to aid one in understanding potential Internet issues that will affect academics, political regulators, industry leaders, and the general public in the future. Equipped with this greater understanding of the way the Internet functions, economic issues and Internet concepts are selectively identified and discussed within the basic structure of interoperability, network externalities and the equitable statistical sharing of Internet resources.

We argue that the challenge to any analysis of the Internet and public policy is that government and industry are not necessarily guided by tightly drawn boundaries. Rather, as technology has evolved, the fortunes and misfortunes of governments, producers, and consumers worldwide are becoming even more closely linked through the Internet. To a large extent Internet activities all consist of exchanges of information and collective goal setting while maintaining high levels of competition. The Internet industry is embedded in a complex and rapidly changing transactional environment in which firm-specific and industry-wide complementarities exist. As transactional relationships increasingly evolve on a global level, the effectiveness of the Internet will largely depend upon an awareness of the economic logic of network structures.

2. The Impacts of Information Technologies on Innovation Dynamics and Labor Demand
Thomas Gries and Stefan Jungblut

Information technologies (ITs) give one of the most important impacts on technological change and economic development. The capability to innovate and successfully implement ITs has turned out to be one of the decisive factors to realize advantages offered by the growing information society. At the macroeconomic level advances in productivity as well as substantial job opportunities are commonly expected as a result of IT diffusion. However, in contrast to economic reasoning both effects are not yet observable. The diffusion of ITs has not led to the expected productivity growth on aggregate. To get a better understanding of this subject the paper intends to develop an endogenous growth model to analyze the impacts of IT diffusion on employment and growth. The process of growth is driven by innovation activities as well as the accumulation of physical and human capital. The model predicts that firms continuously adjust their technological capabilities in order to efficiently match the human capital endowments of the workforce. Technological capabilities on the other hand determine the structure of labor demand and the steady state rate of aggregate growth. The model shows that ITs affect aggregate growth in two opposite directions. At the one hand ITs increase innovation activities. But ITs also increase the demand for human capital necessary for innovation and production activities. Both effects counteract. As a result the overall impact of ITs on growth is ambiguous. We show that only economies with sufficiently educated workers are able to gain from IT diffusion in terms of growth opportunities. Although competition will force firms to implement ITs, the aggregate rate of growth decreases unless the economy sufficiently increases investments in human capital.

3. Information Technology, Endogenous Human Capital Depreciation and Unemployment
Thomas Gries and Henning Meyer

In this paper we analyze certain impacts of information technologies [ITs] on unemployment. It is well known that all sectors and activities are affected by the introduction of new ITs. This technological change goes along with the requirement to adjust education. Employees entering the labor market not only have to be able to use the newest ITs available, but have to adjust their skills continuously to newer technologies, too. To be able to analyze the effects of the introduction of ITs on unemployment we use a model with a Putty-Clay technology. Two types of labor with different abilities to adjust to new ITs are considered. As a result information technologies do not only create jobs. Instead employees who are not able to keep up with the innovation process will become unemployed simultaneously. Especially older workers are affected by this mechanism. Therefore, a continuous introduction of new ITs may be a major reason for the rising unemployment of older workers.

4. Spatial and Organizational Patterns of the Transfer of New Economic Knowledge: A Survey of the Literature and Some Preliminary Results from a Case Study
Peter Liepmann

New economic knowledge and innovations are prerequisites to dynamic efficiency. They are particularly relevant under the condition of intensive world-wide competition. Firms in locations with underdeveloped technological infrastructures need assistance by institutions which transfer new economic knowledge between organisations and across space. Linear, complementary, and feedback models of the innovation process are considered to describe the potential scope for transfer activities. Recipient firms should have F&E personnel of their own to adapt new economic knowledge from external sources to firm-specific applications. Otherwise they will have to rely on specific new economic knowledge which is already applicable without alterations. There are appropriability restrictions for transfer activities when private, tacit, and specialised new economic knowledge is concerned. These restrictions may only be overcome by various forms of long-term co-operation and trust relations. The paper surveys theoretical and empirical work on spatial and organisational patterns of the transfer of new economic knowledge and reports preliminary results from a regional case study.

5. Taxing Electronic Commerce
Marko Köthenbürger and Bernd Rahmann

Electronic commerce is expected to increase tremendously in the next years. As electronic commerce is an exchange of goods and services, it is also subject to value added taxation. Hence, the question of how a tax system should be designed to include these activities arises. We address this question by reviewing the two basic cross-border commodity taxation systems and the associated pros and cons in terms of efficiency and information requirements. A discussion of the application of these taxation principles to electronic commerce is presented in section 4 and 5. We conclude that the origin principle is likely to be the more appropriate tax system to deal with electronic commerce. Unfortunately, the political applicability of this tax system is limited as the question of tax revenue distribution among countries is still unsettled.

6. Survey of Telework Activities in Europe
Wilhelm Dangelmaier, Dirk Förster, Volker Horsthemke, and Stephan Kress

The phenomenon telework is nowadays known in all parts of the European Union. Especially the flexibility of telework in the dimensions time and location of task execution makes it an innovative form of work organisation. It is developing rapidly and today there are already more than 2 million Europeans who practice telework in one form or another (1.25 million in 1994). Nevertheless, there still seems to be a long way to go because reality has often outperformed expectations. Estimations still differ a lot and had to be revised many times (especially in Europe, where Telework is scattered disproportionately over the distinct states with its different development stages).

The following chapters sum up the results of an internet survey on telework activities in Europe. This survey is embedded in the COBIP project which analyses the usage of workflow tools in the management of telework. The survey's aim was to gather up-to-date information about telework-related projects in organizations. The whole study was to be on a European scale with focus on the European Union members. It was obvious that the survey could neither be representative nor could statistically sound due to the nature of the sources available. Therefore, it was to be, and is, only a random sample of currently undertaken telework projects in Europe. After a short historical introduction the actual penetration of telework will be analyzed. Then most recent projects will be examined according to different criteria of huge contemporary importance based mainly on an internet research. These analyses will make it possible to predict the near future of telework and compare it with latest development tendencies.

7. Worldwide Learning with Java and New Information and Communication Technologies
Winfried Reiss

This paper together with the underlying set of Applet-based Java frames in an HTML-file shows the possibility of using Java as a basis for interactive economics teaching.

Relying heavily on the object-oriented structure of the Java language and on the extensive library of routines, it is fairly easy to construct a series of lessons in which users have to decide on possible answers, input points into charts, and do their own calculations and derivations. These lessons can also include simulations including tâtonnement processes.

As I want to present an interactive computer based training program, a paper based description is, however, inadequate; one should test it or have it demonstrated.

8. Java for the Web – Economic Implications
Ralf Menkhoff

This article demonstrates, that programming languages are important not only for, e.g., computer scientists but also for economists. With the growing importance of the web new challenges and opportunities emerge in both software production and software utilization. Hence, I will show some important characteristics of an economically "ideal" programming language for the web and whether Java meets these properties. Moreover, I try to work out fundamental economic implications of using Java as a web-based programming language. In order to derive the inferences I will choose three different outlooks: the perspectives of producers, users, and traders.

No attempt is made to fuel the discussion about total cost of ownership (TCO). The analysis is limited to Java and directly related technologies. Competing technologies like, e.g., ActiveX (a development of Microsoft) will not be considered.

9. Learning Management Science in Hyperspace
Astrid Blumstengel, Stephan Kassanke, and Leena Suhl

The paper discusses approaches of learning an interdisciplinary subject like Operations Research/Management Science. The ability to apply quantitative methods in business has to be learned by training similarly to learning a craft. We argue that this learning process can be supported by case studies complemented with a computer based hypermedia learning environment. We report about experiences from the development and use of ORWelt, a hypermedia learning environment for OR/MS. The project team consists of researchers and varying groups of students who develop parts of the learning environment in a cooperative approach. If adequate support is provided this software development model is a way to address lack of resources, while at the same time providing valuable educational experience for students. We present an outlook on extending the learning environment to include other tools as well.

10. Semantic Integration of Emergent Online Communication
Wilfried Böhler

We argue that semantic integration of emergent online communication - which links information that usually is not thought of as related - will lead to resistance by specialized organization members who can perform complex jobs with a minimum of supervision. Symbolic connections provided by referential opacity and tacit information will encourage evasive behavior if interactive tasks provide information as part of an internal database design that cannot be modified easily. Therefore, if the network authors decide to maintain flexibility of response, workflow design must follow two policies: (1) it must adopt the interaction pattern of a sparsely connected network; (2) it must restrict the number of customized applications.

11. No Laws in Cyberspace? [Das Internet, ein rechtsfreier Raum?][1]
Dirk Michael Barton

The rapid development of the Internet and its possibilities for global communication and information exchange has initiated an extensive discussion about unsolved legal problems. Of relevance are especially the fields of economic law, e.g. copyrights, (data) privacy, and fair trade law, the criminal liability of access- and content-providers concerning illegal contents, and, last but not least (international) contract law with issues like validity of electronic signatures.

On the one hand, jurisdiction is faced with the overwhelming dynamics of the development process. On the other hand, the Internets' global character and the worldwide availability of information published there make international agreements desirable.

Until now, the latter was complicated by differences in national legal systems. For example, a German Internet-Provider was forced to lock the access to illegal (in Germany) contents. Due to technical reasons the access was locked in the US, too, and therefore attacked massively as an offence against the freedom of expression of opinion.

Of course, national law has to continue protecting ethic values and individual rights and interests, but the enormous potential of Internet economics has to be considered, too.

However, these are conflicting objectives: Many legal systems do not strictly avenge, e.g., violation of copyrights (like software-piracy), while German law is

---

[1] This article is written in German because it argues from a specific German point of view. Nevertheless there are some aspects of 'global importance' in it, which are presented in this extended abstract. For further information the interested reader may contact the author.

rather restrictive in this area. Because Internet publishes contents worldwide and immediately, companies have to regard the most restrictive legal system, in order to assure invulnerability against prosecution. It is not enough, if prohibited contents are not in German, or labeled as "not for Germany" to act legally.

At least as explosive is the publication of (e.g. nazi-) propaganda or pornographic material, which is allowed in many states due to the freedom of opinions, but illegal in Germany, because the Internet makes those contents accessible for children. Therefore both content-providers and access-providers can be held responsible according to German laws and – at least on German grounds – be prosecuted. Thus, some German lawyers take the view that a legally punishable act is given if the offender acts deliberately by publishing illegal contents in Germany. However, this is often difficult to prove and will lead to a kind of "anarchy in Cyberspace".

With regard to the German legal system, providers are, of course, always responsible if they create prohibited contents (it is still not sure, whether they are responsible if they *link* such contents). When they only provide Internet-access, there is still no clear jurisdiction in Germany, therefore companies take a high risk with Internet-activities there. Nevertheless, a safe assumption is that providers are obliged to control contents, if it is technically practicable and reasonable, especially when already names of addresses and newsgroups indicate prohibited contents.

All in all, a commercial utilization of the Internet in Germany faces many legal difficulties. In the next few years a clearly defined legislation has to be found. A great deal of research will be necessary to fulfil this task.

List of Contributing Authors

Dr. Dirk Michael Barton   Professor of Business Law
(Dirk_Barton@notes.uni-paderborn.de)

Dr. Astrid Blumstengel   Research Assistant in Business Computing
(blumstengel@hotmail.com)

Dr. Wilfried Böhler   Professor of Business English
(Wilfried_Boehler@notes.uni-paderborn.de)

Dr. Wilhelm Dangelmaier   Professor of Business Computing, especially Computer-Integrated Manufacturing (CIM)
(whd@hni.uni-paderborn.de)

Dirk Förster   Research Assistant in Business Computing, especially CIM
(foerster@hni.uni-paderborn.de)

Dr. Bernard Michael Gilroy   Professor of International Business Studies
(Mike_Gilroy@notes.uni-paderborn.de)

Dr. Thomas Gries   Professor of Economics
(gries@econ.uni-paderborn.de)

Volker Horsthemke   Research Assistant in Business Computing, especially CIM
(Volker_Horsthemke@notes.uni-paderborn.de)

Dr. Stefan Jungblut   Assistant Professor in Economics
(Stefan_Jungblut@notes.uni-paderborn.de)

Stephan Kassanke   Research Assistant in Business Computing
(kass@uni-paderborn.de)

Marko Köthenbürger   Research Assistant in Economics
                              (Marko_Koethenbuerger@notes.uni-paderborn.de)

Stephan Kress   Research Assistant in Business Computing,
                              especially CIM
                              (kress@hni.uni-paderborn.de)

Dr. Peter Liepmann   Professor of Economics
                              (Peter_Liepmann@notes.uni-paderborn.de)

Ralf Menkhoff   Research Assistant in Economics
                              (Ralf_Menkhoff@notes.uni-paderborn.de)

Henning Meyer   Research Assistant in Economics
                              (Henning_Meyer@notes.uni-paderborn.de)

Dr. Bernd Rahmann   Professor of Economics
                              (Bernd_Rahmann@notes.uni-paderborn.de)

Dr. Winfried Reiss   Professor of Economics
                              (Winfried_Reiss@notes.uni-paderborn.de)

Dr. Leena Suhl   Professor of Business Computing
                              (suhl@uni-paderborn.de)

All authors are members of the

Department of Economics
University of Paderborn
Warburger Str. 100
33098 Paderborn, Germany
http://www.uni-paderborn.de
Phone: +49-5251-60-0

A Primer on Internet Economics[1]

Bernard Michael Gilroy

1 Introduction

One of the major economic developments in the world economy of the last decade has been the complementary globalization of production and the rapid development of information and communication technology as exhibited through the emergence of the Internet. The preliminary analysis presented here is guided by the belief that although the Internet has received a great deal of publicity, there still remains areas of vacuum with regard to research on the economics of the Internet and a more wide-spread understanding of the prime issues involved. After a brief history of the evolution of the Internet industry in section 2, a segmentation map of the Internet industry is presented in order to aid one in understanding potential Internet issues that will affect academics, political regulators, industry leaders, and the general public in the future. Equipped with this greater understanding of the way the Internet functions, economic issues and Internet concepts are selectively identified and discussed within the basic structure of interoperability, network externalities and the equitable statistical sharing of Internet resources.

2 A Brief History of the Internet Industry

Originally, the Internet was conceived during the 1960's by military research with the goal of guaranteeing stable communication in the event that parts of the communication system were destroyed (Lammarsch & Steenweg 1995, p. 3). The United States Ministry of Defense developed a decentralized computer network based on "store-and-forward" software. Messages could be broken down into smaller components, with each individual package receiving the electronic address of the recipient. Such information packages could then be processed by the system and routed to the final destination through any of the channels of the network, and software on the receiving computer would reassemble the packages into one message (Maier & Wildberger 1996, p. 4). Shortly after the initial introduction of this "Advanced Research Project Regency Network" or simply "ARPANET", other governmental agencies, universities, colleges and corporate R&D departments were permitted access (Klau 1995, p. 31). Although the protocol allowing this information transmission (TCP/IP) had been developed in 1974, real commercial usage of the Internet is a relatively new phenomenon of the 1990s (for a recent survey on electronic commerce see e.g. Anderson 1997).

[1] The author wishes to thank Ludwig Nastansky for his helpful comments.

Nowadays the Internet's communications properties are increasingly affecting economic transactions in basically all industries. As the Internet has no centralized authority, it is difficult to give accurate statistics regarding user numbers (Hansen 1996, pp. 52ff.). Millions of computers in more than 40 countries, however, are electronically connected to the world's largest digital network (Anderson & Choobineh 1996, p. 22). Estimates place the number of worldwide users at some 60 million and growing (Ghosh 1998, p. 2). Approximately four million users in Germany have access to the Internet, and market observers forecast that by the year 2000 the number will rise to around ten million (Glanz 1997, p. 129). The Internet represents unprecedented opportunities not only for consumers, but also for businesses of all sizes. Commercial connections are currently the fastest growing component of the Internet (Hauenstein 1996, p. 25). Even the smallest company, by connecting to the Internet generates an international presence, allowing data exchange and support services to flow electronically worldwide (Rüdiger 1996).

The user-friendly surface World Wide Web "WWW" was created in 1989 at CERN (Conseil Européen pour la Recherche Nucléaire), a physics laboratory in Switzerland. Acting as a catalyst to network growth, the possibilities to use all facilities of the Internet with just one easy computer application, i.e. a software program called "web browser" (for example, Netscape Navigator or Microsoft Explorer), became a reality. The economic importance of a web browser will be discussed in more detail below. The WWW integrates such economic activities and services as the gathering of information, the transmission of electronic mail, discussion groups, and the downloading of files from remote servers (Nolden 1995, pp. 11ff.).

The main advantage of the WWW is that it enables the user without requiring far-reaching computer knowledge to explore the Internet through connections called hypertext links. Hypertext links are a method of presenting information stored on scattered servers on a global basis, whereby selected parts within the text can be connected to other web sites, providing additional information on the topic (Krol 1995, p. 334). If a page incorporates a hypertext link, the user can simply click on the link and will be taken to the connected page. Every web page on the Internet has its individual address, the so-called Uniform Resource Location (URL). The Hyper Text Transfer Protocol (HTTP) then accommodates the actions necessary for integrating publishing, computing, and broadcasting on the Internet (see e.g. ILC et al. 1996, Nielsen 1995, p. 14). Public use of the WWW was applied to the Internet in 1993 as an interactive system for the dissemination and retrieval of information and multimedia sources such as audio or video sequence files within a document through web pages. Currently, the WWW is the fastest growing Internet resource and it is considered the most attractive service for business usage (Everts 1996, p. 34, Little 1995, p. 35).

3   A Segmentation Map of the Internet Industry

Since the Internet industry is still evolving it is helpful for understanding the economic fundamentals of transactions on the Internet to grasp the scope of the current state of segmentation of products and services within the Internet industry. A basic understanding of the technology is a prerequisite for economic models. Mapping out the industries basic structure will enable companies, as the market matures, to organize their "...potential products and services in context with other companies and in focus within the rest of the industry." (Dayton 1996, p. 1).

The various building blocks of the Internet industry may be classified according to the so-called Open Systems Interconnection (OSI) model developed by the International Standards Organization (ISO) during the past 15 years. Basically, the OSI model permits developers of the network architecture to work on network problems independently and still obtain compatible system solutions. Working through the various successive layers of the network architecture enhanced network functionality is obtained. The OSI model which defines *how the technology of the Internet underlies the segmentation of its products and services* is briefly illustrated in table 1.

Table 1: Understanding the OSI Model			
Layer	Name	Description	Example
7	Application	The communications applications themselves	email, file transfer, client/server applications. Applications such as Netscape & Eudora talk to this layer
6	Presentation	Syntax for data conversion, makes session layer available to application layer.	ASCII, binary conversion, encryption and decryption, sockets
5	Session	Starts, stops and governs transmission order.	Sockets, synchronization
4	Transport	Ensures delivery of the completed message.	TCP, SNA, UDP
3	Network	Routes data to different networks. Forms packets.	IP, x.25, IPX, AppleTalk, Routing
2	Data Link	Transmits from node to node. Divides bits into frames.	Ethernet, Token ring, Frame Relay, Bridging
1	Physical	The connection medium. The hard, physical connection	RTS, CTS, RS-232, copper, fiber, wireless
Source: Dayton 1996, p. 3, orig. in ISO 1985			

Layers 1 and 2 above characterize the primary foundation of the Internet. Originally, the regulated monopolies of telephone and cable companies controlled these segments of the market. As pointed out by Dayton (1996, p. 4), the past market structure and industrial organization has resulted in providers not keeping up with the vast amount of technological innovations in the upper layers. The result being, for example, that although consumer personal computers are now capable of processing bits at intense speeds, most users are still confronted with an Internet experience at a mere 28.8 kBits per second. The upgrading of these primary market segments will be an area of enhanced competition among future providers based upon deregulation efforts in the telecommunication carriers industry (as outlined in greater detail in Antonelli 1995 or the Survey of Telecommunications by Cairncross (1997)). Companies operating in layers 3 and 4 basically deliver TCP/IP packets throughout the network, culminating in customer services such as email, Usenet, ftp, Web, etc. offered by companies operating within layers 5 to 7.

Table 2: A random sampling of companies in each sector						
Name	Hardware	Software	Access	Content	Services	Expertise
Application	Apple, Intel, Dell, Gateway	Netscape, Microsoft, Quarterdeck	EarthLink, Netcom, Sprynet, GNN	AOL, CompuServe, Prodigy, CNN, WSJ	Yahoo, Excite, Infoseek, Lycos	CKS, Digital, Planet, USWeb
Presentation	Sun, SGI, HP, IBM, DEC, Intel	Netscape, Microsoft, Interworld	EarthLink, Netcom, Sprynet, GNN, Best	AOL, CompuServe, Prodigy, BBN	Cybercash, CompuServe, BBN, I/Pro, Netcount RSA	CKS, Digital Planet, USWeb
Session	Sun, SGI, HP, IBM, DEC, Intel	Netscape, Microsoft, Interworld, Xing, Real Audio	EarthLink, Netcom, Sprynet, GNN, Best	AOL, CompuServe, Prodigy, BBN	BNN, CompuServe, I/Pro, Netcount	CKS, Digital Planet, USWeb
Transport	Cisco, Bay, 3Com, Wellfleet	FTP, Netmanage, Network Telesystems	Netcom, UUNET, PSINet, Concentric, MCI, BBN, Sprintlink	AOLNet (ANS), CompuServe, Sprintnet, BBN	BBN, CompuServe, Network Solutions	Anderson, EDS, Perot, BBN
Network	Cisco, Bay, 3Com, Wellfleet	FTP, Netmanage, Network Telesystems	Netcom, UUNET, PSINet, Concentric, MCI, BBN, Sprintlink	AOLNet (ANS), CompuServe, Sprintnet, BBN	BBN, CompuServe, Network Solutions	Anderson, EDS, Perot, BBN
Data Link	USR, Ascend, Cascade, Stratacom, AT&T	NorTel, AT&T	MCI, TCI, Sprint, Worldcom, AT&T	MCI, TCI, Sprint, Worldcom, AT&T	MCI, TCI, Sprint, Worldcom, AT&T	Anderson, EDS, @Home, AT&T
Physical	USR, Ascend, Cascade, Stratacom, AT&T	NorTel, AT&T	MCI, TCI, Sprint, Worldcom, AT&T	MCI, TCI, Sprint, Worldcom, AT&T	MCI, TCI, Sprint, Worldcom, AT&T	Anderson, EDS, @Home, AT&T
Source: Dayton 1996, p. 6						

The Internet industry may alternatively be subdivided into *sectors* as in table 2 which classifies the various products and services available on these network layers. Currently, the Internet has six market sectors (Dayton, 1996):

1. Hardware

2. Software
3. Access
4. Content
5. Services
6. Expertise.

Although one may find company cases of overlapping onto different layers in more than one sector, commonly businesses focus their efforts on one or two layers in one sector only.

The OSI model suggests that companies may be more successful if they generally restrict their main operations to activities involving the layers immediately above and below their general lines of business. Expressing this somewhat differently, it may be argued that "...complications in developing and deploying networks and network-based products are directly proportional to the number of layers involved. Conversely, the fewer the layers involved, the simpler and more reliable the networking technology" (Dayton 1996, p. 7).

The economic trade-off on the other side of the coin, however, is that *as the technology becomes more complex and involves additional layers of the Internet a level of greater flexibility and value-added may be achieved.* It is important for companies wishing to position themselves competitively in the Internet market to comprehend the versatility effects of the multiple layers of the Internet. There are plenty of examples of companies such as AT&T's advance into computer hardware and online services, or USWest's interactive video services and MCI's consumer Internet service that have ended as financial disasters. Of new interest here is also the fact that telecommunications and Internet services are commencing to be traded internationally. Normally, the point of production and the point of consumption of a service activity fall together. As international competition increases, however, dumping of telecommunication services may be observed accompanied by an emerging "novel sort of trade war" (Cairncross 1997, p. 4).

Also, as the number of providers increases and new innovative technologies transform the segmentation of the Internet industry creating new industrial boundaries due to collective goal setting between governments and industry in pursuit of market shares, the future regulatory role of the government interface will have to be reconsidered and newly defined (Auster 1990, Gilroy 1998). In Germany, for example, new entrants are often owned by big industrial entities: debitel, which offers mobile-telephone services, is owned by Daimler-Benz (automotive industry) and by Metro (retail industry). Founded in 1992, debitel has already captured 17 percent of the German mobile market, "...partly by pioneering novelties such as marketing through Mercedes-Benz dealerships and offering a hotline for commuters to reserve parking spaces" (Cairncross 1997, p. 6). The constituent parts of such alliance groupings often have valuable knowledge and experience in manipulating different kinds of government regulatory systems.

Another illustrative German example are the private-sector regional energy monopolies such as Veba, Viag, and RWE who are now positioning themselves to compete with Deutsche Telekom. It may be the case that new models of regulation will be needed to deal with such changes. It has already even been suggested to contract out more regulatory tasks to the private sector. "Why not allow a global accountancy firm such as Price Waterhouse or Arthur Anderson to monitor compliance with licenses, for instance, or even to set up procedures for resolving those dreaded disputes about interconnections? The regulators might then confine themselves mainly to setting the rules in advance – which would inspire confidence among investors" (Cairncross 1997, p. 18).

The exchange of data and access to information are not the only fields of economic activity the Internet has to offer. It is becoming increasingly important for businesses to have access to this new media for a variety of reasons such as promoting the corporate image or facilitating business transactions by implementing the online network technology. Online network technology permits, for example, a relatively low-cost monitoring mechanism of economic and political developments in countries targeted by location decisions of multinational enterprises. As such, electronic networking in multinational enterprises may enhance world productivity (Gilroy 1993, Maloff 1995).

4 Economic Issues and Concepts of Internet Economics

After having examined some of the institutional and technological characteristics of the Internet industry in the above sections, the purpose here is to highlight some of the key economic issues and concepts of Internet economics. The literature on Internet economics, although still in its infancy, is already overwhelming. Consequently, the topics discussed here will be highly selective. For more detailed sources of valuable references on Internet economics the interested reader is referred to take a look at the extremely helpful bibliographies by Klopfenstein (1997) and Economides (1998a).

McKnight and Bailey (1997, p. 3) suggest that an economic model of the Internet must identify and include the following aspects:

1. Policy: the Internet promotes *interoperability* so different telecommunication infrastructures can converge and share services.
2. Economic: *network externalities* are realized when the membership of a network grows.

3. Technical: unused network resources like bandwidth and servers should be allocated to users who demand services so there can be equitable *statistical sharing* of resources.

They point out further that since the Internet supports heterogeneity there is necessarily a lacking of a "common metric of analysis". The challenge, in their opinion, is to develop economic models capable of handling the incorporation of the mentioned aspects.

The goal of economic public policy, as usually argued, is to maximize economic efficiency which has three components: (1) allocative efficiency; (2) productive efficiency; and (3) dynamic efficiency (Economides 1998b). Allocative efficiency requires goods and services to be sold at prices close to production costs. Productive efficiency demands that goods be produced in the most efficient manner possible. Dynamic efficiency compels innovation and growth maximization. The important economic insight here is that generally, these goals may be in conflict, leaving no "optimal" policy solution that maximizes all of them simultaneously. The dynamics of the Internet industry suggests that simple static models of economic analysis as known to date may miss the essence of the market and lead to social losses if prematurely applied for public policy before we have a deeper understanding of where the Internet is going.

If the Internet is to become the *Information Superhighway* of the future it will depend upon providing *network connectivity or interoperability* to users. As illustrated in figure 1 below, networks are composed of links that connect nodes. Internet Service Providers (ISPs) are in the rapidly emerging business of providing network connectivity to users. Since many components of a network are necessary for the provision of a typical service, network components are often complementary to each other.

Decreases in the costs of transmission due to new technologies such as fiberoptic lines, satellites and sinking switching costs along with steadily falling prices of microchips and integrated circuits have transformed the telecommunications industry from a natural monopoly to an oligopoly (Economides 1997, p. 6).

An important economic issue with regard to interconnection is *resale*. New entrants either have to build their own networks; or they can offer their services across the incumbent's network, paying it a fee. Naturally, by reducing their own service pricing schedule existing companies such as Deutsche Telekom may deprive potential new entrants of the margin needed to warrant the construction of their own networks. Such a *limit-pricing strategy* of an established firm and one possibly with high pre-entry capacity levels can discourage entry and slow down the level of industry innovation (see e.g. Tirole 1990, p. 367ff.). Since networks exhibit positive consumption and production externalities, new entrants may be more or less forced to deal with the dominant national telecommunications carrier. It has been pointed out that, "Almost every new entrant complains that the interconnection charges bear no relation to their true cost. Many grumble that interconnection charges account for around 40% of their operating costs" (Cairncross 1997, p. 14).

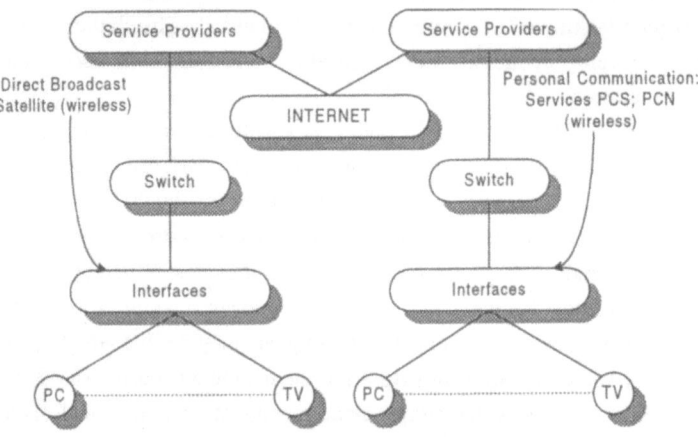

Figure 1: An information superhighway
(Source: Economides 1997, p.2)

Let us take a brief look at the logic of the "dominant firm model" and the reason for a limit-pricing strategy. Assume that the industry consists of many relatively new small firms and one large dominant firm. For example, the German Deutsche Telekom or the American AT&T and their rivals in the interstate telecommunications industry. Even though Deutsche Telekom or AT&T may no longer be technically a pure monopoly, monopoly power may exist given that one firm is dominant and a competitive fringe exists (Solberg 1992, pp. 574ff.).

The essential operational assumption of the dominant firm model is that, without regulation, the dominant firm can set the price and allows the follower firms to sell as much output as they wish at this price. Thus, the minor firms act as price-takers, whereby the dominant firm creams off the remaining part of the market demand. Given that the follower firms can sell as much as they wish at the price established by the dominant firm, they are faced with a horizontal demand curve and perfectly competitive situation. The follower firms view the dominant firm's price as their marginal revenue, and profits are maximized where their marginal cost equals marginal price. This may be illustrated by figure 2.

In figure 2 the industry demand curve is D. $\sum X_j$ represents the sum of the individual supply of minor firms. This curve is *not* to be interpreted as the market supply curve. Instead, the $\sum X_j$ curve characterizes that part of the market supplied by minor firms. Minor firms sell their output so that at any price the common pricing rule, price equals marginal cost, is valid. The dominant firm now supplies the remainder between market demand and the quantity supplied by the minor firms. The dominant firm's average revenue curve AR_d is obtained by subtracting the quantity supplied by the minor firms from market demand.

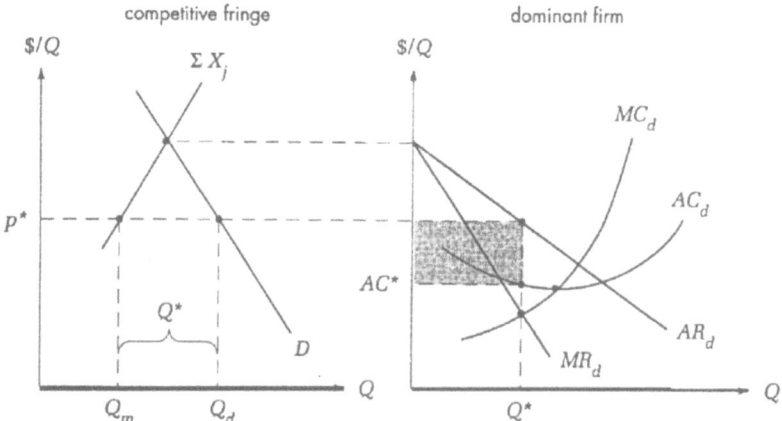

Figure 2: An industry with a dominant firm
(Source: Solberg 1992, p. 575)

At or above price p_0, the minor firms supply all the quantity demanded. At prices beneath p_0, the minor firms supply the part of the market demand determined by their marginal cost curves. The dominant firm supplies the remainder. In accordance with the cost curves AC_d and MC_d, the dominant firm now sets price at p^*, where $MR_d = MC_d$, with output at Q^*. The minor firms view price p^* as constant to them and collectively supply the quantity Q_m. Total units supplied equals $Q_m + Q^*$, which equals the quantity demanded Q_d, and the market is in equilibrium at price p^*.

In the short run, this solution appears stable. According to Cairncross (1997, p. 9), "...the new entrants usually nestle in under the lee of the giant, making a tidy living, but ensuring that their hefty rivals does so too. Over time, the new entrants will help to drive prices inexorably towards costs. But for the moment, look at them as a source of new marketing ideas and new technologies, rather than aggressors in a price war that might well destroy them." However, if the price set by the dominant firm leads to economic profits for the minor firms, potential new entrants will emerge. Additionally, if there are economies of scale present, minor firms will wish to expand their operations. This will shift the dominant firm's AR curve to the left, decreasing the market share and profit of the dominant firm. Consequently, public regulators are faced with the problem of finding an answer to the question: "how do they give the incumbent an incentive to co-operate while still allowing new entrants to make money?" (Cairncross 1997, p. 13).

A second important concept in Internet economics is *network externalities* (see. e.g. Liebowitz & Margolis 1995). The fundamental reason for the emergence of network externalities is the complementarity between the components of a network. Expressed somewhat differently, network industries reward size. The more economic agents connected to a network, the greater the value of being part of the network. A telephone or fax machine, or even a credit card, is basically worthless unless it is plugged into or accepted in a (globally) interconnected network. The value of a telephone or fax machine increases with the number of *expected* units installed. The demand curve slopes downwards but shifts upward with increases in the number of units expected to be installed (Economides 1997, p. 6).

Such positive network externalities emerge when a commodity is more valuable to a user the more users adopt the same commodity. Such externalities may be *direct network externalities* as in the case of a telephone network with n subscribers, the addition of the $(n + 1)^{th}$ subscriber allows for $2n$ additional types of calls to be made (from the new subscriber to all old subscribers and vice versa). Or the externality can be an *indirect network externality* based upon increasing returns to scale in production, so that a greater variety of complementary products can be supplied at lower prices when the network grows. Such "virtual networks", as Economides (1997, p. 1) terms them, arise when two complementary components are required to make a valuable good or service. Typical examples are the combination of a computer operating system and applications software that run under the operating system, video cassettes compatible with a dominant video system, or a popular automobile being serviced by more dealers. The size of a relevant network may be firm-specific as in the car dealership case, or industry-wide as in the cases where technical hardware standards are important.

Users on the demand side of a market affected by network externalities, due to their *interdependent utility functions*, must attempt to anticipate which technology will be widely used by others. Consequently, difficult coordination problems founded upon conflicting consumer preferences and technologies commonly emerge. Such coordination problems often lead to two inherent inefficiencies: *excess inertia* (users postpone adopting a new technology) and *excess momentum* (consumers rush to an inferior technology for fear of getting stranded).

On the supply side, given the presence of network externalities, standards (i.e., a choice of a particular technology to be adopted by all) are often mandated by the government or by private bodies such as industry committees. On both sides, actions by firms and consumers to adopt various technologies give rise to product diversity games of timing. The two polar cases of which are wars of attrition and preemption games (see e.g. Tirole 1990, chap. 10).

Given the presence of network externalities, it may be shown that perfect competition is inefficient:

> The marginal social benefit of network expansion is larger than the benefit that accrues to a particular firm under perfect competition. Thus, perfect competition will provide a smaller network than is socially optimal, and for some relatively high marginal costs perfect competition will not provide the good while it is socially optimal to provide it. One interesting question that remains virtually unanswered is how to decentralize the welfare maximizing solution in the presence of network externalities (Economides 1997, p. 9).

The need for some form of welfare enhancing network price discrimination gives rise to the third major issue: *equitable statistical sharing of Internet resources.* McKnight and Bailey (1997) define equitable statistical sharing as the ability for networks to allocate bandwidth (transmission capacity) to users based upon the users' needs. Although much has been written about Internet pricing, this is still a relatively new area of research. To date, three common pricing models characterize the access debate and the scarcity of Internet transmission resources:

1. Flat-rate pricing: One rate is charged to the user regardless of actual use or type of connection.
2. Capacity-based pricing: Presently, many Internet users pay a fee to connect while they are not billed for each bit sent but are charged for different types of connections.
3. Usage-sensitive pricing: Users pay a portion of their Internet bill for a connection and a possibly varying portion for each bit sent and/or received.

Pricing questions extend, however, far beyond the market for Internet bandwidth and stretch out into more fundamental important areas as exploring new frameworks for rethinking patent and copyright laws in the Digital Age (Barlow 1994) or attempts at developing an economic model for the trade in free goods and services on the Internet (Ghosh 1998). Along these lines of thought a variety of complex and economically interesting questions emerge. For instance, as digital technology is increasingly detaching information from the physical dimension, how should "virtual" copyright and patent laws be designed. "If our property can be infinitely reproduced and instantaneously distributed all over the world without great cost, without its even leaving our possession, without our knowledge, how can we protect it?" (Barlow 1994, p. 84). How is it going to be possible to get payment for intellectual property rights on the Internet? And, if an efficient pricing mechanism can not be found, what will assure the continued creation and distribution of such information on the Internet? What are the economic essentials of unbounded information creation and missing or not clearly defined property rights?

It may be argued that in the past one did not get paid for ideas produced, but for the ability to deliver them into (physical) reality. That is, the economic value was in the conveyance and not in the thought conveyed. "In other words, the bottle was protected, not the wine." (Barlow, 1994, p. 84). Digital technology seems to be obliterating the legal jurisdictions of the physical world as we once knew it and replacing them with the unbounded and largely lawless waves of cyberspace with a new "Metabottle" expressed as complex and highly liquid patterns of ones and zeros. Governments will also have to further clarify liability for material conveyed on the Internet as recent public cases of the distribution of pornographic- and nazi-propaganda material over the Internet suggest.

What solutions will emerge to answer questions like "how to get paid in cyber-space?" Will there be a sort of compensating re-emergence of Internet ethics and accepted norms that successfully sanction the ordering template of society? Or will the future protection of your intellectual property depend on your ability to control your relation to the market? Barlow (1994) suggests that future control will probably be based on restricting access to the freshest, highest bandwidth information protected by a technological solution of cryptography ("Crypto Bottling", i.e. any purely technical method of property protection such as a decoder or encryption), as opposed to institutionalized ethics of some legal social contract defining property rights which inherently always will be hanging behind the developments of new technological innovations.

As already mentioned above, laws of increasing returns based upon familiarity is an important asset in the Internet industry. The best way to raise the demand for your product may simply be to give it away free. One is reminded of the historical strategy of the famous American oil magnate Rockefellar who distributed kerosene lamps free of cost to the Chinese, thereby creating an enormous demand for their complementary input kerosene produced from the oil of Rockefellar's refineries. The current antitrust proceedings against Microsoft is illustrative of a similar situation. The U.S. Department of Justice alleges that Microsoft is attempting to extend its monopoly of the Operating Systems market to the market for Internet browsers. Microsoft is providing its browser Internet Explorer free, i.e. it is alleged to be charging too little, not charging too much as usually the case in such monopoly legal battles. The apprehension being that as Microsoft spreads its dominance from one area of software to the next, Microsoft will stop innovating (see e.g. Choi, Stahl & Whinston 1997, Taylor 1998, Krugman 1998, Economides 1998d, and the online documentation of the latest independent information on the current Microsoft legal battle by Economides (1998c)). For a general discussion of the relevant aspects of competition policy on innovation confer further Langenfeld & Scheffman 1988). Basically, since it takes time and effort for a user to install a competing browser, Microsoft has an advantage (of raising rival's costs) if its browser is already installed by the PC manufacturer. Economic analysis demonstrates that a monopolist has an incentive to raise the costs of the rivals (Salop & Scheffman 1983) and to degrade the quality of the monopolized good, thereby generally reducing the level of industry competition and social welfare (see e.g. Economides 1998d).

Let us now briefly examine the fact that much of the economic activity on the Internet involves value but no money. The amount of freely accessible resources on the Internet still greatly outweighs all commercial resources at the moment. As pointed out by Ghosh (1998), it is basically impossible to put a price on the value of the Internet's free resources, at least in part because they exist because they do not have prices attached. They exist in a *market of implicit transactions*. The exchange of knowledge on the Internet is essentially an act of trade. What are the motivations of what Ghosh (1998) terms the "economics of gossip", i.e. the "free" distribution of operating systems such as Linux or Web server software, Newsgroups, HTML (the language of the web), mailing-lists and on-line chatting sessions? It may be argued that there is no specific economic inherent value in a product. Value lies in the willingness of economic agents to consume a good or service, and this potentially exists in anything that individuals can produce and pass on.

Internet transactions that are not based upon explicit price-tags, may still represent an implicit sales transaction. The involved agents are implicitly selling their work to purchase the work of others – e.g. in a discussion group – or to buy the satisfaction of popularity and enhanced reputation in the "attention economy" which may be convertible into currency or better access to things of value at a later date (Goldhaber 1997, Lanham 1997). "Without the intermediary of money, there are always two sides to every transaction, every transaction is potentially unique, rather than being based on a value derived through numerous similar trades between others – i.e. the price-tag. ...Life on the Internet is like a perpetual auction with ideas instead of money" (Ghosh 1998, pp. 5-6). Based upon the trade principle of reciprocity, i.e. the process of give and take,

"...the economy of the Net begins to look like a vast tribal cooking-pot surging with production to match consumption, simply because everyone understands – instinctively, perhaps – that trade need not occur in single transactions of barter, and that one product can be exchanged for millions at a time. The cooking-pot keeps boiling because people keep putting in things as they themselves, and others, take things out" (Ghosh 1998, p. 10).

5 Conclusion

The Internet industry is embedded in a complex and rapidly changing transactional environment in which firm-specific and industry-wide complementarities exist. As argued above, the challenge to any analysis of the Internet and public policy is that government and industry are not necessarily guided by tightly drawn boundaries. Rather, as technology has evolved, the fortunes and misfortunes of governments, producers, and consumers worldwide are becoming even more closely linked through the Internet. To a large extent Internet activities all consist of exchanges of information and collective goal setting while maintaining high levels of competition. As transactional relationships increasingly evolve on a global level, the effectiveness of the Internet will largely depend upon an awareness of the economic logic of network structures.

References

Anderson, C. (1997, May 10th-16th). A Survey of Electronic Commerce. In: Search of the Perfect Market. *The Economist*, pp. 1-26.
Anderson, M. & Choobineeh, J. (1996). Marketing on the Internet, Information Strategy. *The Executive's Journal*, 4, pp. 22-29.
Antonelli, C. (1995). Technological Change and Multinational Growth in International Telecommunications Services, *Review of Industrial Organization*, 10(2), pp. 161-180.
Auster, E. R. (1990). The Interorganizational Environment: Network Theory, Tools and Applications. In: F. Williams, D. Gibson (Eds.), *Technology Transfer: A Communication Perspective* (pp. 171-191). Newbury Park, California: Sage Publications.
Barlow, J. P. (1994, March). The Economy of Ideas: A framework for rethinking patents and copyrights in the Digital Age (Everything you know about intellectual property is wrong). *Wired*, pp. 84-129.
Cairncross, F. (1997, September 13th-19th). A Survey of Telecommunications: A Connected World. *The Economist*, pp. 1-42.
Choi, S.-Y., Stahl, D. O. & Whinston, A. B. (1997, December 10th). Is Microsoft a Monopolist? *Brazilian Electronic Journal of Economics*, pp. 1-8. Available:
<http://www.beje.decon.ufpe.br/soon.htm> (1998, September 21).
Dayton, S. (1996). *Making Some Sense of the Madness: The Natural Evolution of the Internet Industry* (pp. 1-8). Available:
<http://www.earthlink.net/special/marketevol.html> (1998, September 23).
Economides, N. (1997, December 10th). The Economics of Networks. *Brazilian Electronic Journal of Economics*, pp. 1-32. Available:
<http://www.beje.decon.ufpe.br/economides.htm> (1998, September 21).
Economides, N. (1998a). *Bibliography on Network Economics* (pp. 1-59). Available:
<http://raven.stern.nyu.edu/networks/biblio.html> (1998, September 21).
Economides, N. (1998b). *The Economics Of Networks: Interview mit N. Economides (Part 1|2|3)*. Available:
<http://raven.stern.nyu.edu/networks/part1.html> (1998, September 21),
<http://raven.stern.nyu.edu/networks/part2.html> (1998, September 21),
<http://raven.stern.nyu.edu/networks/part3.html> (1998, September 21).
Economides, N. (1998c). *The Current Microsoft Legal Battles.* Available:
<http://raven.stern.nyu.edu/networks/ms/top.html> (1998, September 21).

Economides, N. (1998d). *Raising Rivals' Costs in Complementary Goods Markets: LECs Entering into Long Distance and Microsoft Bundling Internet Explorer.* Forthcoming in: Annual TPRC volume. Available: <http://raven.stern.nyu.edu/networks/ms/top..htm> (1998, January 26).

Everts, V. (1996, January). Weltweiter Hypertext: Das World Wide Web. *Internet magazin special,* pp. 32-35.

Ghosh, R. A. (1998, July 29th). Cooking Pot Markets: An economic Model for the Trade in Free Goods and Services on the Internet. *Brazilian Electronic Journal of Economics,* pp. 1-17. Available: <http://www.beje.decon.ufpe.br/ghosh/cooking.htm> (1998, September 21).

Gilroy, B. M. (1993). *Networking in Multinational Enterprises: The Importance of Strategic Alliances.* Columbia: University of South Carolina Press.

Gilroy, B. M. (1998). International Competitiveness, Multinational Enterprise Technology Clubs and the Government Interface. In: K.-J. Koch, Klaus Jaeger (Eds.), *Trade, Growth, and Economic Policy in Open Economies* (pp. 13-30). New York: Springer.

Glanz, A. (1997). Business Digital: Managementinstrumente im digitalen Markt. In: K.P. Boden, M. Barabas (Eds.), *Internet – von der Technologie zum Wirtschaftsfaktor* (pp. 129-137). Heidelberg: dpunkt.

Goldhaber, M. (1997). *The Attention Economy: The Natural Economy of the Net,* First Monday, 2(4), Available: <http://www.firstmonday.dk/issues/issue2 4/goldhaber/index.html> (1998, September 21).

Hansen, H. (1996). *Info-Highway – Geschäfte via Internet & Co.* Wien: Orac.

Hauenstein, Th. (1996). Chancen und Risiken eines Internet-Engagements. *Io Management,* 65(9), pp. 25-27.

ILC et al. (1996). *ILC-Glossary of Internet Terms.* Available: <http://www.matisse.net/files/glossary.html> (1997, January 8).

ISO (1985). *Information Processing Systems – Open Systems Interconnections – Basic Reference Model.* International Standard 7498.

Klau, P. (1995). *Das Internet- der größte Informationshighway der Welt.* Bonn: IWT.

Klopfenstein, B. C. (1997). Internet Economics: An Annotated Bibliography. *Journal of Media Economics,* 11(1), pp. 33-48.

Krol, E. (1995). *Die Welt des Internet.* Bonn: O'Reilly/Int. Thompson.

Krugman, P. (1998). *Soft Microeconomics: The squishy case against you-know-who, Slate – The Dismal Science* (pp. 1-5). Available: <http://web.mit.edu/krugman/www/soft.htm> (1998, April 23).

Lammarsch, J. & Steenweg, H. (1995). *Internet & Co.: Elektronische Fachkommunikation auf akademischen Netzen,* 2nd Edition. Bonn: Addison-Wesley.

Langenfeld, J. & Scheffman, D. (1988). Innovation and U.S. Competition Policy. *Aussenwirtschaft,* Special Issue on Technology and Public Policy I/II, pp. 45-95.

Lanham, B. (1997). *The Economics of Attention.* Available: <http://sunsite.berkeley.edu/ARL/Proceedings/124/ps2econ.html > (1998, September 21).

Liebowitz, S.J. & Margolis, S.E. (1995). Are Network Externalities a New Source of market Failure? *Research in Law and Economics,* 17, pp. 1-22.

Little, A. (1996). *Management in vernetzten Unternehmen.* Wiesbaden: Gabler Verlag.

Maier, G. & Wildberger, A. (1995). *In 8 Sekunden um die Welt: Kommunikation über das Internet.* Bonn: Addison-Wesley. Available: <http://www.bingo.baynet.de/internet/netzbuch/netzbuch.html> (1998, September 21).

Maloff, J. (1995). The Virtual Corporation. *Internet World,* 6(7), pp. 46-51.

McKnight, L. & Bailey, J. P. (1997, December 10th). Global Internet Economics. *Brazilian Electronic Journal of Economics,* pp. 1-13. Available: <http://www.beje.decon.ufpe.br/mcknight.htm> (1998, September 21).

Nielsen, J. (1995). *Multimedia & Hypertext: The Internet and Beyond.* Massachusetts: Academic Press Inc.

Nolden, M. (1995). *Das World Wide Web im Internet.* Frankfurt/Main: Ullstein.

Rüdiger, A. (1996). Das Web schlägt alles. *Business Computing,* 4, p. 83.

Tirole, J. (1990). *Theory of Industrial Organization.* Cambridge, Massachusetts: The MIT Press.

Salop, S. C. & Scheffman, D. (1983). Raising Rival's Costs. *American Economic Review*, 73, pp. 267-271.

Solberg, E. J. (1992). *Microeconomics for Business Decisions.* Lexington, Massachusetts: D.C. Heath and Company.

Taylor, K. S. (1998, July 29th). A Commentary on "Is Microsoft a Monopolist?". *Brazilian Electronic Journal of Economics*, pp. 1-4. Available:
<http://www.beje.decon.ufpe.br/taylor/monopolist.htm> (1998, September 21).

The Impacts of Information Technologies on Innovation Dynamics and Labor Demand

Thomas Gries and Stefan Jungblut

1 Introduction

The diffusion of information and communication technologies (ITs) is one of the most important developments in the present process of economic growth and technological change. ITs become increasingly important in almost any kind of economic activity. Therefore, the potential to successfully implement and use ITs has turned out to be a decisive factor to participate in advantages offered by the growing information society.

Most theoretical analysis of the diffusion process of ITs is limited to the micro-economic perspective. However, a number of empirical studies point out that the diffusion and implementation of information and communication technologies are likely to have considerable macroeconomic effects as well. Compared to other key technologies, as for example material- or bio-technologies, ITs are especially important, because they affect almost all branches and sectors of the economy.[1] In addition, ITs are likely to cause considerable modifications of traditional work flows. Therefore it is expected that these technologies have important impacts on the demand for different types of labor. A number of empirical studies indicates that the structure of labor demand strongly shifted in favor of high skilled workers in the OECD countries over the past decade. From the empirical point of view, it is hardly doubted that the diffusion of information technologies tended to speed up this development essentially.[2] In addition, a reverse mechanism seems to exist. The diffusion rate of modern technologies is obviously strongly affected by the educational level and flexibility of the workforce. Both factors determine the efficiency of innovations and advanced techniques. Accordingly, a mutual relationship between innovation activities and the structure of labor supply seems to exist.

The present paper attempts to examine the relationship between information technology related innovation activities and labor demand at a theoretical level. The endogenous growth model is presented in chapter 2. The central idea of the model is that information and communication technologies represent the dominating outcome of technical progress. The technological progress in turn is one of the most important

---

[1] See OECD 1994, p. 133.
[2] See e.g. OECD 1994, pp. 133 and OECD 1996, p.100.

determinants of the process of growth. In addition, real and human capital accumulation are also considered as factors of growth. Two types of workers are distinguished, skilled and unskilled workers, in order to examine the relationship between innovation activities and the structure of labor demand.

The steady-state solution of the model is derived in section 3. In section 4 the impacts of ITs on innovation activities and labor demand are examined. We show that the demand for unskilled labor decreases if periods of high innovation activities will not be accompanied by sufficient accumulation of human capital. Although different effects are associated with the process of diffusion and implementation of ITs, they are always in favor of the skilled. This result does not equally hold for the different effects of ITs on productivity and growth. Instead, the process of IT diffusion can possibly affect these variables in opposite direction. Therefore, the model offers an explanation why the diffusion of information and communication technologies may not lead to higher rates of productivity growth. However, a positive effect will occur, if human capital is relatively abundant. Therefore, the process of innovation and diffusion of ITs must be complemented by educational policies. It is not sufficient to increase the share of skilled workers, but it is also necessary to increase their human capital endowments. Only this strategy guarantees that the increase in productivity and income can be fully realized.

2 The Model

We consider an economy with a large number of households and identical firms. Each household is endowed with one unit of physical labor. The labor services are demanded by firms and used as inputs in production. The aggregate labor endowment of households is constant and denoted $L = \overline{L}$. Two types of labor can be distinguished according to their ability to acquire production related knowledge: skilled and unskilled labor. Unskilled labor L_u may be understood as pure labor while skilled labor L_s offers a service based on production related knowledge, human capital. L_u and L_s are regarded to be constant and $L_u + L_s = \overline{L}$.

Each firm i uses real capital and both types of labor to produce a homogenous, non-storable good. The number of firms is m. The output of a representative firm is denoted X^i. The production function is of the Cobb-Douglas type:

$$X^i = F(K^i, A^i) = K^{i\alpha} A^{i^{1-\alpha}}. \tag{1}$$

K^i denotes the real capital input and A^i the aggregate labor service used by firm $i \in \{1,...,m\}$.

The aggregate labor service depends on labor inputs, L_u^i and L_s^i, technological efficiency, λ^i, and the human capital endowment of skilled labor, h. The aggregation function is assumed to be of the CES type:

$$A^i = A^i(L_u^i, L_s^i, \lambda^i, h) = \left[\beta_u (\lambda^i L_u^i)^{-\rho} + \beta_s (h L_s^i)^{-\rho} \right]^{\frac{1}{\rho}} \qquad (2)$$

with $\beta_u = 1 - \beta_s$. The aggregation function (2) is based on the assumption that technological progress and human capital are complements, i.e. $\rho > 0$. The complementary assumption for technological progress and human capital is comprehensively supported by empirical studies.[3] These studies point out that the diffusion as well as the application of advanced techniques is only possible if sufficiently skilled workers are available as complements. This aspect seems to be especially important for information technologies.[4]

The wage rate per worker of type $i \in \{u,s\}$ is denoted w_j. The aggregate income of households, Y, is the sum of wage income and returns from saving. The returns from saving are given by rW, where W denotes real wealth and r the real rate of return:

$$Y := w_u L_u + w_s L_s + rW. \qquad (3)$$

We assume that the government levies an income tax to finance education. The tax rate is denoted as τ. Thus, the accumulation of human capital is given by

$$\dot{H} = \tau Y,$$

where H denotes the aggregate stock of human capital and $\dot{H} \equiv \partial H / \partial t$. The human capital endowment of the skilled is given by $h \equiv H / L_s$ and accumulates according to

$$\dot{h} = \tau \frac{Y}{L_s}. \qquad (4)$$

The disposable income, $(1-\tau)Y$, is used to finance consumption, C, and savings, S. The saving rate is denoted s and assumed to be constant:

$$C = (1-s)(1-\tau)Y,$$

$$S = s(1-\tau)Y \equiv \dot{W}.$$

We distinguish two types of investment, real capital investment, I_K^i, and investment in technological capital, I_T^i. Total investment expenditure of firm i is given

---

[3] See OECD 1996 for a comprehensive discussion and further remarks.
[4] See OECD 1988, p. 188.

by $I^i = I^i_K + I^i_T$. Real capital investments increase production capacities while investments in technology increase the efficiency of production. The capacity effect,
$\dot{K} \equiv \partial K / \partial t$, is given by

$$\dot{K}^i = I^i_K,\qquad(5)$$

while the production efficiency, $\dot{\lambda} \equiv \partial \lambda / \partial t$, develops according to

$$\dot{\lambda}^i = \frac{I^i_T}{c_T}.\qquad(6)$$

Equation (6) is the innovation function of firm $i \in \{1,...,m\}$. The innovation
function basically states that the speed of technological progress and investments in
technological capital are positively related. c_T denotes the input coefficient of the
innovation process, and $1/c_T$ is the innovation efficiency. The input coefficient
c_T can be varied parametrically to reflect changes in innovation activity as the result
of IT diffusion.[5]

We assume that firms will plan their investment expenditure in order to minimize
the present value of production costs. Current cost, c^i, are given by salaries and capital
services:

$$c^i = w_u L^i_u + w_s L^i_s + rW^i.\qquad(7)$$

We denote

$$\begin{aligned}W^i(t) &= \int_0^t (I^i_T(z) + I^i_K(z))dz \\ &= K^i(t) + c_T \lambda^i(t),\end{aligned}\qquad(8)$$

as the sum of investment expenditure of firm i up to time t. $W^i(t)$ is equal to the current value of real and technological capital by definition.

According to equations (7) and (8) the cost minimization problem of firm i is
given by

$$\min_{L^i_u, L^i_s, I^i_K, I^i_T} \int_0^\infty e^{-rt} \{ w_u L^i_u + w_s L^i_s + r(c_T \dot{\lambda}^i) \} dt\qquad(9.a)$$

s.t.:

$$X^i - F(K^i, A^i) = 0,\qquad(9.b)$$

---

[5] See section 4.

$$\dot{K}^i = I_K^i, \qquad (9.c)$$

$$\dot{\lambda}^i = c_T^{-1} I_T^i, \qquad (9.d)$$

$$I_T^i \geq 0, \qquad (9.e)$$

$$I^i - I_T^i \geq 0, \qquad (9.f)$$

and $K^i(0)$, $\lambda^i(0)$ given.

The cost minimization problem is a restricted problem of optimal control. The control variables are I_K^i, I_T^i, L_u^i, and L_s^i. Equation (9.b) is the restriction for output. Equations (9.c) and (9.d) are the equations of motion for the state variables, K^i and λ^i. Equations (9.e) and (9.f) restrict investments: (9.e) requires technology investments to be nonnegative and equation (9.f) requires technology investments to be less or equal to total investment expenditure. The latter condition is equivalent to $I_K^i \geq 0$.

To solve the cost minimization problem we use (9.a), (9.c), and (9.d) to form up the current-value Hamiltonian

$$H = (w_u L_u^i + w_s L_s^i + r(K^i + c_T \lambda^i)) + \mu_{K1} I_K^i + \mu_{T1} c_T^{-1} I_T^i,$$

with μ_{K1} and μ_{T1} as the costates of (9.c) and (9.d). Then the Langrangean is

$$L = H(\,\cdot\,) - \mu(F(K^i, A^i) - X^i) - \mu_{K2} I_K^i - \mu_{T2} I_T^i. \qquad (10)$$

The Lagrangean combines the Hamiltonian with the restrictions (9.b), (9.e), and (9.f).[6] μ, μ_{K2}, and μ_{T2} denote the Lagrange multipliers of conditions (9.b), (9.e), and (9.f) respectively.

The first order conditions for problem (9.a)-(9.f) can be used to solve for the structure of investment and the demand for both types of labor. With respect to the investment structure corner solutions have to be taken into consideration. Thus, as formally given in table 1, three types of solutions are possible. In Case 1 the rate of return of both types of investment is different. Therefore firms investment in the type yielding a higher return, real capital investment (equation (11.a)) or technology investment (equation (11.b)).

In Case 2 the return is identical and both types of investment will be used (equation (12)). The conditions for labor demand can be derived as

---

[6] See e. g. Kamien & Schwartz 1991, Part II, sec. 10. or Miller 1979, chap. 4.4.

Table 1: Level and structure of investments.

Case 1:		Case 2:
(11.a)	(11.b)	(12)
$r = \mu F_{K^i} > \mu c_T^{-1} F_{\chi^i}$	$\mu F_{K^i} < \mu c_T^{-1} F_{\chi^i} = r$	$\mu F_{K^i} = \mu c_T^{-1} F_{\chi^i} = r$
$I_T^i = 0,$ $I_K^i = I^i,$	$I_T^i = I^i, C$ $I_K^i = 0,$	$I_T^i > 0,$ $I_K^i > 0.$

$$w_j = \mu F_{L_j^i},\tag{13}$$

for $j \in \{u, s\}$.

To close the model we have to use the equilibrium conditions for the product market, the capital market and the labor market respectively. These conditions are given by

$$mX^i = Y,\tag{14}$$

$$mI^i = S,\tag{15}$$

$$mL_j^i = L_j.\tag{16}$$

Equations (14)-(16) can be used to solve for the marginal cost of production, μ, the rate of return, r, and the wage rates, w_j, for $j \in \{u, s\}$.

3 Steady-State Solution

To derive the long-run equilibrium of the economy (steady-state equilibrium) we have to define two functions. These functions will be referred to as the *efficient investment curve* and the *balanced accumulation curve* respectively. The efficient investment curve can be derived by solving (12) for k/h:

$$\frac{k}{h} = \frac{c_T}{L_s/m} \frac{\alpha}{1-\alpha} \frac{\lambda}{h} \left[1 + \frac{\beta_s}{\beta_u}\left(\frac{\lambda L_u}{hL_s}\right)^\rho\right] =: \phi_1(\lambda/h).\tag{17}$$

To derive the balanced accumulation curve we make use of the steady-state condition $\hat{h} = \hat{\lambda} = \hat{K}$, equations (4)-(6), and the equilibrium condition (15).[7]

---

[7] A hat is used to denote growth rates.

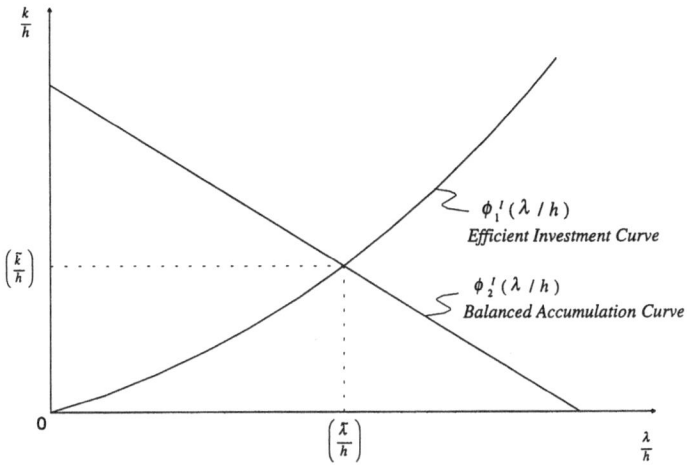

Figure 1: Steady-state solution.

Solving these equation for k/h yields

$$\frac{k}{h} = s\frac{1-\tau}{\tau} - \frac{c_T}{L_s/m}\frac{\lambda}{h} =: \phi_2(\lambda/h). \tag{18}$$

Both steady-state conditions have a straightforward economic interpretation. Equation (17) describes all factor combinations which represent an efficient structure of investment. Equation (18) in turn describes the factor combinations consistent with balanced growth. The long-run equilibrium is given at the intersection of both functions as graphed in figure 1. As can be seen from the figure the steady-state always exists and the equilibrium is unique.[8]

The equilibrium value for the ratio of real to human capital is given by $\tilde{k}/h$, and $\tilde{\lambda}/h$ denotes the long-run equilibrium ratio of technological efficiency to human capital. $\tilde{\lambda}/h$ is one of the most important variables of the model and will be referred to as the *technological intensity* of the production process.

Once k/h and λ/h are determined, the steady-state ratio of wages as well as the steady-state growth rate can be derived as

$$\frac{w_s}{w_u} = \frac{\beta_s}{\beta_u}\left(\frac{L_u}{L_s}\right)^{1+\rho}\left(\frac{\lambda}{h}\right)^{\rho}, \tag{19}$$

---

[8] Formally, the existence and uniqueness is guaranteed by $\phi_1(0)=0$, $\phi_2(0)>0$, $\phi_1'(0)>0$, $\phi_2'(0)<0$, and $\phi_2''(0)=0$.

and

$$\tilde{\gamma} = \tau \left(\frac{k}{h}\right)^{\alpha} \left[\beta_u \left(\frac{\lambda L_u}{h L_s}\right)^{-\rho} + \beta_s\right]^{-\frac{1-\alpha}{\rho}}. \tag{20}$$

Finally, we assume that $\alpha > s(1-\tau)$ is satisfied. This assumption is clearly not restrictive from the empirical point of view, but it is sufficient to make sure that the transversality condition holds.

4 Innovation Dynamics and Labor Demand

One of the most interesting features of information technologies is their wide applicability. ITs can be used in almost all sectors and branches of the economy. This feature undoubtedly speeds up the process of IT diffusion. In addition, empirical studies suggest that the diffusion of ITs is accompanied by a lasting and dramatic drop in real prices and an increasing scarcity of sufficiently qualified workers.[9] In order to see how these factors affect the dynamics of innovation and the structure of labor demand, we have to consider them in more detail.

4.1 Increasing Innovation Efficiency

Decreasing prices of ITs will tend to lower the cost of innovations, c_T. If c_T decreases, the increase in technological efficiency induced by a given investment expenditure, will also increase. This effect becomes clear from equation (6). As a result, the rate of return on technology investments increases relative to investments in physical capital. As a response firms will increase their investment in technologies, I_T^i, and decrease their real capital investments, I_K^i. In addition, the opportunity cost of technology investment will decrease. These effects are captured by an outward rotation of the balanced accumulation curve and the efficient investment curve respectively, as can be seen in figure 2.

The figure shows that the technological intensity increases from $(\lambda \tilde{7} h)'$ to $(\lambda \tilde{7} h)''$. Because human capital is required to complement the implementation of the ITs, the structure of demand for physical labor changes in favor of the skilled. As a result the wage rate for skilled workers *increases* relative to the wage rate for unskilled workers (see equation (19)).

---

[9] See OECD 1988 and OECD 1994.

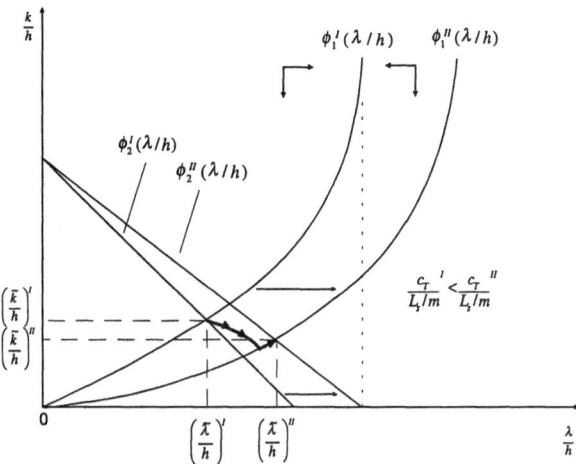

Figure 2: Innovation dynamics, case a.

To analyze the effect of innovation efficiency on growth we have to use equation (20). This equation implies

$$\frac{\partial \tilde{\gamma}}{\partial c_T} \frac{c_T}{\tilde{\gamma}} < 0 . \tag{21}$$

Equation (21) shows that the higher the innovation efficiency associated with the diffusion of ITs, the higher the steady-state growth rate of the economy. This reaction is due to the fact that the growth rate is positively related to the productivity of human capital and the latter in turn increases according to the technological intensity of production.

4.2 Increasing Human Capital Requirements

Empirical studies suggest that ITs are likely to increase the skill intensity of jobs.[10] The skill intensity of labor services is reflected by β_s in the aggregation function (2).

If β_s increases, the importance as well as the productivity of human capital services will increase. Due to the higher productivity the demand for skilled worker increases and a shortage of human capital results. Because human capital is necessary to implement ITs, the return on technology investment decreases. Therefore firms will increase their investment in production capacities relative to innovation activities. As a result of human capital accumulation h increases continuously and λ/h decreases.

---

[10] See OECD 1989, p. 19.

This reaction is shown in figure 3. It is important to note that during the process of adjustment firms do not begin any IT investment activities until the efficient investment curve is reached again, i.e. until the human capital endowment of the skilled is sufficiently high relative to technology. These reactions of the model are perfectly consistent with empirical findings. The OECD notes for example that insufficient human capital endowments are one of the most important obstacles for the successful implementation of ITs.[11] The model confirms this result and makes clear that the sluggish implementation of ITs has to be traced back to too low returns on investment.

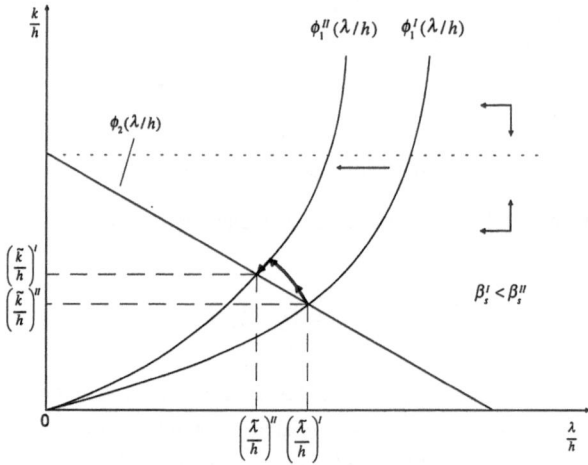

Figure 3: Innovation dynamics, case b.

With respect to the structure of labor demand the model reveals two counteracting effects. On the one hand the demand for skilled workers increases as a result of higher skill requirements in production. On the other hand the demand for the skilled decreases as firms reduce their IT investments. It can be shown that the first effect always dominates the second and

$$\frac{dw_{s/u}}{d\beta_s}\frac{\beta_s}{w_{s/u}}=\frac{1}{1-\beta_s}+\rho\underbrace{\frac{d(\lambda/h)}{d\beta_s}\frac{\beta_s}{\lambda/h}}_{-}>0,$$

where $w_{s/u}:=w_s/w_u$. Thus, according to the model the demand for labor as well as the relative wage rate will increase, if β_s increases. As in the case of higher innovation efficiency, the wage gap between skilled and unskilled workers widens.

---

[11] See OECD 1988.

Again equation (20) can be used to analyze the effect for the steady-state growth rate. It can be shown that

$$\frac{d\tilde{\gamma}}{d\beta_d}\frac{\beta_d}{\tilde{\gamma}}>0 \Leftrightarrow \frac{\lambda L_u}{hL_s}>0.$$

Thus, the impact of higher skill requirements on economic growth are ambiguous. The growth rate of the economy will increase *if and only if* the supply of human capital services, hL_s, exceeds the supply of technology augmented unskilled labor services, λL_u, in absolute terms.

5   Policy Implications

In the preceding sections, the effects of ITs on innovation activities and the structure of labor demand were examined. The analysis showed that the effects on labor demand are unique and in favor of the skilled while the effects on growth are ambiguous. The higher demand for skilled worker tends to increases the income disparity or will increase the unemployment rate among unskilled workers, if labor markets do not work perfectly. Because of both, income and employment disparities as well as insufficient productivity growth, it should be asked which policies are likely to moderate the adverse effects of IT diffusion if they occur. The most obvious possibility with this respect is to increase the share of skilled workers. As a result the supply of human capital increases and the disparity between the demand and supply of labor diminishes. Thus, the tightness of the labor market for the skilled is reduced. Equation (19) makes clear that the ratio of wages decreases as well:

$$\frac{\partial w_{s/u}}{\partial (L_s/L)}\frac{L_s/L}{w_{s/u}}<0.$$

But, for at least two reasons this result should be taken with care. First, a higher share of skilled workers will reduce the excess demand for the skilled only modestly, because the incentive to innovate (to increase λ/h) will increase simultaneously. Second, and probably more important, a higher share of skilled worker will tend to reduce the positive effects on growth. It can be shown that

$$\frac{\partial \tilde{\gamma}}{\partial (L_s/L)}\frac{L_s/L}{\tilde{\gamma}}<0.$$

Because technological progress augments unskilled labor, the productivity enhancing effect of technological innovations decreases according to the number of unskilled workers. This effect in turn decreases the productivity of the skilled and thus, the growth rate of the economy.

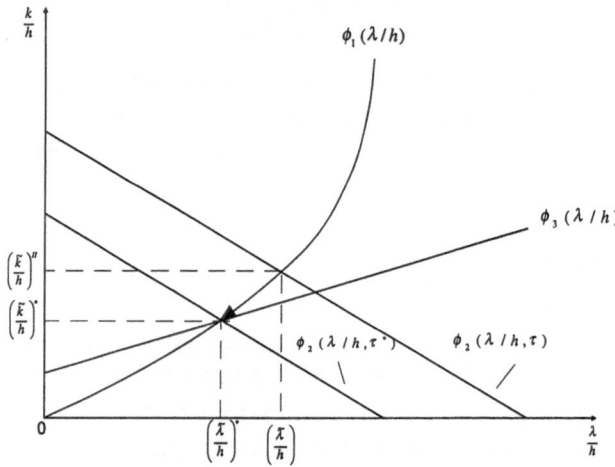

Figure 4: Determination of τ^*.

A second and probably more promising policy option is to adjust the rate of expenditure for education, τ. If τ increases the human capital endowment of the skilled, h, will increase as well. As a result the ratio of wages decreases (see equation (19)). As in the first case it is important to analyze the effects for the growth rate. The reaction of the growth rate is given by

$$\frac{\partial \tilde{\gamma}}{\partial \tau}\frac{\tau}{\tilde{\gamma}}=1-\alpha\frac{s/\tau}{k/h}.$$

It can be proved that this equation implies

$$\frac{\partial \tilde{\gamma}}{\partial \tau}\frac{\tau}{\tilde{\gamma}}>0 \Leftrightarrow \frac{k}{h}>s\frac{\alpha}{1-\alpha}+\frac{\alpha}{1-\alpha}\frac{c}{L_s/m}\frac{\lambda}{h}=:\phi_3(\lambda/h).\tag{22}$$

Equation (22) shows that a higher rate of educational expenditure will increase the aggregate rate of growth only if the ratio of capital intensities is higher than $\phi_3(\lambda/h)$. Thus, in order to maximize the growth rate of the economy the rate of educational expenditure has to be increased until $k/h=\phi_3(\lambda/h)$. Note that both, $\phi_1(\lambda/h)$ and $\phi_3(\lambda/h)$ are independent of τ. Thus, the optimal technological intensity is determined at the intersection of both functions and $\phi_2(\lambda/h,\tau^*)$ implicitly determines the optimal rate of educational expenditure τ^* (see figure 4).

6 Conclusion

The economic development of the industrialized countries over the 80s and 90s is characterized by an increasing diffusion of information and communication related technologies. Technological progress is dominated by ITs in recent years. However, the growth rates of production and income are still modest for most industrialized countries and the commonly expected impulses from IT diffusion cannot be observed up to now. In addition, an increasing demand for skilled relative to unskilled workers can be observed. Empirical studies point out that ITs play a decisive role with this respect.

We developed a theoretical model to analyze the impacts of ITs on innovation dynamics and labor demand. One of the most important findings of the model is that the demand for skilled workers will always increase relative to unskilled labor, if higher innovation activities are insufficiently complemented by human capital accumulation. Because ITs increase innovation activities, the demand for unskilled workers is reduced. The adverse effect for unskilled labor becomes even more important if – as suggested in the empirical literature – ITs alter traditional work flows and increase the skill intensity of jobs. Another important result is that higher IT innovation activities will not necessarily increase productivity and growth. Instead a positive impact on the process of growth can only be expected if human capital is abundant relative to unskilled labor services. Therefore, it is one of the most important implications of the model that the process of innovation and IT diffusion must be complemented by educational policies attempting to increase the qualification of the workforce. The model showed that it is not sufficient to increase the share of skilled workers, but also necessary to increase their human capital endowments. Only in this case the potential increase of productivity and income will be fully realized.

References

Kamien, M. J. & Schwartz, N. L. (1991). *Dynamic Optimization; The Calculus of Variations and Optimal Control in Economics and Management*, 2nd Edition. Amsterdam: North-Holland.

Miller, R. E. (1979). *Dynamic Optimization and Economic Applications*. New York: McGraw-Hill.

OECD (1988). *Employment Outlook, September*. Paris: Organization for Economic Co-Operation and Development.

OECD (1989). *Information Technologies and New Growth Opportunities*. Paris: Organization for Economic Co-Operation and Development.

OECD (1994). *The OECD Jobs Study, Evidence and Explanations; Part I: Labour Market Trends and Underlying Forces of Change*. Paris: Organization for Economic Co-Operation and Development.

OECD (1996). *The OECD Jobs Strategy; Technology, Productivity and Job Creation; Vol. II: Analytical Report*. Paris: Organization for Economic Co-Operation and Development.

Information Technology, Endogenous Human Capital Depreciation and Unemployment

Thomas Gries and Henning Meyer

1 Introduction

Over the past three decades the German economy has been characterized by persistently high and even increasing levels of unemployment. Moreover, aggregate unemployment data suggest that the problem of persistent unemployment has aggravated substantially since the mid-70s. The standardized rate of German unemployment is now at about 9.6 percent while it was less than one percent at the beginning of the 70s. A similar development can be observed for most OECD countries. The unemployment time series plotted in figure 1 supports the view that the unemployment rate has increased over the last 30 years. In recent years, a number of different explanations were developed, most of them attributable to New Keynesian Economics: models of implicit contracts[1], efficiency wage models[2], union models[3], insider-outsider models[4], or hysteresis[5], just to mention a few. Even though the rise and the persistence of (aggregate) unemployment can be explained by these theories, they cannot be used in this paper, because ITs are not considered explicitly as a reason for unemployment.

Further, when explaining the impacts of ITs it is not sufficient to look at aggregate unemployment figures only, individual characteristics such as educational level, seniority, age and gender have to be considered.[6] Table 1 gives a number of disaggregated unemployment measures for the German economy. The data reveal substantial differences in unemployment levels across the labor force. For example, in 1993 unemployment for individuals with less than secondary education was 1.22 times as high as total unemployment while it was well below average unemployment for people with secondary or tertiary education. Furthermore, the unemployment rate for workers aged 55-64 was substantially higher than for prime age workers. Declining age earnings profiles for older workers indicate that this problem is also closely related with relative

---

[1] Azariardis 1975 and Grossman & Hart 1981.
[2] Shapiro & Stiglitz 1984, Foster & Wan 1984, Weiss 1991 and Akerlof 1982, 1984.
[3] McDonald & Solow 1981, Blanchard 1986, Layard & Nickell 1985.
[4] Solow 1985 and Lindbeck & Snower 1988.
[5] Hargreaves-Heap 1980, Blanchard & Summers 1986, 1987, Layard & Nickell 1986, Sneessens & Dréze 1986, Layard, Nickell & Jackman 1991, Cross 1988.
[6] OECD 1996b, c.

human capital endowments. Unemployment in Germany is strongly biased towards the least educated and older section of the workforce and it is likely that both problems are linked. Although in 1993 the total rate of unemployment was roughly the same as in 1983 (see also figure 1) the structural differences of German unemployment clearly increased. Especially the older work force had to face increasing levels of total as well as long-term unemployment.

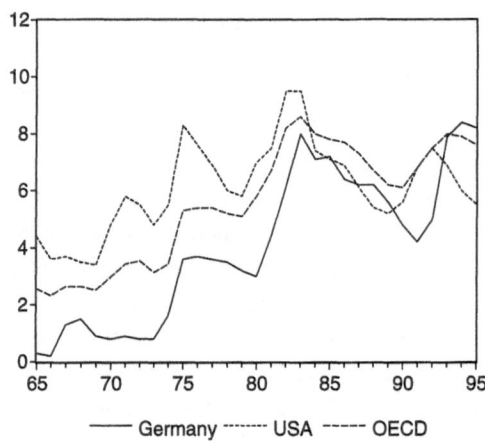

Figure 1: Standardized unemployment rates (percent)
(Source: OECD Employment Outlook, various issues.)

The question of this paper is: How can ITs affect growth and unemployment? First, new ITs permanently change the production process of almost all sectors. "The unique impact of information technologies on the economy is due not only to rapidly falling costs, but also to the fact that almost all sectors and activities can benefit from IT use" (OECD 1994, p. 133). While it is commonly accepted that industrial production changes permanently due to new innovations, other areas of the economy like services or management were considered as less affected. Because new ITs affect these areas as well, this viewpoint has to be changed. ITs do have important growth effects for all sectors of the economy.

Second, ITs change very fast, the product cycles of ITs are very short and the introduction of new ITs goes along with a change in the demand for qualifications. It will be possible to introduce new ITs only, if there are employees who are able to handle them. Therefore, workers have to be educated when entering the labor market, they have to be able to use the newest IT. But, this qualification is not sufficient. Since new ITs are introduced continuously, workers have to adjust their abilities to handle new technologies simultaneously. Workers have to learn their whole working lifetime, they have to permanently adjust their qualifications.

Table 1: Disaggregated unemployment rates (percent), Germany

Year	Total[a]	Education (ratio to total)			Age		Long-term un-employment[c]	
		less than secondary	secondary	tertiary	25-54	55-64	25-54	55-64
1983	7.7	8.5[b]	5.9[b]	5.5[b]	6.3	9.0	2.5	2.0
1993	7.9	9.6	5.9	6.0	6.9	12.6	3.0	5.1

Source: Total unemployment Rate: OECD 1996a; Age, Long-term unemployment: OECD 1995, table 1.8; Education: Statistisches Bundesamt 1982, 1993.
Notes: Data for Education in 1993 refer to West Germany only. The relative unemployment rates for educational groups were calculated as the ratio of the educational group relative to the ratio for all persons who reported their educational status multiplied by the total unemployment rate in column two.
[a] Standardized unemployment rate.
[b] Since unemployment rates for 1983 are not available, the rates are replaced by those for 1982.
[c] Unemployed for one year and above as a percent of the labor force.

To be able to model the effects of ITs, we use a Putty-Clay vintage approach[7] which allows us to identify heterogeneous ITs and qualifications necessary to operate the ITs. At the time of the introduction of a new information technology an optimal factor intensity can be chosen – Putty part of the model. But, afterwards, when a specific IT is in use, adjustments are not possible – Clay part of the model. As a results human capital (the ability to use a certain technology) is linked to that IT and cannot be adjusted to newer ITs.

The human capital model presented in the following section intends to analyze the interaction of ITs and unemployment. In order to analyze impacts of ITs for different parts of the labor force, the model explicitly distinguishes between different labor and human capital groups by using a Putty-Clay vintage approach. Even under neoclassical assumptions of full flexible markets and wages, unemployment may take place. In contrast to the discussion of high wages as the major reason for unemployment in Germany, in the model unemployment is not caused by high wages, but is rather due to the insufficient accumulation of human capital, due to insufficient abilities to adjust to the introduction of new ITs.

---

[7] The Putty-Clay vintage approach goes back to Phelps (1963) and Bliss (1968).

2 A Human Capital Vintage Model

As we are interested in ITs effects for the labor market, we introduce the idea of information technology vintages. IT vintages are the vehicles of productivity growth. Total output at the time t, $Y(t)$, is the sum of all IT output vintages $Y_V(v)$[8]; $(v \leq t)$ which is the output of the IT installed in v.[9] Denoting $m(t)$ as the age of the oldest IT used we arrive at

$$Y(t) = \int_{t-m(t)}^{t} Y_V (v) \, dv \; . \tag{1}$$

Labor supply consists of two types of labor. We assume that workers are heterogeneous with respect to their ability to use new technologies, they are rather flexible or non-flexible. Flexibility implies that workers are able to switch from old to new technologies. In reality there will be a continuous distribution of abilities that leads to a continuous distribution of flexibility. In order to make the point clear we simply distinguish two types of labor, non-flexible and flexible labor: $N^s = N^s_{nf} + N^s_f$. The division into different types of labor is exogenous and fixed.

Non-flexible labor supply N^s_{nf} is divided up into different technology vintages characterized by different human capital endowments. Starting their working life these workers are provided with the most modern human capital. Therefore, they are able to operate the most modern IT at that time. But later, this labor is not able to adjust its human capital stock to new ITs. A certain vintage of non-flexible labor is tied to the respective technology vintage. After leaving education non-flexible labor is not able to use other more modern ITs than those learned originally.

We denote $N^s_{nf,V}(v)$ for labor that entered the labor market at time v. All vintages have the same size and those retiring are replaced by the entering vintages $(N^s_{nf,V}(v) = N^s_{nf}(v))$. Denoting T as the total working lifetime, total labor supply of the non-flexible labor consists of T different vintages. Hence total non-flexible labor supply remains constant:

$$N^s_{nf} (t) = \int_{t-T}^{t} N^s_{nf,V} (v) \, dv = T N^s_{nf,V} \; .$$

---

[8] We index all variables that belong to a certain vintage V. Adding up the outputs of all IT vintages Y_V we receive the total output Y.

[9] It would be more general to denote the vintage output as $Y_V(v,t)$. By letting the vintage output be $Y_V(v)$ we assume that the output of one IT is fixed once it has been installed – Clay part of the model.

The human capital endowment per capita of this labor force – the ability of non-flexible workers to use the most modern IT – is denoted h_V. Human capital H_V of the IT vintage t is given by[10]

$$H_V(t) = h_V(t) \, N^s_{nf,V}.$$

The labor demand derived from all different IT vintages sums up to the total labor demand. A vintage cannot retire partly or be reinstalled after retiring. Therefore we have either $N^d_{nf,V}(v) = N^s_{nf,V}(v) = N_{nf,V}$ or $N^d_{nf,V}(v) = 0$. The total non-flexible labor demand is:

$$N^d_{nf}(t) = \int_{t-m(t)}^{t} N^d_{nf,V}(v)\,dv = m(t)\,N^s_{nf,V}.$$

The full employment condition for non-flexible labor is

$$N^s_{nf}(t) = N^d_{nf}(t) \iff T\,N_{nf,V} = m(t)\,N_{nf,V}.$$

Non-flexible labor is fully employed, if and only if $T = m(t)$.

Flexible labor supply N^s_f consists of different vintages as well, but it is not tied to a certain IT. Flexibility implies that this type of labor can work in every IT vintage. It is possible to reallocate this labor from old to new ITs with no adjustments costs. Assuming that retiring workers are replaced by those entering we have:

$$N^s_f = const.$$

Flexible labor demand is the decisive factor how labor is divided up into different vintages. Because of the flexibility these workers are able to use ITs efficiently. The introduction of new ITs leads to rising productivity of flexible workers. Workers using new ITs are more efficient than workers using older technologies. Thus, ITs are the engine of growth and ITs lead to technological progress. Due to rising productivity the introduction of new ITs augments flexible labor and resulting, flexible labor in efficiency units $\Lambda_V(t)$ is the product of physical units of flexible labor $N^d_{f,V}$ employed in vintage t and the productivity factor $\lambda_V(t)$:

$$\Lambda_V(t) = \lambda_V(t)\,N^d_{f,V}(t).$$

Total flexible labor demand is the sum of all vintages used:

---

[10] To emphasize the character of human capital as a type of capital there is a quasi-rent that describes the return of this factor.

$$N^d{}_f (t) = \int_{t-m(t)}^{t} N^d{}_{f,v} \, (v) \, dv.$$

Flexible labor is employed by the newest $m(t)$ ITs.

The resulting full employment condition for flexible labor is given by

$$N^s{}_f = N^d{}_f (t) \Leftrightarrow N^s{}_f = \int_{t-m(t)}^{t} N^d{}_{f,v} \, (v) \, dv. \tag{2}$$

Flexible labor demand is determined endogenously. As we assume a fully flexible labor market equation (2) will always hold.

When using a *Putty-Clay* IT vintage model we have to distinguish between new and old ITs. Installing a new IT, the inputs can be substituted against each other (Putty part). But afterwards – once an IT is installed – the inputs are fixed (Clay part). Therefore, restrictions caused by the past decisions influence the present and the total output given by equation (1) consists of the sum of different vintage outputs. We assume a Cobb-Douglas production function for Y_V that represents the putty part of the model:

$$Y_V = H_V{}^\alpha \Lambda_V{}^{1-\alpha} . \tag{3}$$

To close the model we have to apply standard techniques that guarantee an efficient allocation.

Efficient factor allocation: Optimal investment in human capital is described by an optimization problem similar to the standard neoclassical theory of investment. Profits from human capital investments are maximized by choosing the optimal factor intensity $\kappa = {H_V}/{N^d{}_{f,v}}$. An efficient human capital investment has to satisfy two conditions simultaneously: *i.* The present value of the human capital investment has to equal the costs of this investment (zero profit condition, the quasi-rent $r(t)$ is determined). *ii.* The human capital intensity has to maximize future profits (profit maximization).

i. Zero profit condition: The profits of an IT installed at time t consists of the revenue given by $Y_V(t)$ minus the costs of flexible labor given by $w(v) \, N^d{}_{f,v}(t)$.[11]$H_V(t)$ must equal the present value of future profits from investment in human capital installed at the time t which works with a specific IT:

---

[11] Once an investment is installed the amount of flexible labor demanded $N^d{}_{f,v}$ is fixed. Therefore it depends on t. But, the wage is not fixed, it grows within the model and depends on v.

$$H_V(t) = \int_t^{t+m(t)} (Y_V(t) - w(v)N^d{}_{f,V}(t)) \exp(-\int_t^v r(z)dz)\, dv. \tag{4}$$

This equation can be regarded as an equation that determines the internal rate of return or quasi-rent $r(t)$. The existence and uniqueness of $r(t)$ will be established in the appendix where the model is solved for the steady-state.

ii. Profit maximization: Writing equation (4) in intensity form, we get:

$$\kappa(t) = \int_t^{t+m(t)} (y_V(t) - w(v)) \exp(-\int_t^v r(z)dz)\, dv.$$

The human capital intensity κ is chosen to maximize the present value of all future profits. Therefore the present value should be stationary with respect to variations in κ alone. The derivative of equation (4) with respect to κ should vanish:

$$\frac{\partial y_V}{\partial \kappa} \int_t^{t+m(t)} \exp(-\int_t^v r(z)dz)\, dv = 1. \tag{5}$$

The conditions (4) and (5) correspond to the ordinary notion of an intertemporal competitive equilibrium.

Since flexible labor is homogeneous and can be employed in any vintage, the wage rate is determined by

$$w(t) = \frac{\partial Y}{\partial N^d{}_f} = \frac{\partial Y}{\partial m} \frac{\partial m}{\partial N^d{}_f} = \frac{\partial Y_V(t-m(t))}{\partial N^d{}_{f,V}(t-m(t))} = y_V(t-m(t)). \tag{6}$$

The wage for flexible labor equals the flexible labor productivity of the oldest technology used.

The quasi-rent $r(t)$ describes the human capital rate of return. $r(t)$ is the internal rate of return of a human-capital investment. The sum of all revenues of a specific human capital vintage is H_V. The earnings of non-flexible labor or the human capital income $(=Y_V(t) - w(v) N_{f,V}(t))$ is discounted by the quasi-rent. Since the wage rate is growing, the efficiency of each vintage decreases, when the technology gets older. Economically human capital depreciates simultaneously. After $m(t)$ periods a human capital vintage retires, because the vintage is fully depreciated and the vintage does not produce any human capital income.[12]

---

[12] Equation (6) is equivalent to $w(t+m(t)) = y_V(t)$. After $m(t)$ vintages have been passed the wage rate equals the revenues of the technology which was installed $m(t)$ vintages before. The revenue is exhausted by the wage costs.

Total expenditure for human capital accumulation H_V is exogenous determined. Denoting τ as the ratio of expenditure for education per GDP we get

$$H_V = \tau\, Y. \tag{7}$$

3   Solution of the Model

We solve the model for the steady-state only. The economy is in steady-state, if human capital H_V grows by the rate $\hat{\lambda} = \dfrac{\dot{\lambda}_V}{\lambda_V}$, and $N^d_{f,V}$ is constant. Using equations (1) to (7) it follows that the retiring age m and the quasi-rent r are constant in steady-state while the remaining variables grow at the rate $\hat{\lambda}$:

$$\hat{\lambda} = \frac{\dot{Y}_V}{Y_V} = \frac{\dot{\kappa}_V}{\kappa_V} = \frac{\dot{Y}}{Y} = \frac{\dot{H}_V}{H_V} = \frac{\dot{w}_V}{w_V} = const.$$

It is shown by Lemma 1 and Lemma 2 in Appendix I that equations (1) to (7) can be reduced to

$$r\frac{\tau}{\hat{\lambda}\alpha}(1-e^{-\hat{\lambda}m}) = (1-e^{-rm}) \tag{*}$$

with the quasi-rent given by $r = \hat{\lambda}(\dfrac{1}{\tau} - \dfrac{1-\alpha}{\alpha})$. Theorem 3 proves that equation (*) has a unique positive solution for m, if $\alpha \neq \tau$. Thus the age of the oldest IT used m^* is implicitly given by this equation. Having a unique positive value for m^* there exist unique values for the other variables of the model in steady-state. These values follow directly from the equations (1) to (7):

Flexible labor:
$$N^d_{f,V} = \frac{N^s_V}{m^*},$$

Factor intensity:
$$\kappa(0) = \lambda_V(0)(\tau\,\frac{1-e^{-\hat{\lambda}m}}{\hat{\lambda}})^{\frac{1}{1-\alpha}},$$

Wage rate:
$$w(0) = \lambda_V(0)(\tau\,\frac{1-e^{-\hat{\lambda}m}}{\hat{\lambda}})^{\frac{\alpha}{1-\alpha}} e^{-\hat{\lambda}m},$$

Total output:
$$Y(0) = \frac{N^s_V}{m^*}\lambda_V(0)\tau^{\frac{\alpha}{1-\alpha}}(\tau\,\frac{1-e^{-\hat{\lambda}m}}{\hat{\lambda}})^{\frac{1}{1-\alpha}},$$

Vintage output:
$$Y_V(0) = \frac{N^s v}{m*} \lambda_V(0)(\tau \frac{1-e^{-\hat{\lambda}m}}{\hat{\lambda}})^{\frac{\alpha}{1-\alpha}}.$$

So far we proved the existence and uniqueness of a steady-state growth path. Even though the transitory dynamics may be interesting as well, we directly turn to economic implications of our findings.[13]

4 Implications

The human capital model developed in the previous section has some interesting implications for the interaction of the introduction of new ITs and employment. Although all markets have neoclassical properties and wages can fully adjust, unemployment occurs: the steady-state value of the discarding age $m*$ of an IT is determined endogenously.[14] $m*$ is dependent on α, $\hat{\lambda}$ and τ only. The last T-$m*$ vintages of non-flexible labor are unemployed, because these workers have depreciated their human capital. These workers were not able to keep up with the skills required to operate new ITs. The non-flexible workers have no chance to be employed again, since they have qualifications which are not demanded any more. The human capital income of a vintage $Y_V(t) - w(v) N_{f,V}(t)$ decreases and finally becomes zero when a vintage retires. Therefore, the condition for leaving the labor market is the zero wage condition. Additional wage adjustment is impossible.

How can we get unemployment even under basically neoclassical assumptions for labor markets with fully flexible wages? In neoclassical standard models production factors can be substituted smoothly for each other. By definition, any adjustment to a new factor intensity is possible. Any restrictions on adjustment are excluded. Accumulated (human) capital can immediately be changed in terms of its intensity without problems and costs. This standard assumption in neoclassical theory is analytically identical with a Putty-Putty approach where the past does not matter. Moreover, it is essential to guarantee the existence of factor market equilibrium. When assuming a Putty-Clay approach the past does matter. Choosing an optimal human capital intensity only the newest ITs are affected. ITs already installed cannot be changed; the history

---

[13] Transitory dynamics and stability analysis is extremely difficult in vintage models. In fact we have not seen any rigorous proof for stability of vintage models so far. Therefore, solving this problem will be left to later work.

[14] This model generates the age of the oldest IT used by adopting an optimal human capital investment approach. Therefore, it does not seem to be reasonable to change the retiring age politically as discussed in Germany. Following this model an (exogenous) increase of the working life time T leads to higher unemployment.

of an investment decision is considered; past IT decisions influence the present. Limitations due to the history of the production process are the reason for unemployment of older worker generated in this model.

These predictions of the model are consistent with the stylized facts of German unemployment presented in the introduction. The empirical data suggest that unemployment rates are indeed higher than average for older workers and people who are characterized by insufficient qualifications. Especially the older workforce – if non-flexible – is characterized by insufficient human capital endowments. Their education is based on outdated IT vintages.[15]

It is interesting to ask, if the model also holds for a wider range of countries. Unfortunately, the empirical picture of unemployment for older workers is quite diffuse. While for a number of countries unemployment rates for older workers are indeed substantially higher than for prime age workers[16], for most countries both rates do not differ substantially. Therefore, we are not yet sure, if unemployment for older workers is likely to be a country-specific phenomenon. Germany and the United States may be good examples for this heterogeneous empirical picture (see figure 2). As stated above the unemployment rate of older workers is substantially higher than the rate for prime age workers in Germany. In the United States, however, the opposite is true. But, even for the United States unemployment of older workers has increased during the past 20 years. Thus, unemployment of older workers is a growing problem in the US as well.

Moreover, older workers generally react more sensibly on incentives for leaving the workforce than prime age workers do. The decision for early retirement instead of being unemployed substantially relieves the labor supply of older workers; it is, however not reflected in unemployment statistics. In the United States, as well as in Germany, participation rates for older workers have continuously declined relative to average participation over the last decades. This development may very well indicate workers' reaction to deteriorated job opportunities and partly reflect involuntary unemployment. Modified unemployment series capturing this effect show that the number of older workers leaving the labor force is very high in Germany and in the United States.[17] Therefore, the mechanisms of the model – human capital depreciates endogenously due to the permanent introduction of new ITs – seems relevant for both countries.

---

[15] In IWD (1997, p. 6), it is elaborated that especially qualified workers are effected by unemployment, if they get older. This result shows that the terms non-flexible and unqualified have to be distinguished.

[16] See e.g. OECD 1995, Table 1.8.

[17] See Appendix II.

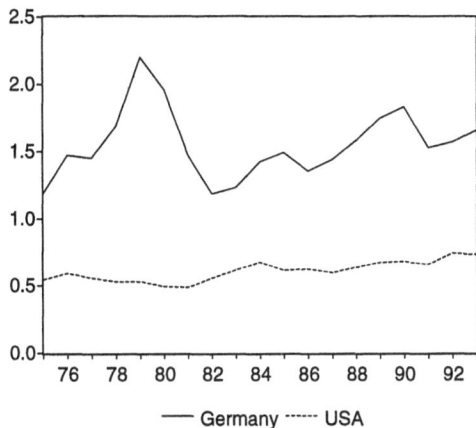

*Figure 2:   Unemployment rates for men, aged 55-64 relative to total unem-
            ployment, Germany and United States, 1975-93*
(Source: OECD Labor Force Statistics, own calculations)

Having a situation with high unemployment rates of older workers, we want to
ask how we can avoid this situation. The model suggest that we have[18]

$$\frac{\partial m^*}{\partial \tau} > 0.$$

Thus, the higher the stock of human capital, the slower human capital depreciates endogenously. Unemployment can be reduced, if more resources are spent for
education. This result shows that it is not sufficient to introduce permanently new
ITs. If new ITs are introduced, workers have to be educated using this new ITs. If
this (first) education, the endowment with human capital is not sufficient, especially
older workers will not be able to keep up with the continuous introduction of new
ITs and get unemployed.

Considering the heterogeneous abilities of workers that lead to flexibility, unemployment can be reduced by education in a second way: Flexible workers are able
to learn new ITs and can switch from old to new ITs. Flexibility implies the ability to
use any IT. Therefore, flexible workers will never get unemployed. On the other hand,
non-flexible workers are able to use the most modern IT only when entering the labor
market. These workers continue using the same IT for their working lifetime till this

---

[18] See Conjecture 4.

specific technology retires. After m^* vintages non-flexible workers get unemployed. The model suggests[19]

$$\frac{\partial m^*}{\partial N^s{}_f} = \frac{\partial m^*}{\partial N^s{}_{nf}} = 0.$$

The retiring age does not depend on the structure of labor supply. Thus, unemployment can be reduced, if workers switch from non-flexible to flexible. Since flexible workers are characterized by the ability to learn new ITs without any costs, the first education should try to build up these abilities. Participating in education workers should learn to adopt new technologies. If education leads to flexibility, workers will get flexible, the number of non-flexible workers will reduce and unemployment will decrease. To summarize, rising the expenditure for education reduces the unemployment period of non-flexible workers $T-m^*$, and improving education by supporting "flexible learning" might reduce unemployment of older workers, because less workers will be non-flexible.

Appendix I

Lemma 1 *If the equations (4), (5) and (6) hold, it follows that the rate of return r will be constant in the steady-state. It is*

$$r(t) = r = \frac{y_V(0) - w(0) + \hat{\lambda}\kappa(0) - \hat{\lambda}y_V(0)(\frac{\partial y_V}{\partial \kappa})^{-1}}{\kappa(0)}.$$

Proof: Defining $g(\kappa, t) := \kappa(t) - \int_t^{t+m(t)} (y_V(t) - w(v)) \exp(-\int_t^v r(z)dz)\, dv$ equation (4) can be written as $g(\kappa, t) = 0$ and equation (5) as $\frac{\partial g}{\partial \kappa} = 0$. Since equation (4) holds identically in t, g is constant as a function of t. Thus the first derivative of g with respect to t is zero. Using again the equations (4) to (5) this reduces to:

$$\frac{\partial g}{\partial t} = 0 \Leftrightarrow r(t) = r = \frac{y_V(t) - w(t) + \kappa'(t) - \frac{\partial y_V}{\partial t}(\frac{\partial y_V}{\partial \kappa})^{-1}}{\kappa(0)}.$$

To show that $r(t)$ is constant we have to show that the nominator and the denominator grow by the same exponential rate. Obviously this holds for the steady-state. Using

---

[19] This result follows by differentiating equation (*).

$\kappa'(t) = \hat{\lambda} \; \kappa$ and $\dfrac{\partial y_V}{\partial t} = \hat{\lambda} \; y_V(t)$, the formula for r follows.

Lemma 2 *In the steady-state the equations (1) to (7) can be reduced to one equation which only depends on m, the age of the oldest technology used. The resulting implicit equation for m is*

$$r\frac{\tau}{\hat{\lambda}\alpha}(1-e^{-\hat{\lambda}m}) = (1-e^{-rm}),\qquad (*)$$

with $r = \hat{\lambda}(\dfrac{1}{\tau} - \dfrac{1-\alpha}{\alpha})$.

Proof: In the steady-state equations (1) and (7) can be reduced to

$$\frac{\kappa}{y_V} = \tau\frac{1-e^{-\hat{\lambda}m}}{\hat{\lambda}}.\qquad (7')$$

Using Lemma 1 and the Cobb-Douglas technology we get

$$r = \frac{y_V}{\kappa}(1-e^{-\hat{\lambda}m}) + \hat{\lambda}(1-\frac{1}{\alpha}).$$

Substituting equation (7') the formula for r follows. In steady-state equation (5) reduces to

$$\frac{\kappa}{y_V} = \alpha\frac{1-e^{-rm}}{r}.\qquad (5')$$

Equating (5') and (7') the implicit equation for the retiring age follows.

Theorem 3 *If* $\alpha \neq \tau$, *there exists a unique, positive m in the steady-state.*
Proof: Using Lemma 2 it follows that in the steady-state equation (*) holds. It has to be shown that this equation holds for one and only one positive m. Let $g_1(m)$ be the left hand side and $g_2(m)$ the right hand side of equation (*). It is sufficient to show that there is a unique point of intersection of these functions. The functions have the following properties:

$$\lim_{m\to\infty} g_1(m) = r\frac{\tau}{\hat{\lambda}\alpha}, \quad \lim_{m\to 0} g'_1(m) = r\frac{\tau}{\alpha}, \quad \lim_{m\to\infty} g'_1(m) = 0, \quad g''_1(m) < 0,$$

$$\lim_{m\to\infty} g_2(m) = 1, \quad \lim_{m\to 0} g'_2(m) = r, \quad \lim_{m\to\infty} g'_2(m) = 0, \quad g''_2(m) < 0.$$

There are two cases to consider:

Case I: $\tau < \alpha$: In this case we get $r\dfrac{\tau}{\hat{\lambda}\alpha} > 1$. Therefore it is

$\lim_{m\to\infty} g_1(m) > \lim_{m\to\infty} g_2(m)$ and $\lim_{m\to 0} g'_1(m) < \lim_{m\to 0} g'_2(m)$.

These properties guarantee the existence with the intermediate value theorem. The concavity of g_1 and g_2 guarantee the uniqueness of an intersection of the functions.

Case II: $\tau > \alpha$: In this case we get $r\dfrac{\tau}{\lambda\alpha} < 1$ and

$\lim_{m\to\infty} g_1(m) < \lim_{m\to\infty} g_2(m)$ and $\lim_{m\to 0} g'_1(m) > \lim_{m\to 0} g'_2(m)$.

The existence of an intersection follows similarly as in Case I. The concavity of g_1 and g_2 guarantee the uniqueness again. The proof of the theorem is now complete.

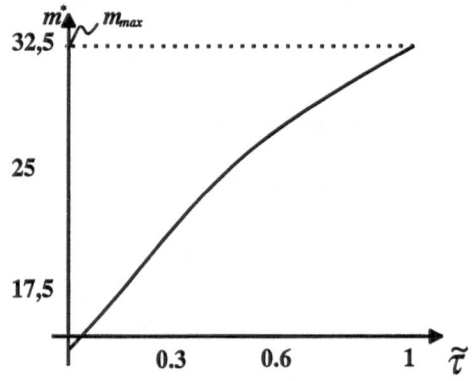

Figure 3: *The relation between m^* and $\tilde{\tau}$ is plotted given $\alpha=0.51$ and $\hat{\lambda} = 0.05$.*

Conjecture 4 *There is a positive relation between the retiring age m^* and τ in steady-state, it is* $\dfrac{\partial m^*}{\partial \tau} > 0$.

Instead of proving the Conjecture we use simulations to analyze the relation between $m^*(\tau)$ for a wide range of parameters for $\alpha, \hat{\lambda}$. For all feasible parameters we get that m^* increases, if τ increases. Parameters are feasible, if the quasi-rent is positive. The *level* of m^* is depending on the parameters, of course. For the simulation we use the software mathematica using a Newton algorithm to calculate the root of equation (*). The representative result is plotted for given values of α and $\hat{\lambda}$ in figure 3.

Appendix II

As argued in section 4 unemployment statistics are likely to underestimate demand deficits for older workers because they do not capture participation effects. In order to see how this effect may influence unemployment, the participation rate of a base year was extrapolated with the rate of change of average participation. The difference between this modified and the original participation rate partly reflects hidden unemployment and was added up to the reported unemployment share. This value was used to calculate a modified unemployment rate. For example, the German participation rate of older workers was 57.7 percent in 1990 while the modified participation rate was calculated at 64.6 percent. Reported unemployment was 9.9 percent of the labor force and 5.7 percent of the total population respectively. Therefore, 15.6 percent of the population or 19.5 percent of the (modified) labor force were calculated as involuntarily unemployed.

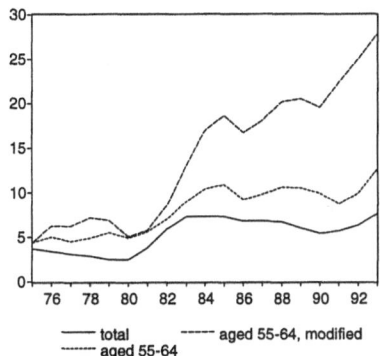 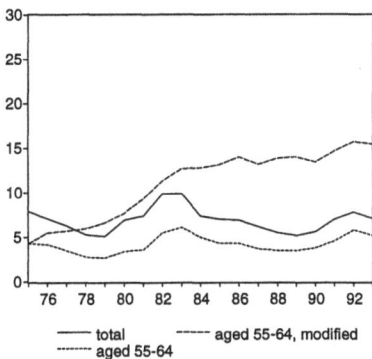

Figure 4.a: Unemployment rates for   *Figure 4.b: Unemployment rates for*
men, Germany 1975-93   *men, United States 1975-93*

(Source: OECD Labor Force Statistics, own calculations)

As can be seen from figure 4, the unemployment series constructed that way differ sharply from the original unemployment series. The series therefore suggest that official statistics do not report deteriorating job opportunities for older workers, because the labor market for older workers is strongly affected by declining participation rates.

References

Akerlof, G.A. (1982). Labor Contracts as Partial Gift Exchange. *Quarterly Journal of Economics*, 97, pp. 543-69.

Akerlof, G.A. (1984). Gift Exchange and Efficiency Wage Theory: Four Views. *American Economic Review*, 74, pp. 79-83.

Azariardis, C. (1975). Implicit Contracts and Underemployment Equilibria. *Journal of Political Economy*, 83, pp. 1183-202.

Blanchard, O. J. (1986). The Wage Price Spiral, *Quarterly Journal of Economics*, 101, pp. 543-65.

46   Gries, Meyer

Blanchard, O. J. & Summers, L. H. (1986). Hysteresis and the European Unemployment Problem. In: S. Fischer (Ed.), *NBER Macroeconomics Annual 1986*. Cambridge, Massachusetts: MIT Press, pp. 15-77.

Blanchard, O. J. & Summers, L. H. (1987), Hysteresis in Unemployment. *European Economic Review*, 31, 288-95.

Bliss, C. (1968). On Putty-Clay. *Review of American Studies*, 35, 105-32.

Cross, R. (Ed.). (1988). *Unemployment, Hysteresis and the Natural Rate Hypothesis*, Oxford: Basil Blackwell.

Foster, J. & Wan, H. (1984). Involuntary Unemployment as a Principal Agent Equilibrium. *American Economic Review*, 82, 287-98.

Grossman, S. & Hart, O. (1981). Implicit Contracts, Moral Hazard, and Unemployment. *American Economic Review*, 71, 301-7.

Hargreaves-Heap, S. P. (1980). Choosing the Wrong Natural Rate: Accelerating Inflation or Decelerating Employment and Growth. *Economic Journal*, 90, 611-20.

IWD (1997). *Informationsdienst des Instituts der deutschen Wirtschaft*, 45.

Layard, R. & Nickell, S. (1985), *Unemployment, Real Wages and Aggregate Demand in Europe, Japan and the US*. Centre for Labor Economics, London School of Economics Discussion Paper No. 214.

Layard, R. & Nickell, S. (1986). Unemployment in Britain. *Economica*, 53, Supplement, pp. 121-69.

Layard, R., Nickell, S. & Jackman, R. (1991). *Unemployment: Macroeconomic Performance and the Labor Market*. Oxford: Oxford University Press.

Lindbeck, A. & Snower, D. J. (1988). *The Insider-Outsider Theory of Unemployment*. Cambridge, Massachusetts: MIT Press.

McDonald, I. M. & Solow, R. M. (1981). Wage Bargaining and Employment. *American Economic Review*, 71, pp. 896-908.

OECD (1994). *The OECD Jobs Study: Evidence and Explanations, Part I: Labor Market Trends and Underlying Forces of Change*. Paris: Organization for Economic Co-Operation and Development.

OECD (1995). *Employment Outlook*. Paris: Organization for Economic Co-Operation and Development.

OECD (1996a). *Employment Outlook*. Paris: Organization for Economic Co-Operation and Development.

OECD (1996b). *OECD Jobs Strategy: Technology, Productivity and Job Creation, Vol. 1 Highlights*. Paris: Organization for Economic Co-Operation and Development.

OECD (1996c). *OECD Jobs Strategy: Technology, Productivity and Job Creation, Vol. 2 Analytical Report*. Paris: Organization for Economic Co-Operation and Development.

Phelps, E. (1963). Substitution, Fixed Proportions, Growth and Distribution. *International Economic Review*, 4, pp. 265-88.

Shapiro, C. & Stiglitz, J. E. (1984). Equilibrium Unemployment as a Worker Discipline Device. *American Economic Review*, 74, pp. 433-44.

Sneessens, H. & Dréze, J. (1986). A Discussion of Belgian Unemployment Combining Traditional Concepts and Disequilibrium Econometrics. *Economica*, 53, Supplement, pp. 89-119.

Solow, R. (1985). Insiders and Outsiders in Wage Determination. *Scandinavian Journal of Economics*, 87, pp. 411-28.

Statistisches Bundesamt (1983), *Bevölkerung und Erwerbstätigkeit, Fachserie 1, Reihe 4.1.2: Beruf, Ausbildung und Arbeitsbedingungen der Erwerbstätigen (Ergebnisse des Mikrozensus)*. Stuttgart: Metzler Poeschel.

Statistisches Bundesamt (1993). *Bevölkerung und Erwerbstätigkeit, Fachserie 1, Reihe 4.1.2: Beruf, Ausbildung und Arbeitsbedingungen der Erwerbstätigen (Ergebnisse des Mikrozensus)*. Stuttgart: Metzler Poeschel.

Weiss, A. (1991). *Efficiency Wages: Models of Unemployment, Layoffs, and Wage Dispersion*. Oxford: Carledon Press.

Spatial and Organizational Patterns of the Transfer of New Economic Knowledge: A Survey of the Literature and Some Preliminary Results from a Case Study[1]

Peter Liepmann

1 Introduction

Competition has increased to a great extent in markets for national and international goods and services: by the introduction and enlargement of the Common Market; by the opening of Central- and East-European countries; and by the general globalization of the markets for goods, services, and resources. The internationalization of competition is requiring a higher degree of adaptability of industries, sectors, and regions: to technological and organizational progress with ever shorter product life-cycles; to cost-cutting and higher productivity by such means as "lean production", "team production", "in- and/or outsourcing"; to the functional division of labor across space; and to an increase of non-price competition, especially in the prevailing oligopolistic markets in which all kinds of informational first-mover advantages are relevant (Demsetz 1982; Marris & Mueller 1980; Koutsoyiannis 1982). In contestable markets these informational leads will only exist temporarily. In markets with barriers to entry they may permit long-term monopolistic behavior and market dominance (Martin 1993; see also Gerosky 1987).

Against this background, the survival of firms in oligopolistic markets (their permanency) will depend on their constant alertness to gain new economic knowledge and to transform it – in the sense of Schumpeter – into a flow of innovations. This may be a difficult task, when new economic knowledge is created within the firm. The same task is even more complex though, when it is created outside the firm, be it in the form of private or public new economic knowledge. That is why transfer institutions as intermediaries between invention and innovation have specific functions in the diffusion of that knowledge.

---

[1] The research underlying this paper has been assisted by grants from the Committee for Research and Academic Education of the University of Paderborn and from the Ministry for Science and Research of the Federal State of North-Rhine Westphalia. The author wishes to thank them both. The empirical field work is being carried out by Jochen Ullrich. The author appreciates valuable comments on earlier drafts of this paper by the participants of the Research Seminar of the Department of Economics and Business Administration of the University of Paderborn. The author also wishes to thank for valuable help received from G. Eberlein, B. M. Gilroy, and W. Rothfritz.

Feldman (1994, p. 2) emphasizes along the lines of Dosi (1980) and Nelson (1988) the distinction between *private* and *public knowledge*: "Private knowledge comes primarily from within firms but it is also found in industry associations, scientific and professional societies, and networks of related firms and support services. Public knowledge is obtained from institutions that support R&D in scientific and technical fields. These are primarily universities but may also include various government science and technology programs. In this view, innovation embodies a broader landscape of social and economic institutions, and relationships than previously conceived." The "broader landscape" mentioned is to be interpreted in a spatial context insofar as new economic knowledge is created external to firms – in specific locations: predominantly in agglomerations – and is diffused across space under restrictions and with lags – if at all (Feldman 1994, pp. 23-24).

Another distinction to be considered is that between *specialized* (person- or organization-specific) and *standardized information*, each of which may either be public or private in the above sense. Specialized new economic knowledge may only be mobile across space after restrictions of privacy are overcome, i. e., after persons or organizations are ready to disclose it (Pred 1977, pp. 19ff.). This type of knowledge may refer to: "...non-routine production activities associated with innovation such as research and development, experimental and prototype manufacturing, and small volume production (which) are increasingly spatially concentrated" (ibid., p. 13). Standardized economic knowledge is developed along with the routinization of production processes. It can be formulated and communicated ("book of blueprints"; Teece 1989, 1992). Thus it makes firms – including high-tech firms – footloose, so that they can choose least-cost locations. Especially multi-plant firms make use of relocating production units. The embodied economic knowledge then becomes spatially mobile, although in a selective way, i. e. restricted to embodied standardized economic knowledge.

Target regions of relocated production units are the peripheries of agglomerations, peripheral regions which are further away (Gerlach & Liepmann 1972), and low-cost countries (Liepmann 1992, pp. 7ff.). Headquarter functions are located in agglomerations that exhibit a developed "*technological infrastructure*" (Feldman 1994, chap. 4): that is research and development departments of universities and firms; concentrations of firms of the same and of related industries (for spill-over effects of new economic knowledge); networks of all kinds of producer services as well as suppliers of capital equipment and intermediate goods. A technological infrastructure offers various knowledge inputs to cope with the uncertainties of innovation processes that are to realize informational first-mover advantages.

In the literature on regional economics a developed technological infrastructure is mostly seen as part of the external and internal economies resulting from an agglomeration of economic activities and contributing to *static efficiency*. But as Feldman (1994, p. 2) correctly points out, it is, moreover, to be seen as contributing to *dynamic efficiency*: "The technological infrastructure promotes knowledge transfer, facilitates problem-solving, and reduces the risks and cost of innovation. Once in place, the technological infrastructure creates a capacity for innovation. Due to the cumulative and self-enforcing nature of knowledge, this capacity or core competence becomes specialized to particular technologies and industrial sectors... As a result of these place-specific concentrations of knowledge, technological advance and competitiveness is enhanced. It is in this way that geography plays an essential role in innovation, and the growth of advanced, capitalist societies". Due to *communication costs* (spatial restrictions of mobility) and to the *selectivity of the transfer of economic knowledge* neither all firms nor all regions of an economy will share the benefits of dynamic efficiency and innovativeness or "progressiveness" (Martin 1988, p 7).

In particular, small and medium-sized firms/enterprises (SMEs) in less-developed regions – in Germany as well as in other countries – face competitive disadvantages in adaptability, dynamic efficiency and innovativeness (Deutscher Bundestag 1997, p. 10; Deutscher Bundestag 1993, p. 6.). These regions are threatened by the shutting-down or spatial relocation of production units or even by general deindustrialization, with complementary effects on regional services, employment, value-added, and tax income (Liepmann & Ullrich 1997; Cohen & Zysman 1987).

As a consequence endogenous regional growth potential is to be strengthened in the newer technology- and innovation-oriented policy for less-developed regions in Germany: by overcoming bottlenecks, especially those pertaining to the human capital of employees, to the stock and flow of new economic knowledge, and to the specialization and competence of management (Köthenbürger & Ullrich 1994). *Technology transfer* is an important element of this type of regional policy. It needs informal interpersonal contacts, networks of co-operating firms, and specialized *transfer institutes,* predominantly for SMEs.

Little is as yet known about the effectiveness of institutes for the transfer of new economic knowledge and technology, which are of major interest in this paper. Although empirical research on inventions and innovations is using a great variety of indicators and methods, these are not applied to transfer institutes in a systematic way. These institutes, nevertheless, are in need of research on their effectiveness to justify their activities and their costs as well as new grants. A long-term collaboration has developed between the Institute for the Transfer of New Economic Knowledge and Technology.in the County of Soest (ITWS) and the author to review the institute's activities. This institute has public and private partners in the board of directors and the board of advisors, i. e. representatives of the University of Paderborn, the County of Soest, of thirteen local communities, and of several firms located in the region.

Transfer institutes which operate in less-developed regions have to overcome spatial restrictions of communication costs mentioned before in order to diffuse new economic knowledge, and to open up the potential for dynamic efficiency of agglomerations for their customers. The term agglomeration in this context stands for all classes of "urban districts" (Vanhove & Klaassen 1987, pp. 188f.) with a competitive technological infrastructure, the term less-developed regions for those with at least a minimum level of industrialization. Any efforts to industrialize a rural region "de novo" ("Nachindustrialisierung"; Tacke 1992, p. 143) would be fruitless, as research on target and instrument efficiency of regional policy has shown (Köthenbürger & Ullrich 1994). A re-industrialization of traditional industrialized regions with structural crises poses different problems that will not be dealt with in this paper. The preliminary empirical results presented below refer to the county of Soest and the somewhat larger "Hellwegregion".

2 Linear, Complementary, and Feed-back Model of the Innovation process

Points of departure for the activities of transfer institutes – such as the ITWS in Soest – can be described more precisely by drawing on models of the innovation process (Feldman 1994; Teece 1989; Dosi 1988).

In the traditional *linear model* the innovation process is – somewhat simplifying matters – structured in the following consecutive stages: scientific-technological discovery (invention); applied research to create a new product or find a more efficient production process; and, finally, introduction of the new product and/or utilization of the productivity gains (product and process innovation). The essential impulse for innovations – technological progress in the sense of Schumpeter – according to this model comes from the discovery stage. New ideas and new economic knowledge are generated and introduced here. New ideas will only be developed further in the following stages of the innovation process to find firm-specific applications and marketable goods or services.

Dosi (1988) analyses the search process for innovations of all kinds in a more realistic way (pp. 1122ff.). To typify his approach one could speak of a *complementary model*. In it new economic knowledge is, on the one hand, created through formalized basic research in laboratories as well as in research and development departments. Complementary to basic research new economic knowledge, on the other hand, is created when goods are differentiated or production processes made more efficient through experience and cumulative volume economies. Although technological progress may be different between firms, industries and sectors, there are four general patterns (Dosi 1988, p. 1125): "...(a) economically expensive and formalized processes of search...; (b) informal processes of diffusion of information and of technological capabilities (e.g., via publications, technical associations, watch-and-learn processes, personal transfers); (c) those particular forms of externalities, internalized within each firm, associated with learning by doing and learning by using; and (d) the adoption of innovation developed by other industries and embodied in capital equipment and intermediate inputs."

Technological progress in the complementary model, thus, results from a complex process of problem solving, in which the problem is not well defined in the beginning. Existing and available information cannot be applied without additional firm-specific adaptations. Neither is there a general algorithm for problem solving which can be deducted from the stock of available information. Problem solving, therefore, presupposes a *"knowledge base"*: a mixture of basic knowledge, of new, firm-specific knowledge and of firm-specific experience knowledge (Dosi 1988, p. 1126).

In the context of transfer institutes it is important to know to what extent a particular knowledge base is combining knowledge that is freely and universally available with knowledge that is embodied in persons or organizations. Dosi (1988, p. 1126) speaks – in addition to the above mentioned distinction between private and public knowledge – of: "...publicness and universality versus tacitness and specificity of... knowledge bases". The latter is neither well defined nor codified; it is differing from one person to the other, although several persons may build it up collectively by experience in a particular organization (firm). In each innovative firm there is a particular balance between public and tacit knowledge, implying a specific *"technological paradigm"* which is guiding innovative efforts. Dosi (ibid.) defines this as follows: "A technological paradigm is both an *exemplar* – an artifact that is to be developed and improved... with its particular characteristics – and a *set of heuristics* (e.g., Where do we go from here? Where should we search? What sort of knowledge should we draw on?)" (p 1127).

Whereas public knowledge tends to be diffused more easily (scientific reputation as an incentive), private and tacit knowledge is ultimately to be marketed so that there is an incentive to avoid unfeasible spill-over effects. Transfer institutes have to take this into account and also the fact that every technological paradigm entails a specific combination of intra-firm and 3 external determinants of innovations.

The *feed-back model* of the innovation process formulated by Feldman (1994, p. 16f.) accentuates interdependence and dynamic learning between and in all stages of the process: discovery, applied research and development, market introduction. The impulse for innovations may come from every stage. Firms use all kinds of internal and external sources of new economic knowledge. The basic determinants have already been analyzed by Coase (1938), further contributions to clarify them stem from Williamson (1995, 1985) and Feldman (1994).

Feldman (1994, p. 16f.) identifies four knowledge inputs which he subsumes – as mentioned in the introduction of this paper – under the term technological infrastructure: (a) basic research of universities which opens up various options for private research and development of firms; (b) applied research and development of firms; (c) tacit knowledge of persons and organizations that is accumulating as a result of work experience and informal learning and is diffusing to some extent through spill-over effects among firms of the same industry or of related industries; (d) finally knowledge that is provided by diverse and often highly specialized producer services. Knowledge embodied in capital equipment and intermediate goods should be added as another relevant input.

All these knowledge inputs (re-)distribute uncertainties of the innovation process and may even reduce them for a group of related institutions and firms as a whole. As an implication, these inputs also reduce costs of the innovation process and/or increase its effectiveness. Besides, a synchronization of its stages is necessary when product life-cycles are becoming shorter and shorter in worldwide oligopolistic competition. Under these conditions the early identification of new options for innovation is essential for the survival of firms so that research and development specialists, internal and external to firms, have to collaborate with marketing, production, and finance specialists (Teece 1989, pp. 35-42; Freeman 1989).

Spatial concentration of a respective technological infrastructure in agglomerations or urban districts are stimulating the innovation process. Regional specialization of the generated knowledge inputs occurs. Their utilization according to any firm-specific technological paradigm requires permanent trial and error, questioning, evaluation, and face-to-face contacts. As a best-case scenario, regional innovation networks or complexes may develop (Stöhr 1985) with a high and differentiated level of the supply of knowledge inputs. These do not only add to each other, but also interact with positive feed-backs. To take advantage of any of the resulting large volume economies, SMEs in particular should collaborate with competitors and suppliers as well as with distributors and customers. As Gomes-Casseres (1996, p. 214) somewhat provocatively puts it: "...polygamy is often better than monogamy", meaning by polygamy all kinds of alliances of firms, which change the organizational level of competition, but do not necessarily reduce its intensity.

The above survey of models of the innovation process leads to the identification of some points of departure for the activities of transfer institutes like the ITWS in Soest.

On the one hand, public knowledge and information about scientific and technological discoveries are transferable insofar as there are markets such as those for patents, licenses, and trade marks or freely available publication media, e.g. journals. On the other hand, private and tacit knowledge and information about results of applied research and development will not be disclosed without precautions, if innovation rents are expected. The reasons for market failure in the case of private information are well known. There are, however, incentives for owners of private knowledge to engage in long-term contracts, or joint ventures, or alliances with interested firms, or to insist on financial commitments of collaborating competitors, suppliers, distributors, and customers (Williamson 1985). By these organizational means unfeasible spill-over effects and costs of parallel research and development can be avoided as well as prospects of marketability improved (Levin et al. 1987, pp. 805ff.).

These organizational means may cause a loss of control for the individual firm, but they also lead to gains in flexibility, dynamic efficiency and competitiveness for the collaborating group as a whole. Although there is some danger of anti-competitive behavior in the case of big firms, this need not be so, when SMEs are concerned. They, in particular, are in need of collaboration, especially in oligopolistic markets, in unstable and reactive or even turbulent environments. As Emery and Trist (1965/69) well point out for turbulent environments, some kind of matrix-organization to control strategic and environmental uncertainties enhance the chances of survival.

Creditor banks and consultants probably are in a better position than transfer institutes to assist in the organization of collaborations and alliances. If transfer institutes have been able to built up long-term trust relations with the firms concerned, they may – even in the case of private and tacit knowledge – be at least in a position to act as intermediaries between inventions and innovations. Transfer institutes are probably more successful in establishing contacts with experts, consultants, services etc., which assist firm specific research and development especially in the case of SMEs. A close compliance with property rights is essential to avoid unfeasible spill-over effects, when firm specific, private and tacit knowledge is to be improved or even a new technological paradigm introduced. More general transfer activities in this context may be to organize seminars or other kinds of qualification programs to enhance the human capital of employees or managers.

Summing up, one main restriction for transfer activities into less-developed regions is the fact that the relevant knowledge is integral to technological infrastructures, which are concentrated in agglomerations and urban districts. Another main restriction is the fact that the relevant knowledge to a great extent is private and tacit, that in this case spot markets fail, and that some kind of institutionalized collaboration to internalize unfeasible spill-over effects and/or long-term trust-relations are preconditions for any transfer.

3 Spatial Diffusion of New Economic Knowledge: A Survey of Empirical Studies

Traditional growth theory assumes an unrestricted diffusion of new economic knowledge within the boundaries of an economy. Agglomeration economies (external effects), communication costs and selectivity of information flows, which explain much of the spatial concentration of firms of one or more industries in urban districts (and no-where else), are ignored. Although Krugman (1991, pp. 1-11 and p. 53f.) therefore emphasizes the importance of regional studies, he at the same time suggests to do empirical research on external effects only as far as these are visible and measurable. In his view, though, spatial flows of new economic knowledge are "...invisible; they leave no paper trail by which they may be measured and tracked, and there is nothing to prevent the theorist from assuming anything about them that she likes" (ibid.). This view is unjustified to the extent that there exists any kind of a relationship between knowledge inputs and indicators for innovations and that this relationship shows up in regression analyses.

First of all Jaffe (1989) cannot trace explicitly the diffusion flows of private, specific and tacit knowledge of persons or organizations (the "transport mechanism (of) informal conversations"; ibid., p 957). Nevertheless, he is able to demonstrate at the level of the Federal States of the US: (a) that there is a direct relationship between research activities of universities and the frequency of patents held by firms, which are used as indicators for new economic knowledge; (b) that university research is stimulating firm research and that, therefore, also exists an indirect relationship between the two variables; (c) that these findings of direct and indirect spill-over effects especially refer to the pharmaceutical, the chemical, and the electric industries.

In a follow-up study Jaffe, Trajtenberg and Henderson (1993), also use patent citations as an indicator of innovations. In this way they include lagged spill-over effects in the form of specific patent applications. The authors confirm: a spatial concentration of such effects; they increase at the beginning and later on decline; they link different "technological neighborhoods" of the original patent and its specific applications; there is no significant difference in the case of original patents developed in universities or in firms. To meet the criticism of patents or patent citations as indicators of innovations (e.g. by Cohen & Levin 1989, pp. 1062), Acs, Audretsch and Feldman (1992) use data of all published innovations (in the sense that they have in fact been introduced in the market). They in general confirm Jaffe's (1989) results and especially find a strong relationship between university research and electronic innovations.

Finally, Audretsch and Feldman (1996) look at the relationship between spatial concentrations of industrial firms and urban districts. They rank industries according to their research and development intensity (relation of R&D expenses and sales). Innovative firms are supposed to have a high percentage of qualified employees. Transport cost and capital intensity should positively influence the spatial concentration of firms. The authors then test differences in the spatial concentration of industries. They confirm – even after controlling for the effect of the pre-existing concentration of industrial firms – the following hypothesis: "The propensity for innovative activity to cluster will tend to be higher in industries where new economic knowledge plays a more important role. Presumably, it is in such industries where new economic knowledge which generates innovative activity is transmitted tacitly through what has been described as knowledge spillovers. Therefore, innovative activity is more likely to occur within close geographic proximity to the source of that knowledge, be it a research laboratory, the research and development of a corporation, or exposure to the knowledge embodied in a skilled worker" (ibid., p. 638). Consequently those industries tend to cluster geographically that are under competitive stress to innovate.

Summing up, the "broader landscape" to be considered in studying innovative activities is confirmed by the above findings. There are spill-over effects from public and private institutions performing basic research. A favorable precondition for innovations is the socio-economic environment of agglomerations and urban districts. The determinants of innovations transcend the organizational boundaries of single firms, the capabilities of single researchers, or the risk preference of single pioneer firms (Feldman, Florida 1994, p. 226f.). This is on one hand opening up scope for inter-firm collaboration and for potential activities of transfer institutes, but is on the other hand also constraining them, because the relevant information often is private, tacit and specialized as well as spatially concentrated. The higher the competitive stress (rivalry) in industries to innovate, the more concentrated they will locate in space, at least with their headquarter functions.

4 External and Internal Sources of New Economic Knowledge: Determinants and Survey of Empirical Results

Firms with their respective technological paradigms permanently have to make decisions: (a) whether they realize their paradigms with internal research resources; (b) whether they instead – or additionally – make use of external research leading to public knowledge; or (c) whether they rely on private and tacit knowledge that is transferred by spill-over effects and is embodied in persons, capital equipment, and intermediate goods. In each of these cases there is the incentive of appropriating any new

economic knowledge, of applying it in firm-specific product and/or process innovations, and of marketing it. Decisions regarding internal and/or external research resources are dependent on various criteria which will be described below. Explanations
provided by the transactions costs approach are well known (Williamson 1975, 1985)
and, therefore, will not be explicitly repeated here.

On the one hand, *external research sources* are utilized: when there are financial or other resource constraints for internal research; when uncertainties of research
and development are to be shifted or – in the case of complementary internal research
– to be partitioned; when external research can be carried out with economies of scale
or scope (Den Hertog & Thurik 1993, p. 279f.). On the other hand, *internal research
sources* are utilized: (a) when there are complementary work processes, especially in
the research, production and marketing divisions or when complementary main resources and capital equipment are used in production; (b) when a loss of control in
appropriating the returns of research is anticipated; (c) when potential careers of scientists and engineers in the internal labor market, predominantly in research and development departments, enhance their motivation and work performance (Audretsch,
Menkveld & Thurik 1996, p. 520f.). In addition, one has to recall that frequently there
is (spot-)market failure in the case of external new economic knowledge and that the
required knowledge is highly person- and firm-specific. When human capital specificity increases within the firm, though, principal-agent or "hostage" problems may arise.
However, new contributions to the feasibility of team organization demonstrate that
these problems can be solved (Appelbaum & Batt 1994).

Den Hertog and Thurik (1993, pp. 282ff.) analyze data of 446 Dutch firms engaging in internal and/or external research activities. They use as explanatory variables: size of firms; market structure and growth; capital intensity; profit rate; growth
of individual firm sales and qualification of employees. The size of a firm should
positively be correlated with internal research activities, because big firms command
larger internal and external financial resources (a variant of the Schumpeterian hypothesis). Also big firms may more easily be able to utilize various sources of scale
and scope economies in internal research. Market concentration and capital intensity
lead to and result from non-price competition for ex post market power; to this end
internal research activities are favored to gain informational first-mover advantages
with supra-normal profit rates and to avoid unfeasible spill-over effects of new economic knowledge. Growing – as against stagnating – markets do not offer incentives
for collaboration or even collusion, e.g. in collective external research. Growth of individual sales provide cash flows to engage in internal research. Qualified employees
are a precondition for this option.

The regression results obtained by Den Hertog and Thurik (1993, pp. 285ff.) do not confirm all their expectations. They demonstrate, though: that on the one hand external research activities decrease with the size of the firm and increase with their individual growth of sales; that on the other hand internal research activities are positively correlated with market concentration, more so with market growth and the share of qualified employees. Against the background of the technology-oriented regional policy in Germany the results of Den Hertog and Thurik can be summed up as follows (ibid., p. 288): SMEs will probably make use of external sources of research and development to a larger extent than big firms; in particular, this will apply to those SMEs which produce for less concentrated markets and have a relatively high capital intensity.

In a follow-up study with the same set of data Audretsch, Menkveld and Thurik (1996, p. 524) come to the following results: (a) External sources of new economic knowledge are utilized more intensively when the respective firm also engages in internal research; (b) firm size does not significantly explain the use of external sources; (c) a high share of qualified employees influences external research activities negatively (firm-specific human capital); (d) a high capital intensity influences them positively (presumably because it prevails in firms with standardized products and production processes and, therefore, without unfeasible spill-over effects). The distinction between "high-" and "low-tech industries" leads to some more interesting results as cited below.

Summing up, the authors' findings confirm Dosi's complementary model of the innovation process. Internal research and development activities appear to be a precondition for the use of external sources. External subcontracting of research contributes to positive spill-over effects of new economic knowledge. In the authors' own words: "To engage in both kinds of R&D there seems to be need for a critical mass. Either the firm needs to develop a certain amount of R&D effort, or the firm needs to be in an environment with ample technological opportunities. The results show that the more R&D employees a firm has, the higher is the probability that the firm engages in *both* internal and external R&D. The results also show that in high-tech industries internal and external R&D tend to be complements, and in low-tech industries they tend to be substitutes" (Audretsch, Menkveld & Thurik 1996, p. 528). Any transfer of new economic knowledge – in the case of high-tech firms – would consequently have to be adapted to the respective technological paradigm. Any transfer – in the case of low-tech firms – would have to aim at firms with a high capital intensity and a low share of qualified employees.

Köthenbürger and Ullrich (1994) deliver a comprehensive survey of theoretical and empirical studies on the transfer of new economic knowledge in Germany. Three studies are of particular interest here. The first study was undertaken by Staudt, Bock and Mühlemeyer (1992). They confirm the dependence of SMEs in North-Rhine Westphalia on external sources: partly on consulting and transfer institutions, but mainly on personal contacts to customers, suppliers and competitors. The authors conclude (ibid., p. 990f.) that the services offered by consulting and transfer institutions do not yet meet well the demand for them by SMEs. The second study was undertaken by Hahn, Gaiser, Héraud and Muller (1994) who compare industries in the regions of Alsace and Lake Constance. They arrive at quite similar conclusions.

The third study is the innovation panel of Mannheim which is carried out by the Centre of European Economic Research and is mainly investigating SMEs (defined as having less than 250 employees). 50% of the SMEs reviewed do not innovate, 25% innovate by making use of external sources of new economic knowledge, and the remaining 25% innovate by using internal sources. Although the majority of the SMEs reviewed are prepared to realize informational leads in competition, various restrictions would have to be overcome in the first place: mainly deficits in managerial and research and development capabilities, learning costs, and financial restrictions (Harhoff et al. 1996, p. 13).

The same study also demonstrates that the adoption of new economic knowledge is facilitated by the exchange of experience between firms, by investing in capital equipment with embodied technological progress, and by recruiting qualified employees. Technology transfer is concentrating on German sources (collaboration with customers also includes foreign partners). In contrast to big firms there are hardly any inter-firm alliances or joint ventures. SMEs mainly adopt "mature" technologies, but also results of applied and basic research. The most important external sources of new economic knowledge are universities, followed by public and private research institutions. Spatial proximity between universities and firms as well as complementary internal research of firms facilitate transfer activities. A collaboration promises higher returns, when long-term partnerships and trust relations have been developed. Yet the discontinuous time pattern of innovative activities of SMEs frequently restricts continuous collaboration. They have – because of financial constraints – to sell a new product in the first place before they can plan the next innovation. The demand for transfer services will therefore be "bumpy" (Harhoff et al. 1996, pp. 17, 90).

Although big firms utilize university contacts to a greater extent than SMEs do – as for instance Link and Rees (1990) show – SMEs could do better in order to make internal research more effective. Therefore, specialized transfer institutes would have to help non-innovating SMEs to develop a technological paradigm for themselves. They would also have to convince innovating SMEs of the advantages which complementary internal and external sources of new economic knowledge promise.

5 Preliminary Results from the Case Study "ITWS"

5.1 Purposes and Activities of the ITWS

The Institute for the Transfer of New Economic Knowledge and Technology in the County of Soest (ITWS) was founded in 1992 as a kind of public-private partnership (so-called "An-Institut" of the University of Paderborn). It has the purpose of facilitating transfer between the University of Paderborn, in particular the affiliated School Soest, on the one hand, and local communities as well as firms and individuals, on the other hand. The target region of its activities is the County of Soest and the somewhat larger "Hellwegregion". Target customers foremost are SMEs. Access to research and transfer institutions outside the target region is to be opened up.

From 1992 until the end of 1996 transfer activities of the ITWS comprise 396 cases, in which research and development projects were initiated or guided, or various services rendered. The activities mainly concern customers from the service sector and from the industries dominating the regional economy. The respective firms are located in the County of Soest (56%), outside the county and in North-Rhine Westphalia (37%), in other German Federal States (6%) and in the European Community (1%). Customers are SMEs (55%) and bigger firms (28%), as well as private and public research and development institutions.

Transfer activities to a considerable extent concern highly specialized services of the Laboratory for Surface Analytics (31%), which is run by the ITWS itself. That is why customers frequently are service firms, e.g. consultants, independent engineers, other laboratories and research and development institutes. The laboratory services can be interpreted partly as basic, partly as applied research. They are covered by official definitions of transfer activities, because they are not provided with direct commercialization purpose (Abramson et al. 1997, p. 1f.). The laboratory itself is integrated into a network of related research institutions within North-Rhine Westphalia, the Working Group of Surface Analytics.

5.2 Questionnaire for Interviews with Customer Firms

The preliminary results presented below relate to customer firms each of which was interviewed for two to three hours (at management level). Interviews of actual and potential "suppliers" of new economic knowledge and technologies and of a regional control group of firms (without transfer experiences) are envisaged. To structure the interviews a questionnaire was designed. It comprises 5 groups of questions:

- General indicators of the firm: location, organizational structure, sales, employees by qualification and function;
- research and development activities within the firm: expenses, status of employees before recruitment, projects, information sources, status of collaboration;
- innovations: status of market introduction, motives, internal or external impulses, restrictions;
- backward and forward linkages: inside/outside target region, in- and/or outsourcing;
- finally collaboration with the ITWS: first/later contacts, contact media, transfer activities provided, evaluation of transfer spectrum, collaboration, alternatives, effects, problems etc.

5.3 Preliminary Results from the Pre-test

5.3.1 Sales and Employees

The pre-test was conducted with three mechanical engineering and three metal-processing firms. The youngest firm was founded in 1993, the others are older (in three cases older than 10 years). Their location is in the target region (in one case outside). According to traditional indicators such as sales and employees all 6 firms belong to the group of SMEs (they have less than 50 million of sales and less than 200 employees; three are classed as small, the other three as medium-sized).Overall sales and employment figures had a positive trend between 1990 and 1997 (employment + 25%). Insofar, the firms reviewed are positive exceptions from the general recession in the early nineties, during which manufacturing employment in the County of Soest declined by 5%.

Table 1: Employees by qualification and size class of firms		
size class of firm qualification	3 small firms sales less than 10 mil employees in %	3 medium-sized firms sales 10 to 50 mil employees in %
in vocational training	6	3
unskilled	24	31
with certificate of vocational training	36	55
with certificate as foreman or technician	15	4
with certificate of university education	19	7
total of size class	**100**	**100**

Table 1 summarizes the qualification structure of the employees by size class of firms. All the pre-test firms appear to have a relatively high share of employees with a certified qualification. The small firms also exhibit a high level of academic education of their employees.

5.3.2 Research and Development

Table 2 summarizes the occupational function of the employees of the pre-test firms. It reveals that all pre-test firms engage in internal research and development (R&D): according to the interviews mainly in applied research and product development. The R&D intensity (relation of expenses for R&D and sales) is 22% in the case of the small firms and 5% in the case of the medium-sized firms. The partners interviewed expect the difference to narrow in the coming years.

Table 2: Employees by occupational function and size class of firms		
size class of firm ⟍ qualification	3 small firms sales less than 10 mil employees in %	3 medium-sized firms sales 10 to 50 mil employees in %
research and development	19	5
production and manufacturing	37	78
producer services	21	4
marketing and administration	23	12
other services	-	1
total of size class	**100**	**100**

The R&D personnel is mainly recruited from the own staff with certified vocational training (51%), from other firms (33%), and from public research institutions (16%). Predominantly the medium-sized firms collaborate with external – public and private – R&D institutions, with independent engineers and with consultants. The older the respective firm, the more frequent are the reported collaborations. The pre-test firms state as restrictions of collaborations (excluding those with the ITWS): specificity of required R&D, danger of unfeasible spill-over effects of new economic knowledge, and lack of long-term trust relations. In most firms the ITWS is the first collaboration partner. For the future they anticipate a heterogeneous demand for R&D consultation. The potential spectrum of consultation seems to widen with the size of firm.

Summing up, close attention will have to be paid to the qualification structure of employees and to their status before recruitment when the remainder of firms which collaborated with the ITWS (and the control group) is interviewed. The relative weights of transfer services and spill-over effects by recruited R&D employees as well as of internal R&D activities may be decisive for any kind of innovations and dynamic efficiency, as is explained in the complementary and the feed-back models of the innovation process. All pre-test firms are engaging in R&D transfer activities. There are some indications that size and/or age of the firm may be relevant determinants for these activities.

5.3.3 Innovations

The pre-test firms introduced 36 innovations in the period 1990-97 (the small ones 16, the medium-sized ones 20). Discontinuation of innovation projects in 2 firms was caused by problems of adapting production technology, of marketing and of obtaining subsidies. The innovations are generally motivated: in the case of the small firms by succession and differentiation of products, by sales promotion and market share; in the case of the medium-sized firms – rather differently – by productivity gains, flexibility and product quality standards. Internal impulses for innovations originate from the management and the F&E department in the case of small firms, in the case of medium-sized firms also from the marketing department. External impulses are reported to originate from collaborating and competing firms, from suppliers and customers, from fairs, conferences, and contacts with scientific research. Restrictions for innovations in both size classes relate to the costs of innovation, to uncertainties about market trends, and to problems in developing marketable products or in undertaking the necessary re-organization of the production process.

The reported preliminary findings suggest that there is ample scope for integrating supply and production management into the innovation process (i. e. for applying the "complete" feed-back model of the innovation process). Japanese and US firms demonstrate – with various forms of organizing team production – that they are able to realize significant innovation potentials in these spheres. Frequently, however, preconditions to do just that are a fundamental re-organization of the production and work process and high, long-term investments (Appelbaum & Batt 1994).

5.3.4 Regional Backward and Forward Linkages

Backward (supplies) and forward (sales) linkages are determinants of regional effects, which may be enhanced by the transfer of new economic knowledge. A strong regional export base contributes to regional income, whereas supplies from outside the region (imports) diminishes it. Intra-regional division of labor saves – otherwise arising – transport and communication costs and strengthens regional competitiveness.

Against this background the small pre-test firms on an average have 110 suppliers with a slightly positive trend to be observed in the past and expected in the next years. The medium-sized firms on an average have 275 suppliers without any observable or expected trend. The share of regional supplies (region defined here as a concentric ring around the town of Soest with a radius of 50 km) amounts to 20% and less (higher in the case of raw materials, lower in the case of services and capital equipment). The pre-test firms have 5 to 3600 customers. Their number tends to increase with firm size. Regional sales on the average of all firms amount to 27%, exports to

European countries and the "rest of the world" to 25%. Those interviewed expect an increase of exports.

These preliminary findings suggest that the regional development in the County of Soest may, to a large extent, be determined exogenously. In the context of regional economic policy, therefore, the transfer of new economic knowledge would also have to aim at developing the intra-regional potential of the division of labor and specialization. This may require intensive collaboration with various institutions engaged in local and regional economic policies. Inter-firm networks of collaboration and alliances, with strong backward and forward linkages, could – as stated earlier in this paper – add to the dynamic efficiency and competitiveness of SMEs.

5.3.5 Collaboration with the ITWS

First and subsequent contacts between the pre-test firms and the ITWS are mostly made by their management, but partly also by some of their employees (represented by their respective trade union). Transfer activities of the ITWS cover the whole spectrum described above: consultations, general and special seminars, laboratory services, initiation and guidance of R&D. The ITWS also made contacts between the majority of these firms and third parties such as scientific specialists of the University of Paderborn, research institutes, laboratories, and industry associations.

Without going into details here, the ITWS is evaluated by the interview partners positively. This has reportedly to do with the competence of the staff members of the institute and the specialized information they provide. Besides, this has to do with the relatively low costs of services the ITWS uses to invoice, low in comparison to alternative, profit-orientated transfer institutes and consultants (that is why all the pre-test firms would object privatization of the ITWS). Finally it has to do with the spatial proximity of the ITWS and the implicated low communication cost. For some of the pre-test firms only earlier contacts with alternative transfer institutions and specificity of the required new economic knowledge prevented more frequent contacts with the ITWS.

The transfer activities of the ITWS, on the whole, have positive employment effects. Mostly they are accompanied by adaptations of production and work processes, i. e. by adaptation costs. Nevertheless, the majority of the pre-test firms report that the transfer is adding to their dynamic efficiency (product quality, flexibility, competitive prices, and shorter production time). Whether these effects justify long-term subsidies for the ITWS, with public financial means, cannot be answered before the envisaged empirical study has been completed.

6 Conclusions

The reported preliminary findings of the case study ITWS are consistent with the complementary and the feed-back models of the innovation process as well as with the determinants utilizing internal and external knowledge inputs. The spatial and organizational origins of the knowledge inputs for the pre-test firms are not yet investigated. The same applies to the categorization of the inputs as specialized vs. standardized or as private vs. public.

The reported findings are not necessarily statistically representative for all the transfer activities of the ITWS. Any generalization may, therefore, be distorted. In the following steps of the study special attention will be paid to:

- the function and relevance of indirect transfers of new economic knowledge (i. e. by using other persons or service institutions as intermediators);
- the transfer character of the laboratory services of the ITWS;
- the function of seminars as providing post-graduate education and/or an opportunity for first or subsequent contacts with the ITWS;
- the character of the transfer activities of the ITWS (including its laboratory services) as public goods, as mixed public-private goods, or as private goods and – as an implication – to the justification of the allocation of public funds as subsidies vs. the option of charging market prices for transfer services;
- the options of establishing networks of collaborating firms as well as transfer institutions, i. e. of a matrix organization especially for SMEs, to cope with highly reactive and turbulent environments, and to realize individual and collective flexibility, specialization, and dynamic efficiency.

New information and communication technologies will undoubtedly add to the effectivity of transfer services. They may even induce the transformation of the regional economy into one with information-intensive industries and rapid productivity gains, or in the words of Freeman (1989) lead to the adoption of a fundamentally new "techno-economical paradigm" comparable only to the long waves of the Schumpeterian process of creative destruction. The extent to which this may happen, though, crucially depends on the transferability of the relevant new economic knowledge and technologies, on their standardization, publicness and marketability on the one hand vs. their specialization, tacitness and privateness on the other hand. To avoid unfeasible spill-over effects in the case of the latter type of information, long-term collaboration and trust relations have to be established in the first place.

References

Abramson, H. N. et al. (1997). *Technologietransfer-Systeme in den USA und Deutschland.* Karlsruhe and Washington, D. C.: National Academy of Engineering and Fraunhofer Gesellschaft.

Acs, Z. J., Audretsch, D. B. & Feldman, M.P. (1992). Real Effects of Academic Research: Comment. *American Economic Review*, 82, pp. 363-67.

Appelbaum, E. & Batt, R. (1994). *The New American Workplace – Transforming Work Systems in the United States.* Ithaca and London: ILR Press/Cornell University Press.

Audretsch, D. B., Menkveld, A. J. & Thurik, A. R. (1996). The Decision Between Internal and External R&D. *Journal of Institutional and Theoretical Economics – JITE*, 152, pp. 519-30.

Audretsch, D. B. & Feldmann, M. P. (1996). R&D Spillovers and the Geography of Innovation and Production. *American Economic Review*, 86, pp. 630-40.

Cohen, St. S. & Zysman, J. (1987). *Manufacturing Matters – The Myth of the Post-Industrial Economy.* New York: Basic Books.

Cohen, W. M. & Levin, R. C. (1989). Empirical Studies of Innovation and Market Structure. In: R. Schmalensee and R.D. Willig (Eds.) *Handbook of Industrial Organization* (pp. 1059-1107). Amsterdam et al.: Elsevier Science Publishers B.V.

Demsetz, H. (1982). Barriers to Entry. *American Economic Review*, 72, 47-57.

Den Hertog, R. G. J. & Thurik, A. R. (1988). Determinants of Internal and External R&D: Some Dutch Evidence. *De Economist*, 141, pp. 279-89.

Deutscher Bundestag (1997). *Rahmenplan der Gemeinschaftsaufgabe "Verbesserung der regionalen Wirtschaftsstruktur" für den Zeitraum 1997 bis 2000/2001.* Drucksache 13/7205. Bonn: Deutscher Bundestag.

Deutscher Bundestag (1993). *Raumordnungsbericht (1993). Unterrichtung durch die Bundesregierung.* Drucksache 12/6921. Bonn: Deutscher Bundestag.

Dosi, G. (1988). Sources, Procedures, and Microeconomic Effects of Innovation. *Journal Of Economic Literature*, 26, pp. 1120-71.

Emery, F. E. & Trist, E. L. (1965/1969). The Causal Texture of Organizational Environments. Reprinted in: F.E. Emery (Ed.), *Systems Thinking, Selected Readings* (pp. 241-57), Harmondsworth: Penguin Education.

Feldman, M. P. (1994). *Knowledge Complementarity and Innovation.* Boston: Small Business Economics.

Feldman, M. P. & Florida, R. (1994). The Geographic Sources of Innovation: Technological Infrastructure and Product Innovation in the United States. *Annals of the Association of American Geographers*, 84, pp. 210-29.

Freeman, C. (1989). Die Verbreitung neuer Technologien in Unternehmen, Wirtschaftsbereichen und Ländern. In: A. Heertje (Ed.), *Technische und Finanzinnovation – Ihre Auswirkungen auf die Wirtschaft* (pp. 67-89). Oxford and Frankfurt.

Gerlach, K. and Liepmann, P. (1972). Konjunkturelle Aspekte der Industrialisierung peripherer Regionen – dargestellt am Beispiel des ostbayerischen Regierungsbezirks Oberpfalz. *Jahrbücher für Nationalökonomie und Statistik*, 187, pp. 1-21.

Geroski, P. A. (1987). Do Dominant Firms Decline? In: D. Hay, J. Vickers (Eds.), *The Economics of Market Dominance* (pp. 143-67). Oxford: Basil Blackwell.

Gomes-Casseres, B. (1996). *The Alliance Revolution – The New Shape of Business Rivalry*, Cambridge, Massachusetts et al.: Harvard University Press.

Hahn, R., Gaiser A., Héraud, J.-A. & E. Muller (1994). Innovationstätigkeit der Unternehmen und regionales Umfeld. *Raumforschung und Raumordnung*, pp. 193-202.

Harhoff, D., Licht, G. et al. (1996). Innovationsaktivitäten kleiner und mittlerer Unternehmen, Ergebnisse des Mannheimer Innovationspanels. Schriftenreihe des ZEW, Bd. 8, Baden-Baden: Nomos Verlagsgesellschaft.

Jaffe, A. B., Tratjenberg, M. & Henderson, R. (1993). Geographic Localization of Knowledge Spillovers as Evidenced by Patent Citations. *Quarterly Journal of Economics*, 108, pp. 577-98.

Jaffe, A. R. (1989). Real Effects of Academic Research. *American Economic Review*, 79, 957-70.

Koutsoyiannis, A. (1982). *Non-Price Decisions – The Firm in a Modern Context.* London et al.: Macmillan.

Köthenbürger, M. & Ullrich, J. (1994). *Innovationsorientierte Regionalpolitik – am Beispiel des Instituts für Technologie- und Wissenstransfer im Kreis Soest (ITWS).* Diploma thesis, University of Paderborn.

Krugman, P. (1991). *Geography and Trade.* Gaston Eyskens Lecture Series. Cambridge, Masachusetts: MIT Press.

Levin, R. C., Klevorick, A. K., Nelson, R. R. & Winter, S. G. (1987). Appropriating the Returns from Industrial Research and Development. *Brookings Papers on Economic Activity*, 3, pp. 783-820.

Liepmann, P. & Ullrich, J. (1994). *Sektoraler Strukturwandel im Bezirk der Industrie- und Handelskammer Ostwestfalen zu Bielefeld – Tertiärisierungstendenzen der Beschäftigung.* Arbeitspapiere des Fachbereichs Wirtschaftswissenschaften der Universität-Gesamthochschule Paderborn, Neue Folge Nr. 47, Paderborn.

Liepmann, P. (1992). Externes Unternehmenswachstum und regionsexterne Kontrolle – Ein Beitrag zur Fusion Siemens-Nixdorf. *Jahrbücher für Nationalökonomie und Statistik*, 210, pp. 1-17.

Link, A. N. & Rees, J. (1990). Firm Size, University Based Research, and the Returns to R&D. *Small Business Economics*, 2, pp. 25-32.

Marris, R. & Mueller, D.C. (1980). The Corporation, Competition, and the Invisible Hand. *The Journal of Economic Literature*, 18, pp. 32-63.

Martin, St. (1988). *Industrial Economics – Economic Analysis and Public Policy.* New York et al.: Macmillan Publishing Comp.

Martin, St. (1993). *Advanced Industrial Economics.* Oxford et al.: Blackwell.

Nelson, R. R. (1988). Capitalism as an Engine of Growth. In: G. Dosi et al. (Eds.), *Technical Change and Economic Theory.* London: Francis Pinter.

Piore, M.J. & Sabel, C. (1984). *The Second Industrial Divide: Possibilities for Prosperity,* New York: Basic Books.

Pred, A. (1977). *City-Systems in Advanced Economies: Past Growth, Present Processes, and Future Development Options.* London: Hutchinson.

Staudt, E., Bock, J. & Mühlemeyer, P. (1992). Informationsverhalten von innovationsaktiven kleinen und mittleren Unternehmen – Ergebnisse einer empirischen Untersuchung in Nordrhein-Westfalen. *Zeitschrift für Betriebswirtschaft*, 62, pp. 989-1008.

Stöhr, W. B. (1985). *Territorial Innovation Complexes, Interdisciplinary Institute of Urban and Regional Studies.* University of Vienna.

Tacke, A. (1982). *Stagnation der Industrie – Krise der Region.* Frankfurt et al.: Campus Verlag.

Teece, D. J. (1989). Inter-organizational Requirements of the Innovation Process. *Managerial and Decision Economics*, Special Issue, pp. 35-42.

Vanhove, N. & Klaassen, L. H. (1987). *Regional Policy: A European Approach,* 2nd Edition. Aldershot et al.: Avebury.

Williamson, O. E. (1975). *Markets and Hierarchies: Analysis and Antitrust Implications.* New York: The Free Press.

Williamson, O. E. (1985). *The Economic Institutions of Capitalism.* New York: The Free Press.

Taxing Electronic Commerce

Marko Köthenbürger and Bernd Rahmann

1 Introduction

The evolution of new information technologies in the last two decades has fundamentally changed the way society interacts. Computers can be found in many applications and the exchange of information via computer networks solves problems which were difficult or even impossible to solve without the use of modern information technology. Decentralized production as well as office systems, via electronic information exchange are good examples of how the organization of transactions changed due to the existence of computer networks. In general, companies use the information network for coordinating the production and distribution of goods and services more effectively. Another prominent example is the Internet. It enables the worldwide exchange of information at relatively low transaction costs. One of the most significant uses of the Internet is in the field of commerce. Many goods and services can already be bought on the Internet and are accessible worldwide by customers. Information services produced in one country can now be exported to any country without incurring extensive transaction costs.

To some extent, this new form of commerce is different to traditional ways of commerce. Especially, there are some prerequisites which are crucial for the development of electronic commerce. Besides technological prerequisites, numerous commercial, as well as legal aspects, become important for electronic commerce. Examples include the provision and regulation of information infrastructure, the protection of intellectual property rights, and the taxation of this new type of commerce.[1] Therefore, public arrangements dealing with these issues have an important impact on the evolution of electronic marketplaces.

The taxation of electronic commerce has become a central legal issue. The European Union, as well as the United States, have agreed on not hindering the usage of electronic services and the corresponding infrastructure by imposing special taxes on electronic commerce transactions. Electronic commerce should be taxed in the same way as traditional commerce. However, this agreement implicitly assumes that electronic transactions can be taxed like any non-electronic transactions.

---

[1] A more detailed list of commercial and legal aspects is given in OECD 1997a, Garcia 1995, Spaanderman & Ypsilanti 1997 and Mansell 1996.

The question under consideration in this paper is whether electronic commerce can be taxed at all and if so, how the basic principles of commodity taxation can be applied to it. In short, the paper describes the implication of electronic commerce on the ability of the state to raise revenues. Therefore, the paper is organized as follows: in section 2 a brief overview on electronic commerce is given. Some technical and economic aspects of electronic commerce are presented.

Section 3 reviews normative principles of taxation commonly accepted in the theory of public finance. The application of these principles to the taxation on electronic commerce is analyzed in section 4. Finally, section 5 summarizes and draws some conclusions.

2 Electronic Commerce

As already mentioned, electronic commerce is experiencing a growing popularity among customers. A wide range of products can be bought over the Internet. The worldwide net of consumers has access to computer software, entertainment products, information services, professional consulting, financial services, business statistics and even medical diagnostics. The supply and demand of these services over the Internet increases rapidly as the Internet enables new types of commercial transactions and serves as a substitute for traditional types.

2.1 Types of Electronic Commerce

Table 1: Types of commerce

Activity	Purchase	Payment	Delivery
Traditional Commerce:			
Tangibles	face-to-face	face-to-face	face-to-face
Services	face-to-face	face-to-face	face-to-face
Disintermediated Commerce:			
Mail order	mail/ phone	check/ credit card	common carrier
Electronic buying	on-line	on-line	common carrier
Electronic commerce	on-line	on-line	on-line

Source: McLure, 1997

Commerce occurs in different ways as table 1 shows. Traditionally, the exchange of goods and services was organized in a non-electronic way. The purchase, the payment, as well as the delivery occurred on a face-to-face basis. Mail ordering enabled the customer to order products by mail or phone and to pay by either check or credit card. The delivery was done with the help of common carrier. The evolution of electronic commerce changed this dramatically. Basically, two types of electronic commerce can be distinguished. On the one hand, tangible products can be sold using the Internet. This is normally done by sending an order to the seller over the Internet or

by browsing through a virtual catalogue and ordering products by clicking the catalogue. The products are delivered to the customer by using common carriers. Except
for the way the order is placed, this kind of electronic commerce is similar to traditional types of commerce such as mail ordering. Therefore, this is also called electronic buying. However, when talking about electronic commerce, most people have a
different kind of transaction in mind: the sale of intangible products. In this context
intangible products are digitized information transmitted over the Internet.[2] Examples
of this type of product include computer software, electronic books, business statistics,
and newspapers. As this type of electronic commerce differs more from the traditional
exchange of goods and services, it is likely to be the more interesting type of commerce with respect to the way taxation occurs.

2.2 Economic Aspects of Electronic Commerce

Electronic commerce experienced a tremendous growth in the last years and is
expected to continue to expand rapidly. The OECD (1997c, p. 14) estimates an annual
growth rate of over 200%. However, measuring the dynamics of electronic commerce
is difficult for a number of reasons. First, a commonly accepted definition of electronic
commerce has not been agreed upon yet.[3] Second, even with a precise definition sales
figures cannot be obtained as easily as in the case of traditional commerce. One reason
is that separating electronic from traditional commerce is rather difficult especially in
case of firms engaging in both kinds of commerce.[4]

Table 2 presents a list of total sales estimates given by the International Data
Corporation, Forrester and Yankee. Differences in estimates can be attributed to the
above mentioned measurement difficulties.

Table 2: Internet sales in million of US$		
Institution	1995	2000
International Data Corporation (IDC)	1,000	117,000
Forrester	518	6,579
Yankee	850	144,000

Source: OECD 1997c

The table shows that electronic commerce will become more important in the
future and therefore, potential problems for the state taxing such companies must be

---

[2] Intangible products are also called "content".
[3] The definition of electronic commerce given in section 2 is widely accepted but not the standard.
Organizations such as the European Commission and the OECD use different definitions, and consequently, the diversity of definitions leads to a huge variability of growth estimates.
[4] For a more in depth analysis of measurement difficulties see OECD 1997c.

analyzed in detail before a serious fiscal problem arises. An economic explanation for the increasing use of electronic commerce can be given by assessing the resources necessary for the organization of the transaction. If the costs for negotiating, writing and enforcing a contract (transaction costs) are high, the transaction is likely to be organized within a hierarchy (e.g. a firm). Low transaction costs call for a market solution.[5] Electronic commerce offers the possibility to conduct transactions with lower transaction costs since gathering information, finding market actors, placing orders, negotiating and executing transactions will become easier (Picot et al. 1997). Information about market participants can be accessed more easily by browsing through the Internet. The placing of orders and the execution of the transaction can be organized directly. The evolution of electronic cash systems will contribute to a further reduction in transaction costs. Consequently, electronic commerce and, in general, information and communication technology favors markets as a coordinating mechanism. For transactions formerly carried out within a hierarchy, a market organization will become more attractive which will intensify the increasing use of electronic commerce.

2.3 Technical Aspects of Electronic Commerce

In this section, a brief overview is given on what the Internet is and how it works. This is only done as far as the explanation provides a better understanding of the implications of electronic commerce for taxation. The Internet is a worldwide net of computers which consist of a number of autonomous subnets. These nets, in turn, may contain further numerous autonomous nets. The subnets are connected to each other and, therefore, communication among them is possible. Three kinds of subnets can be characterized: the so-called intranet, networks run by scientific or educational institutions, and networks run by commercial providers. First, the intranet is a net used for intra-firm data communication. Different computers within an organization are connected to each other and communicate without using a public network. It is not necessary that all computers must be located at one geographical location. Computers at different locations, e.g. subsidiaries of a multinational firm, can form such a private network (intranet). Second, a variety of networks are used for scientific and educational services. They are run by universities, science foundations, and other non-

---

[5] The general framework for analyzing this issue is given by the New Institutional Economics (NIE) and especially by transaction cost theory. Besides transaction costs, the specificity of the transaction and the uncertainty of the environment determine the organization of the transaction. For simplicity, we only focus on transaction costs. For a detailed presentation of NIE and electronic markets see Malone, Yates & Benjamin 1987 and Picot, Bortenlänger & Röhrl 1997.

commercial institutions. The third kind of network is used for commercial purposes. Service providers rent networks and offer access to these nets to their customers.

Besides this view, the Internet can also be described as a collection of resources which can be used by those who have access to the physical net. These services can partly be used free of charge (e.g. email, search engines). Other services provided over the Internet are priced such as electronic banking, the provision of business statistics, and electronic journals. The latter kind of services are of interest as these belong to electronic commerce. Due to the fact that the subnets are autonomous, some form of a common language is necessary for communication between them. The common standard for intersubnet communication is the communication protocol TCP/IP (Transmission Control Protocol/Internet Protocol) while a variety of other protocols are used in subnets. The TCP/IP is responsible for routing data through the net. In order to understand the routing process, some knowledge about routing technology is necessary. The Internet uses packet-switching technology. That means data streams are transmitted over the Internet by breaking them up into packets which are routed independently to its destination. The information necessary for routing is contained in the header of each packet so that at each router (nodes in the net) the packet can be sent to the next node according to the destination. At the final destination, the TCP/IP is responsible for reassembling the packets to the original data stream. Therefore, in contrast to a circuit switching technology, a connection between the origin and destination does not have to be set up before the data stream can be transmitted and closed after transmission.[6]

Up to now, data streams sent over the Internet are not encrypted. If a third party is able to reassemble the packages to its original data stream, information is accessible to outsiders and the integrity of the data is not assured. However, integrity and privacy protection are considered as essential ingredients to any commerce system (Peha & Strauss, 1997). Therefore, it is likely that the encryption of data streams will become the standard.

3 Principles of Taxation

It is widely agreed upon in public finance that a tax system should be designed according to the following principles[7]:

- Administrative simplicity: The tax system should be simple to administer. It should be easy and inexpensive for tax authorities to determine and collect the tax in order to reach high net revenues.

---

[6] For further explanations of technical aspects see Halsall 1996 and MacKie-Mason & Varian 1994.
[7] For a discussion of these principles see any introductory book in public finance, e.g. Rosen 1998.

- Low compliance cost: The private sector should not be burdened with too many obligations by the collection and clearance of the tax in order to minimize tax avoidance.

- Economic efficiency: The tax system should finance the budget with a minimum of economic distortions. This principle is explained in more detail in section 3.1.

- Equity: In general, society's notion of equity should be reflected by the tax system. This principle is operationalized by the concept of vertical and horizontal equity. Horizontal equity requires that similar transactions are taxed similarly. A violation of this principle would be, for example, a consumption tax regime which treats consumers with identical consumption differently. While horizontal equity refers to similar transactions vertical equity means that different transactions should be taxed differently. One application of this concept is the income tax system of almost all countries as households with a higher ability to pay are taxed higher.

In practice, it is difficult to pursue all principles simultaneously as a variety of tradeoffs exists among them. Equity versus efficiency is the most discussed tradeoff in the literature of public finance but is only of minor interest in this context. Here, the relevant tradeoff exists among efficiency and low compliance cost. This tradeoff can best be explained if the process of taxation is understood as a state action which takes place in an asymmetric information environment.

In general, the state has little information concerning the characteristics and behavior of the tax payer making it difficult to define and control a tax base. The state tries to overcome the information asymmetry by increasing the requirements for reporting the tax base which, in turn, leads to higher compliance cost. The principle of economic efficiency is subject to many approaches of designing a tax system. The basic results of the efficient taxation approach are summarized in the next two sections.

3.1 Commodity Taxation and Economic Efficiency - General Results

Taxation is not only a pure transfer of resources from the private sector to the state, but it also affects the behavior of the tax payer. In general, a change in behavior due to taxation can be distinguished in an income and a substitution effect. The former describes changes in behavior due to a decrease in income whereas the latter refers to changes in behavior resulting from a substitution of a higher taxed good for a lower taxed good. The substitution effect is the source of distortions arising from the tax system as it alters the relative attractiveness of consumption and production activities that would otherwise prevail without taxation. Therefore, the efficient taxation (ET) approach seeks to minimize these distortions for raising a given amount of tax revenues.

A tax system with no distortions arises if all goods are taxed at the same rate (first-best tax system). As the relative attractiveness of consumption is unchanged, taxation does not lead to substitution effects. Distortions are minimized to zero. Unfortunately, not all goods can be taxed in practice (e.g. leisure). Under this restriction on tax instruments, it is no longer optimal to levy a uniform tax rate on all goods. Non-uniform taxation leads to lower distortions (second-best tax system). The ET theory suggests a tax system which taxes goods with low substitution possibilities at a higher rate than goods with high substitution possibilities. This rule of thumb ensures a relatively low overall substitution effect and distortion. For the special case of perfect substitutes, the ET approach recommends taxing both types of goods in the same manner. Otherwise a perfect shift from the more taxed to the less taxed good would arise resulting in higher welfare losses compared to the taxation of imperfect substitutes. The tax would be used in a discriminating manner which is not the intention of a tax with a pure financial character.

3.2 Efficient Commodity Taxation of Cross Border Transactions

So far, we have analyzed how commodity taxation system should be designed in order to achieve economic efficiency by implicitly assuming that only one national tax system exists. A problem arising in international trade, is to decide whose country's tax system to apply. In this section, different value added tax (VAT) policy options are presented which can be applied to the taxation of cross-border commodity transactions.[8] The question of which tax regime to apply is again a question of economic efficiency. In this context economic efficiency is defined as trade and location neutrality. This means that the tax system should not give incentive to exporters and importers to change their trade and location decisions for tax avoidance reasons. But before the efficiency implications are analyzed in detail, the two basic VAT-systems are introduced.

3.2.1 The Destination and Origin Principle

In the literature, two basic international commodity taxation principles can be distinguished, the destination principle and the origin principle (Frenkel, Razin & Sadka 1991). Under the destination principle commodities are tax exempted in the exporting country and are taxed according to the VAT-system in the importing country. Therefore, this principle ensures that all commodities are taxed similarly in the country in which they are consumed. Therefore, border tax adjustments are necessary. Commodities

---

[8] Here, we concentrate on the technique of value added taxation as this is the most applied technique of taxing consumption.

crossing the border are tax exempted in the country of origin and are taxed at the VAT-rate of the country of destination. This requires fiscal frontiers for detecting which commodities are exported and not subject to domestic taxation. The same system is necessary to identify imports for taxation. Traditionally, border controls serve as fiscal frontiers. However, border tax adjustments do not necessarily require physical borders. Even with an abolition of border controls, the information can be provided by the first production or distribution stage in the country of destination or the last production or distribution stage in the country of origin. Accounting books of a company can be used by fiscal authorities in order to access the information necessary for implementing the tax system. Consequently, this system may even be implemented in an economic union with different VAT-systems but no border controls.

Under the origin principle commodities are taxed in the exporting country and are tax exempt in the importing country. In contrast to the destination principle, commodities are taxed in the country of production regardless of where they are consumed. Therefore, border tax adjustments are not necessary for this commodity taxation system. One feature common to both systems is the identification of a physical location of exporters and importers. If, for a given cross-border transaction, the origin country is not known the origin principle cannot be applied. The same holds true for the destination principle. The lack of being able to identify a destination country makes it impossible to implement the destination principle.

As mentioned above, an optimal commodity tax system of cross border transactions should not affect the trade and location decision of firms and households. Private decisions should be driven by commercial and not by tax avoidance reasons. Though the design of a tax system follows the neutrality principle, it is not always possible to eliminate all distortions arising in the context of taxation. A tax regime eliminates some distortions but creates new ones which are not present in other tax regimes. Therefore, the designing of a tax system means facing a tradeoff of distortions and finding an optimal tax system with a minimum of distortions. In the next section, a variety of distortions are listed which arise within the two basic commodity tax systems presented above and must be taken into account when deciding between them.

3.2.2 Distortionary Effects of the Destination and Origin Principle

In this section, we analyze whether the two VAT systems have any of the following distortionary effects:

- distortion of trade flows,
- distortion of location decision, and
- transfer pricing.

A VAT system is trade distorting if exporters or importers have an incentive to deviate from their pre-tax trade decision. To be more precise, consider a simple trade model. Imagine that a homogenous good can be bought in a foreign country as well as in the domestic country. The price of the foreign good in the domestic currency is P_F and of the domestic good P_D. The corresponding VAT-rates are τ_F and τ_D. If tax rates are zero, a consumer will buy the foreign good as long as P_F is lower than P_D and vice versa. The introduction of an origin-based VAT may change the consumer's decision. The after tax prices of the goods are now P_F $(1+\tau_F)$ and P_D $(1+\tau_D)$. For $\tau_F > \tau_D$, it becomes possible that the after tax price of the foreign good exceeds the after tax price of the domestic good although P_F is lower than P_D.

Therefore, under the origin principle a distortion of trade flows may arise. The destination principle does not have these undesirable effects. The after tax prices under the destination principles are P_F $(1+\tau_D)$ and P_D $(1+\tau_D)$. If P_F is lower than P_D, then this also holds for the after tax price and vice versa. Distorting trade effects do not arise under this principle.

So far, the analysis is only done for absolute prices. After all, resource allocation depends on relative rather than absolute prices. Therefore, the results derived above are even more general. The relative after tax commodity price $[P_F (1+\tau_D)]/[P_D (1+\tau_D)]$ under the destination principle and $[P_F (1+\tau_F)]/[P_D (1+\tau_D)]$ under the origin principle reveal that relative prices are unaffected under the destination principle in contrast to the origin principle. Consequently, trade flows are even more distorted under the origin principle as indicated only by absolute prices.[9]

An additional distortion has to be taken into account if firms and households are mobile. If the origin principle applies, firms have an incentive to relocate the firm in a country with low VAT rates. This lowers the after tax price for the consumer and increases the competitiveness of the firm. Under the destination principle, firms do not have this incentive as the VAT rate is determined by the place of consumption and not of production. Though a destination based VAT system is neutral with respect to the firm's location decision, it gives rise to the relocation of households or at least to buying goods and services in countries with lower VAT rates. While the former is one of many incentives for households to relocate, but definitely not the dominant reason, the

---

[9] In this section, we abstract from flexible exchange rate accommodate price level changes which lead to the equivalence of a destination- and origin-based VAT system in a free trade environment. This is done for three reasons: first, we want to keep the analysis as simple as possible, second, within the EU a flexible exchange rate system does not exist, and third, the equivalence result rests on the flexibility of prices (e.g. wages) which does not hold true in the short run. For an in depth analysis of this issue see Genser, Haufler & Sørensen 1995 as well as Lockwood, de Meza & Myles 1995.

latter is more relevant for the design of a commodity taxation system. Direct consumer purchases (cross-border shopping) is a common practice especially in regions close to countries with lower VAT rates. It becomes more attractive with the abolition of border controls. With direct consumer purchases, the destination principle becomes partially ineffective and elements of the origin principle apply.

Transfer pricing is another source of distortion which arises with the existence of multinational firms (MNF). Through strategic transfer pricing, MNF can transfer value added to countries with low VAT rates and thereby, reduce the VAT liability. To analyze the incentive of transfer pricing, consider a MNF with the parent company in the domestic country and a subsidiary in a foreign country. The subsidiary produces solely an intermediate good I which is exported to the parent company at price P_I. The parent company uses the good I as an input to produce the final good X and sells X at a price P_X in the domestic market. The VAT rate in the domestic country is τ_D and τ_F in the foreign country. If the destination principle applies, the total tax liability T of the MNF amounts to $T = \tau_D (P_X X - P_I I) + \tau_D P_I I$ which simplifies to $T = \tau_D P_X X$. By changing the transfer price P_I, the MNF cannot change the tax liability T and, therefore, cannot use P_I for tax avoidance reasons. Under an origin-based VAT system, the tax liability T is given by $T = \tau_D (P_X X - P_I I) + \tau_F P_I I$ which equals $T = \tau_D P_X X + (\tau_F - \tau_D) P_I I$.

In this case, the tax differential $\tau_F - \tau_D$ plays a crucial role. The transfer price P_I influences the total tax liability and can be strategically set in order to reduce T. If τ_D is lower than τ_F, T can be minimized by transferring value added to the domestic country. To achieve this, the transfer price is set at a low level. The reverse holds true for a domestic VAT rate τ_D exceeding the foreign VAT rate τ_F. A high transfer price of P_I shifts the tax base to the foreign country.[10]

4 Application

In this section, a synthesis of section 2 and 3 is given. It analyzes how a commodity tax system for electronic commerce can be designed on the basis of the above presented taxation principles.

The fundamental questions for taxing electronic commerce can be characterized as:

• In which way do distortionary effects of commodity taxation regimes differ when applied to electronic commerce from those arising in taxing traditional commerce?

---

[10] Different VAT systems are not the only incentive for transfer pricing. The capital income system, as well as the market form in different countries, provide an incentive to transfer the tax base to the most preferable country; see on this Genser & Schulze 1997 and Schjelderup & Sørgand 1997.

- Which additional problems exist in defining and identifying a tax base in the case of electronic commerce?

The two questions are addressed separately. Therefore, first, distortions arising from taxing electronic commerce are presented while abstracting from identification and control problems. To be more precise, it is assumed for simplicity that the physical location of sellers, buyers, servers and hosts, as well as the value of each transaction, is known to all parties interested in the information. In the second part of this section, problems in detecting electronic transactions for third parties (e.g. the state) and to identify the individuals involved in the transactions are analyzed. In particular, possibilities in detecting the origin and destination of data streams from the perspective of the seller and buyer of intangible goods are of interest here.

4.1 Distortionary Effects of Taxing Electronic Commerce

The basic information necessary for the application of any commodity system is the destination and origin of goods and services. This becomes even more important for cross-border transactions as this information is the deciding factor in which commodity taxation regime is relevant for the transaction. The location of the importer and exporter are usually taken as the destination and origin. But in the case of electronic commerce this question cannot be answered clearly.

If the origin principle applies, two definitions of destination are possible: the location of the server on which the web-site of the seller can be found and the location of the seller. The former is extremely vulnerable to distortions. In this case, the seller can relocate the website on a server in a low-VAT country. The transactions costs for this substitution effect are relatively low compared to VAT-differentials between countries. For illustration, even within the European Union, tax differentials amounted to 10% in 1997.[11] Taking countries outside the European Union into account, the tax differential will be even larger. This substitution possibility is likely to be used heavily as it enables the supplier to offer their products at a lower after tax price or to realize higher profits.

If the origin of an intangible is determined by the location of the seller, basically, the same kind of distortions arises as in the case of traditional commerce. The seller has an incentive to relocate the firm leading to a reduction of the VAT liability. It should be noted that the relocation of firms for tax avoidance reasons is only one determinant of a firm's location decision. But the relocation of a firm offering intangibles (e.g. a software firm moving from France to Germany) can be organized with

---

[11] In 1997, the VAT rate (regular rate) in Germany was 15% and in Sweden 25%; Bundesministerium der Finanzen (Federal Ministry of Finance) 1997.

lower transaction costs as the relocation of a firm with production facilities offering tangibles. Another kind of distortion arises within MNF. As mentioned above, transfer pricing is one strategy of MNF to reduce the tax liability. Taxing electronic commerce according to the origin principle may lead to a transfer of value added to a low VAT country. Tax authorities try to limit transfer pricing by determining the "correct" value of the transaction within MNF by finding equivalent transactions carried out between independent firms (OECD, 1997b). In general, this strategy is also available to MNF offering tangibles. However, in the case of exchanging intangibles, it will become increasingly difficult for tax authorities to identify equivalent transactions and therefore, to limit the scope of transfer pricing. In addition, it will become more attractive to offer intangibles only from subsidiaries in low VAT countries. From the perspective of the seller, intangibles have the advantage that consumers do not care so much about the place in the world from where they receive, for instance, the software package as transportation costs do not exist. Therefore, a relocation of the supply on intangibles form one subsidiary to another subsidiary will not have an effect on demand but enables the supplier to offer them at a lower price.

Under the destination principle, two definitions of destination can again be distinguished. The location of the host and of the customer can be used as the destination of an intangible. If the former applies, consumers will chose a provider with a host in a low tax country. As providers will anticipate this reaction, they will remove their hosts to low VAT countries. Therefore, this definition of destination cannot be regarded as a workable solution as it creates massive distortions. Even if one considers the case that providers would not react in the above mentioned way, customers could avoid high VAT by obtaining access to the Internet while staying in a foreign country with a more favorable VAT rate for the customers. This is simply a type of cross-border shopping arising with intangibles. The location of the customer defined as the destination creates fewer problems. In this case, distortions can only occur if the customer changes locations to a low VAT country. As already mentioned in section 3.2, it is not very likely that this is the dominant reason for a household's location decision.

Consequently, compared with taxing tangibles under the destination principle, intangibles will not create new distortions. From the perspective of a tax designer pursuing economic efficiency, the destination principle in combination with the definition of destination as the location of the customer would be the most preferred tax system for electronic commerce. This tax regime would also pass the test of administrative simplicity and low compliance costs but only because of the assumptions concerning the availability of all tax relevant information mentioned above.

The interesting question now is how the evaluation of the different tax systems changes if the information requirements of each system are taken into account. This may affect the administrative simplicity and compliance costs of the different tax regimes, possibly leading to tradeoffs between these principles and economic efficiency.

4.2 Identification and Control Problems in Taxing Electronic Commerce

Taxing cross-border activities requires information concerning the import and export of goods and services. Traditionally, border controls provided the necessary information and enabled the state to implement an origin or destination-based tax system. With the removal of border controls in some countries fiscal frontiers replaced them and provided the necessary information.

Applied to intangibles even with border controls, international transactions are difficult to identify. The reason is twofold. First, data streams are sent over the Internet using packet-switching technology. The only way to get information about imports and exports is to reassemble the packages to the original data stream which is almost impossible for the millions of packages sent per hour. Second, even if it is possible to reassemble the original data stream the state does not have any information about the value of the transaction which is the basis of a commodity taxation system. Data streams containing the intangible are normally separated from data streams for the underlying payment of the intangible. The two reasons represent an even higher barrier for the state to collect taxes if data is encrypted. Encryption is made to protect the integrity of the data and the individual privacy. A state which is able to reassemble packages cannot use the data unless it has access to the appropriate keys in order to decrypt it. But this would counteract the intention of encryption: the protection of integrity and privacy. Therefore, it seems to be unlikely that this instrument will be made available to the state. Consequently, border controls cannot be used to detect imports and exports of intangibles. The question arising now is whether fiscal frontiers provide the necessary information to implement a cross-border commodity taxation regime.

Under the destination principle, the location of the consumer determines the relevant tax system. Since the whole range of information necessary for taxation cannot be obtained during the flow of data, the origin or destination of an intangible is the only thing left to identify the whole transaction. If the consumer would report all electronic commerce activities to the domestic fiscal authorities, a destination-based tax system could be implemented. However, this would require the consumer to pay taxes voluntarily as the state faces difficulties to draw samples for tax auditing purposes and therefore, to credibly threaten consumers with fines in the case of tax evasion. On the other hand, the supplier of intangibles could be obliged to report the destination to the state. Hellerstein (1997) proposes to impose the obligation on the supplier to make reasonable efforts in determining the customer's address and to report them to the state. For the case of intangibles which depend on personal information of the customer (e.g. medical diagnostics) it seems likely that the supplier will have access to the address. But many intangibles are exchanged without any need for knowing who receives the intangibles (e.g. business statistics, electronic books). The seller will face difficulties determining the destination and will bear compliance costs if he is obliged to do so.[12] Compliance costs are even higher, as under this tax system, the supplier must have information about the relevant VAT rate in each country and must remit the tax to the customer's state. Thereby, it should be kept in mind that excessive compliance costs provide an incentive to the supplier for tax evasion.

Under the origin system, the customer may have difficulties to determine the origin of the supplier. Perhaps, he is able to determine the location of the server. But this must not coincide with the location of the firm. If origin is defined as the location of the server, the seller may have access to this information. It induces much more compliance costs identifying the location of the firm. Additionally, the customer would have to report the origin of the intangibles purchased to the state which again requires the customer to pay taxes voluntarily. The supplier, as the source of information, seems to be the more workable approach. All commercial activities are recorded by the supplier and can be used for taxation as the listing of sales is sufficient for implementing an origin-based VAT system. In general, the system is vulnerable to tax evasion by not listing all electronic commerce activities. But this is also possible for tangibles and is not a characteristic of intangibles.

Problems also arise in MNF in detecting intrafirm exchange besides the already mentioned difficulty in finding equivalent transactions for limiting transfer pricing (Owens, 1997). Private intranets are widespread in MNF making it more difficult or impossible to distinguish intangibles produced in a firm from those received from other related firms. Due to the information asymmetry, value added can now be transferred more easily to low VAT countries. Taking informational requirements of an origin and destination based taxation system into account, the origin principle seems to be the more appropriate system. It will lead to lower compliance costs and higher administrative simplicity.

---

[12] Hellerstein (1997) proposes a tax system primarily based on the destination principle. Under the proposed tax system, the vendor is obliged to make "reasonable and good faith efforts to determine the purchaser's billing address" (Hellerstein 1997, p. 597). However, the problem for administering this tax system is giving a precise definition of "reasonable and good faith efforts". Consequently, even if a clear cut definition is found both tax principles are applied depending on the effort level of the vendor.

5 Further Implications

In the last section, problems in taxing electronic commerce were presented. The analysis reveals a tradeoff between economic efficiency, on the one hand, and administrative simplicity and low compliance costs, on the other. So far, the analysis only refers to intangibles. However, if an appropriate tax system to tax intangibles exchanged electronically is found, the impact on tangibles must also be considered. Depending on the economic relationship between intangibles and tangibles, two polar cases can be distinguished: the case of complements and substitutes. For illustration, an electronic book may serve as a substitute for printed books, whereas electronic books and hardware are complements.

The theory of efficient taxation (ET) presented in section 2 provides insight into how the relationship between electronic intangibles and tangibles should be reflected in the tax system. In the case of substitutes, a different tax treatment of both goods (e.g. electronically exchanged intangibles are taxed lower than tangibles) changes the relative price of the goods leading to a substitution of tangibles for intangibles. The distortionary character of different tax treatment results in a loss of welfare. In the case of perfect substitutes, different taxation of both goods leads to a perfect shift from tangibles to intangibles. The distortionary character of the tax system increases. Therefore, the theory of efficient taxation recommends an equal tax on both goods. An unequal tax treatment would also violate the taxation principle of horizontal equity as consumption activities satisfying the same needs are taxed differently. How likely is it that both types of goods are taxed in the same manner? If, for instance, electronic commerce is taxed according to the origin principle (due to information requirements as presented in the last section) and tangibles on a destination basis (the dominant taxation principle in the European Union), it is likely that both types of goods are taxed differently. Distortions created by the unequal tax treatment must be balanced against a reduction of distortions due to the application of the origin- rather than the destination principle. In contrast, if the destination principle (destination defined as the location of the consumer) is applied, electronically exchanged intangibles and tangibles are taxed at the same rate. However, this principle can only be implemented if the above mentioned information requirements are fulfilled.

In the case of complementary goods, the demand of these goods is not influenced by relative prices. Consequently, a change in relative prices does not lead to a substitution effect and hence, welfare losses. The only effect left is the income effect which is not welfare reducing from the perspective of the economy as a whole.

Another policy option discussed in the literature is the Bit-tax (Beck & Prinz 1997). Under this tax regime, the amount of data transferred is subject to taxation. However, this policy option is not a substitute for a cross-border taxation system as data transfer itself is not an indicator for an electronic exchange of goods and services. The Bit-tax also taxes transactions with no underlying commercial aspect (e.g. email). Additionally, this tax instrument gives rise to tax avoidance strategies as the volume of data transfer can easily be changed without changing the information transmitted.

6 Conclusion

In this article, the implications of electronic commerce for commodity taxation have been analyzed. This has been done on the basis of taxation principles, which should guide any tax system: economic efficiency, low compliance costs, administrative simplicity, and equity. These principles have been applied to design a tax system for cross-border electronic commerce transactions.

The tax system designer faces two fundamental problems: identification of distortions and how the information requirements of different commodity taxation regimes are fulfilled. While abstracting from the latter problem, the following conclusions can be drawn. An origin-based VAT system for taxing electronic commerce causes massive distortions no matter how the origin is defined (as the location of the seller's firm or the server). A destination-based VAT system has the advantage of creating low distortions if destination is defined as the location of the customer. Additionally, this tax regime generally ensures an equal taxation of electronic commerce and tangibles. Ignoring the former problem and taking only information requirements into account, the result changes. The origin system is now superior to the destination system.

In sum, the analysis reveals a tradeoff between economic efficiency, on the one hand, and low compliance costs and administrative simplicity, on the other. The destination principle causes less distortions but high compliance and administrative cost whereas the origin principle must be favored on the basis of the availability of information necessary for implementation, but creates high distortions. Therefore, in the face of information requirements the origin principle can only be implemented.

In general, policy proposals must be simple and perceived as fair from the viewpoint of public decision makers. A policy reform increasing economic efficiency is not taken into consideration as a reform option if the resulting consequences, other than efficiency, are regarded as not acceptable. A potential barrier for the implementation of the origin principle arises from the issue of tax revenue distribution among countries. Normally, under an origin-based commodity tax system, tax revenues accrue to the country of origin. This could become a serious issue in the political debate. As firms have an incentive to relocate the server or the firm, a concentration of commodity tax revenues in a few countries is not unlikely. In order to gain broad political acceptance of the origin principle, the "one-country" distribution rule must be replaced by other rules favoring a more equal distribution of tax revenues. Unfortunately, such a rule has not been negotiated yet.

References

Beck, H. & Prinz, A. (1997). Should All the World be Taxed? Taxation and the Internet. *Intereconomics*, 32 (March/April), pp. 87-92.

Bundesministerium der Finanzen (Federal Ministry of Finance) (1997). *Die wichtigsten Steuern im Vergleich* (The Most Important Taxes in International Comparison). Bonn: Bundesministerium der Finanzen.

Fox, W. F. & Murray, M. N. (1997). The Sales Tax and Electronic Commerce: So What's New? *National Tax Journal*, 50(3), pp. 573-592.

Frenkel, J., Razin, A. & Sadka, E. (1991). *International Taxation in an Integrated World*, Cambridge, Massachusetts: MIT Press.

Garcia, D. L. (1995). Networking and the Rise of Electronic Commerce: The Challenge for Public Policy. *Business Economics*, 30(4), pp. 7-14.

Genser, B. & Schulze, G. G. (1997). Transfer Pricing under an Origin-based VAT System. *Finanzarchiv N.F.*, 54, pp. 51-67.

Genser, B., Haufler A. & Sørensen, P. B. (1995). Indirect Taxation in an Integrated Europe: Is There a Way of Avoiding Trade Distortions Without Sacrificing National Tax Autonomy?. *Journal of Economic Integration*, 10(2), 178-205.

Halsall, F. (1996). *Data Communications, Computer Networks and Open Systems*, 4th Edition. Harlow: Addison-Wesley.

Hellerstein, W. (1997). Transaction Taxes and Electronic Commerce: Designing State Taxes that work in an Interstate Environment. *National Tax Journal*, 50(3), pp. 593-606.

Lockwood, B., de Meza, D. & Myles, G. D. (1995). On the European Union VAT Proposals: The Superiority of Origin over Destination Taxation. *Fiscal Studies*, 16(1), pp. 1-17.

MacKie-Mason, J. K. & Varian, H. (1994). Economic FAQs About the Internet. *Journal of Economic Perspectives*, Vol. 8., No. 3, pp. 75-96.

Malone, Th. W., Yates, J. A. & Benjamin, R. I. (1987). Electronic Markets and Electronic Hierarchies. *Communication of the ACM*, 30(6), pp. 485-497.

Mansell, R. (1996). Designing Electronic Commerce. In: R. Mansell and R. Silverstone (Eds.), *Communication by Design – The Politics of Information and Communication Technologies* (pp. 103–128). Oxford University Press.

McLure, Ch. E. Jr. (1997). Electronic Commerce, State Sales Taxation, and Intergovernmental Fiscal Relations. *National Tax Journal*, 50(4), pp. 731-749.

OECD (1997a). *Electronic Commerce – Opportunities and Challenges for Government*. Paris: Organization for Economic Co-Operation and Development.

OECD (1997b). *Transfer Pricing Guidelines for Multinational Enterprises and Tax Administration: 1997 Update*. Paris: Organization for Economic Co-Operation and Development.

OECD (1997c). *Measuring Electronic Commerce: Committee for Information, Computer and Communications Policy*. Paris: Organization for Economic Co-Operation and Development. Available: <http://www.oecd.org> (1998, February 22).

Owens, J. (1997). What Chance for the Virtual Taxman? *OECD Observer*, 208, pp. 16-19.

Peha, J. M. & Strauss, R. P. (1997). A Primer on changing Information Technology and the Fisc. *National Tax Journal*, 50(3), pp. 607-621.

Picot, A., Bortenlänger, C. & Röhrl, H. (1997). Organization of Electronic Markets: Contributions from the New Institutional Economics. *Information Society*, 13(1), pp. 107-123.

Rosen, H. S. (1998). *Public Finance*, 5th Edition. Homewood, Illinois: Irwin/McGraw-Hill.

Schjelderup, G. & Sørgard, L. (1997). Transfer Pricing as a Strategic Device for Decentralized Multinationals. *International Tax and Public Finance*, 4, pp. 277-290.

Spaanderman, J. & Ypsilanti, D. (1997). Infrastructures for Electronic Trade. *OECD Observer*, 208, pp. 13-15. .

Survey of Telework Activities in Europe[1]

Wilhelm Dangelmaier, Dirk Förster, Volker Horsthemke, and
Stephan Kress

1 Introduction

It was in the early 1970s when the concept of telework came about for the first
time in the agglomeration area of Los Angeles. When the oil crisis hit many economies people became aware about the amount of fuel used for commuting. In 1973 Jack
Nilles proposed working at home as a way of cutting fuel consumption and saving
time.[2] His idea was to ban commuting to the data-highway and he called it telecommuting.[3] Although it is often stated telecommuting would be the American equivalent
for the European telework, Nilles himself defines telecommuting as a form of teleworking. He adds that it is difficult to distinguish between these two words because
many languages do not have an accurate translation for the word 'telecommuting'.[4]

When Alvin Toffler picked up on the idea of telework in the 1980s, he advo-
cated the concept of the electronic village as the main place of production in the future
and had a receptive audience. In Europe especially Scandinavian countries (Denmark
and Sweden) were fascinated by his ideas which caused immense public discussion.
Scientific investigation forecast a tremendous future. However, telework was not as
successful as expected in the 1980s. Although some of the pilot projects and experiments were promising remote working was economically irrelevant. Especially technology caused a lot of problems because its capacity was restricted and the necessary
information network was not yet dense enough. This and other aspects made telework
too inefficient at that time.

The same happened to the early German projects, where telework was first
mentioned in 1982 at Siemens. Although this was a successful project it was tried to
legally prohibit telework in Germany in 1983. Managers were not flexible enough to

---

[1] This survey is embedded in the "COBIP" project. The COBIP project ("Telework co-ordination
Services for co-operative Business Processes") is located within the Telematics Application Programs
of the European Commission (UR 4002 – SECTOR 6).
[2] See Kirchmair 1996, p. 48-49: Jack Nilles analyzed the relation between company and branch. He
distinguishes between centralization (workplaces are kept or brought back to the parent company),
fragmentation (parent company sets up branches), dispersion (branches are divided into smaller entities), diffusion (individual workplaces).
[3] Telework is the British expression. Synonyms that can be found: work at home, teleworking (mainly
UK) télétravail, télématique and travail à distance (F), Telearbeit, Telematik, Distanzarbeit, Fernarbeit
(D), see also Huber 1987, p. 18.
[4] See Nilles 1994, pp. 11-12.

adopt and manage telework, the economical and technological barriers were too high and the public was not yet convinced of its advantages. Although the ideas persisted, it did not expand to the extent that was initially envisioned.

Telework finds itself in a state of certain unpredictability. Its development has been overestimated in the early 1970s, when the theory came to light, almost forgotten in the late 1970s, when business was expected to implement the theoretical construction, praised again in the early 1980s and kept on the simmer in the late 1980s. Lately it is found to be on the increase again.

Estimations still differ a lot and had to be revised many times. Often it was stated that telework would be the only thinkable form of organization that could persist into the future. Nevertheless, there still seems to be a long way to go because reality has outperformed expectations. The public now knows more about telework and is becoming interested in the opportunities it offers. In addition, managerial doubts are ebbing. Both is surely partly due to the governmental programs aimed to spread knowledge about telework. Technological premises are given, too, and they are advancing so that forecast is positive again. Even when technological infrastructure is given, its initiation frequently has to be catalyzed either by innovative companies introducing pilot projects or by state support. Telework is scattered disproportionately throughout Europe, and the distinct countries are on different development stages. Before we will have a closer look at which part of the EU is on which development stage, the latest figures presented in the literature referring to this issue will be shown.

2 Organizational Forms of Telework

There are many ways of defining telework and it would be difficult to find one term that fits every demand. Telework is a relatively new field of investigation which constantly undergoes a process of fast development and frequent change. Telework is not a job, but a method of organizing work which is built around the processing of information. The individual or group of people carrying out the work, is physically remote from the employer for whom it is being done and uses modern information and communication technology to transfer the product of work.[5]

Telework can be regarded as a special kind of teleco-operation. It deals with the carrying-out of tasks and processes that are not limited to the company's boundaries. It is a defining characteristic that this teleco-operation is computer-supported, making use of Information and Communications Technology (ICT). Teleco-operation can be divided into an inter-organizational and an intra-organizational type. Inter-organizational teleco-operation refers to telework involving the co-operation of two or more

---

[5] See Stanworth 1991b, p. 215; Huber 1987, p. 10.

different companies. This kind of co-operation can, for example, be implemented in engineering fields. Intra-organizational teleco-operation describes all forms of teleco-operation within a company's organization. It also includes "extreme" types of tele-work such as mobile offices. The intra-organizational forms of teleco-operation are the matter of this survey (see figure 1).

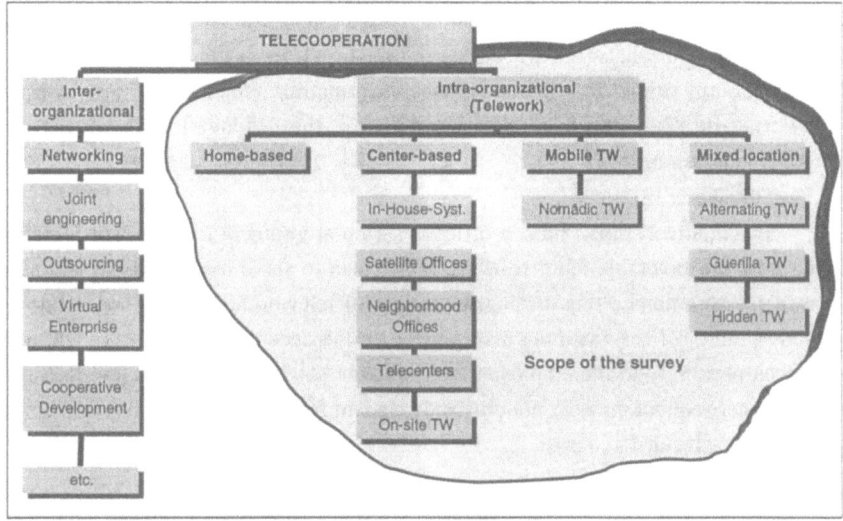

Figure 1: Inter- vs. intra-organizational level of telework

Telework (which will now be used as a synonym for intra-organizational teleco-operation) is that kind of contractually agreed work that is fulfilled off-site, i.e., the employee is at least temporarily dislocated from the company's in-house offices. It can be carried out as home-based, center-based, mobile telework or in a mixed location pattern and is characterized by the use of public means of communication and the corresponding technological devices.[6]

- Home-Based Telework

Home-based telework is either done exclusively or predominantly at home, but it does not exclude that some of the working-time is spent visiting clients and employers.[7] Yet, it includes that the teleworker theoretically does not have to be present in the company. Every regular weekly presence in the company, for example, fits better the definition of alternating telework.

---

[6] See bmbf 1996.
[7] See Kirchmair 1996, p. 11.

- In-house-system

The word 'remote' does not always mean far away. That is why some authors tend to say that teleworkers can have their workplace under one roof with the rest of the company.[8] In that case the worker is doing telework when he uses the information and telecommunication systems rather than personal contact to communicate with his fellow workers and superiors. However, the in-house-system regarded as a form of intranet between separated sites of a specific company would be very close to what Jack M. Nilles defines as 'teleworking' – not only office-based but any kind of work that uses information technology.[9] An in-house-teleworker in a branch communicating with e.g. the headquarters is, on the other hand, also a remote worker.

- Satellite Offices

If a relatively small branch office is set up at a remote location, specifically to open up more favorable labor markets, rather than to serve local customers, it seems reasonable to embrace this under the heading of telework. These branch offices are called satellite offices when the main aspect for the decentralization of the workplace has been proximity to the employees.[10] Moreover, satellite offices often are set up as profit centers so that they are not only independent from the company but also responsible for their results.[11]

- Neighborhood Offices

Several remote workers employed by various supporting companies have their workplaces in the same building. These neighborhood centers are situated close to the home of the remote worker and bring information and communication facilities close to them. Neighborhood centers can include commercial business service centers as well as 'dedicated' centers set up by a particular work organization for exclusive use of their own workers.[12]

- Telecenter

A telecenter is a sort of neighborhood centers. They provide a mix of commercial and altruistic services, often associated with rural settings. Telecenters are more like a meeting-place of remote workers providing them the necessary equipment and, moreover, offering them jobs as well as services such as computer education and ad-

---

[8] See Kirchmair 1996, p. 49.
[9] See Nilles 1994, pp. 11-12.
[10] See Stanworth 1991a, pp. 9-10; Dostal 1985, p. 468.
[11] Profit-center: 'Das Profit-Center ist ein Anreizsystem mit einer betont marktorientierten Ausprägung'. See Freese 1992, p. 374.
[12] See Picot, Reichwald & Wigand 1996, p. 373; Kirchmair 1996, p. 49; Stanworth 1991a, p. 10.

vanced training. They can be established by one or more companies, institutions, the government or as independent enterprises.[13]

- On-site Telework

On-site telework is similar to mobile telework. Nevertheless, there is a major difference: the on-site teleworker has an office-based workplace, but this workplace is located in the client's company. Customer-site based telework is common as advisers, consultants, long-term maintenance men, software developers, systems specialists, etc. have worked like this for many years. Any worker doing his/her job in the client's company who is connected to his/her parent company is an on-site teleworker. Normally, the job is related with a certain project and the remote worker changes his location after the termination of the project.[14]

- Mobile Telework

Mobile telework needs no workplace. All the employee needs are voice, document and data transferring facilities (e.g. a laptop, a modem, a fax, and a cell-phone). Consequently, the teleworker can work at any place and any time and, usually, is not equipped with any stationary workplace.[15]

- Alternating Telework[16]

Alternating telework involves the combination of remote and office-based work, within the typical working week. The employee does not only work as a remote worker but he also has a centralized workplace. Thus, he spends part of his working week in the company's building and part at home. How much he stays in either of the places depends on the contractual agreement between employer and employee.[17]

- Guerilla Telework

Stanworth uses the word 'overflow pattern' to describe telework which is used as in addition to the normal working week. Mainly managers have laptops or computer set-ups at home to keep them constantly abreast of changing world markets. They can link up their equipment wherever they are and whenever they want. Unfortunately they are never really 'off duty'.[18]

- Hidden Telework

This kind of telework is done in addition to the normal working week, too. The main difference between hidden and guerilla telework is that the hidden teleworker is no executive, does not take part in any telework-program and sometimes is not even

---

[13] See Stanworth 1991a, p. 10; Kirchmair 1996, p. 51.
[14] See bmbf 1996, pp. 7-8.
[15] See Rieker 1995, p. 200; Stanworth 1991a, pp. 13-14.
[16] 'Alternating' telework is known as well as 'mixed location pattern', 'alternate' or 'nomadic' telework.
[17] See Stanworth 1991a, p. 8; Kirchmair 1996, p. 50; Geenen 1992, p. 7.
[18] See Rieker 1995, p. 200; Stanworth 1991a, p. 7.

linked up to the company's information technology network. He simply takes work home to get it done there unofficially.[19]

3 Penetration of Telework

The estimated potential of telework is immense which comes probably from the good US-performance in telecommuting, the US-American equivalent term of tele-working. About 9 million US American residents were telecommuting in 1994/95. That is quite a high number, considering that the total workforce of the USA is smaller than that of the EU.[20] The EU, on the other hand, is said to have a potential of about 10 million teleworkers that will be reached in the year 2000. The present number, how-ever, is only about 2 million.[21]

There is a huge discrepancy between different calculations, as well. Spanish statistics, for instance, expect only 2 million European teleworkers in 2000 and Kirchmair even mentions that at the same time there will be just 11.7 million tele-workers worldwide.[22] Assessments often had to be adjusted when real performance turned out to be lower. For 1990 for example the envisioned total of teleworkers for the UK was 2.2 million compared to a real amount of 5,000.[23] The difference in 1995 was already smaller: estimated 4 million vs. 1.23 million true teleworkers.[24] In other words, it is true that telework is growing at a fast speed, but still 'augurs' tend to be exaggerating a tad in their forecast.

It is almost impossible to give undoubtedly correct figures because estimates are being made in various ways, i.e. measures differ. Though recent estimates come close enough to the real figures because enthusiasm is decreasing and it is being taken into account that telework's evolution is no sudden explosion but a long-term progress. In addition, more and more figures coincide so that the reliability for the sake of this investigation is given.

The following table (see table 1) shows the most recent available 1994 figures that demonstrate the present dissemination of telework in many European countries. Compared with the USA (4.54%) European telework (1%) is still nearly insignificant. Solely Sweden (3.77%), Finland (2.5%) and the UK (2.2%) come close. Whereas, compared with Japan, Europe is still one step ahead because Japan is said to have close

---

[19] See Picot, Reichwald & Wigand 1996, p. 387.
[20] See ETO 1996.
[21] See Die Welt 1994, p. 13; Elola 1997, p. 52; and ETO 1996.
[22] See Elola 1997, p. 52 and Kirchmair 1996, p. 57.
[23] See Stanworth 1991b, p. 215.
[24] See Stanworth 1991b, p. 215; see also: Blake 1994, p. 26.

to 0% teleworking workforce.[25] In fact, Anglo-Saxon countries are more open to this form of organization.

Table 1: Estimate of the number of teleworkers in Europe in 1994[26]				
Country	Population > 15 years	Workforce	Teleworkers	Teleworkers as % of Workforce
Austria	7,000,000	3,278,000	8,195	0.25
Belgium	8,202,000	3,770,000	18,044	0.48
Germany	67,733,000	36,528,000	149,013	0.41
Denmark	4,287,000	2,637,000	9,800	0.37
Spain	31,741,000	12,458,000	101,571	0.82
France	45,775,000	22,021,000	215,143	0.98
Finland	5,000,000	2,400,000	60,000	2.50
Greece	8,415,000	3,680,000	16,830	0.46
Italy	48,361,000	21,015,000	96,722	0.46
Ireland	2,611,000	824,000	15,000	1.40
Luxembourg	378,400	165,000	832	0.50
Netherlands	12,365,000	6,561,000	80,000	1.22
Poland	7,846,000	4,509,000	25,107	0.56
Sweden	7,003,271	3,316,000	125,000	3.77
United Kingdom	46,544,000	25,630,000	563,182	2.20
EU	284,258,400	148,739,000	1,484,439	1.00
USA**	206,310,400	121,600,000	5,518,560	4.54

A further interesting result is the difference between the number of companies offering telework and the percentage of teleworking population (see table 2). 0.47% of the French workforce is employed by 7% of the companies. Thus, there are more French companies than French citizens who are interested in telework. In opposition to that, 7.4% of the British companies (just 0.4% more than in France) employ 1.21% of the workforce. The British have a more open-minded attitude towards telework than British enterprises. The German public (0.22%) seems not be as interested in telework as German companies (4.8%), and the average Italian company interested in telework outperforms almost all of its European fellows: 16.7 teleworkers per company. It seems that the few Italian teleworkers are all employed by a small number of companies.

About 1.25 million European teleworkers took pleasure in the opportunities of their new jobs in 1994. It seems that they accept their work because the 1996 figures show close to 2.2 million teleworking population. A little more than 1 million of them

---

[25] The most recent figures count 0% teleworkforce in Japan. This is unlikely as it is an eager supporter of telework (see BMWi 1996, chap. 6).
[26] See Korte & Wynne 1996, p. 28; empirica 1994a, p. 7; empirica 1994b, p. 5; Bertin & O'Neill 1997; EC 1997; PA Consulting 1994.

are employed in the United Kingdom, 450,000 in France, 325,000 in Germany, around 260,000 in Spain and 222,000 in Italy. 252,000 teleworkers are scattered throughout the rest of the EU.

Table 2: Dissemination of telework in Europe in 1994[27]						
	Germany	France	United Kingdom	Italy	Spain	Average
Companies						
% of companies with telework	4.80	7.00	7.40	2.20	3.60	5.00
Teleworkers/Company	6.10	8.30	16.90	16.70	9.80	11.40
Population						
% of teleworking population	0.22	0.47	1.21	0.20	0.32	0.48
Absolute # of teleworkers	149,000	215,000	563,000	97,000	102,000	225,200

Telework in practice does not necessarily mean that it only can be found in big industrial companies like IBM, which was, by the way, one of the first to introduce telework on a large scale in Spain. IBM España has a workforce of 1.400 and half of it are teleworkers.[28] Although telework in Spain is still on the stage of initiation, Spanish residents are innovative regarding telework. The Monasterio Cisterciense de Santa María de Valbona, a convent situated in Lleida (Spain), regards teleworking as a 'blessing', offering teleservices to the mundane world. Five of the 20 nuns opted for telework instead of doing gardening. Between 9:15 – 13:00 they are at their clients' disposal, elaborating scores in the computer and manuals for computer companies. Telework offers them the opportunity to keep pace with modern development without breaking their convent's rules that oblige them to stay within the territory of their cloister.[29]

4 Survey of Telework-Projects in the EU

4.1 Methodology of the Survey

202 projects – mainly found on Internet pages – have been analyzed. Almost none of the projects contained information about all of the criteria mentioned in the following chapter, but a project had to inform about at least three criteria[30] to be selected. The Internet provides the most recent – but unfortunately already pre-selected-information about telework. Especially linguistic constraints were faced as English is not the only language used in the Internet. Chiefly sources in English, German and Spanish were perused. Some pages in French, Dutch and Danish could also be ana-

---

[27] See empirica 1994a, p. 7; empirica 1994b, p. 5.
[28] See Elola 1997, p. 59.
[29] See Elola 1997, p. 55.
[30] Note: Country and start-date of a project were further selection criteria.

lyzed. Investigation was moreover restricted to the word "telework" rather than tele-commuting as telework applies to 95% to non-European regions.

The survey is an unrepresentative random test of accidentally, not methodologically found projects. Many times very few criteria were mentioned in a project's description. A representative survey could only be obtained carrying out a large scale investigation which would include interviews with employers and employees. The interrogation would have to be related to the survey's specific demands. The "Bundesministerium für Arbeit und Sozialordnung" carried out a representative survey in Germany in 1997.[31] Aside from its restriction to German telework its aim was to investigate mainly the legal framework so that it was little useful for the elaboration of this survey. The objective of this survey is to study how telework is received in the media Internet which is said to be the mirror of telework's current situation. Furthermore, the purpose is to make a future prediction in order to find out whether an Internet random test is suitable for a more ambitious investigation and whether the figures are reliable. Last but not least, the information about telework in Europe found in literary sources will be updated by the results detected in the Internet.

Table 3: Survey-overview (total amount of projects: n = 202)						
Criteria	Organizational Form	Task Structure	Occupational Classification	Employment Status	Monetary Sponsorship	Life-Cycle
Σ of projects	193	89	107	125	195	193

In table 3 it is illustrated how often a specific criterion was stated in a project's description. Some programs contained more than one attribute of the same criterion so that the total amount of the attributes does not necessarily coincide with the amount of projects (the letter "n" – in tables and figures – refers always to the number of projects and not to the number of attributes).

4.2 Limitations

A typical drawback of Internet recherché is that it is often not possible to assess the expertise of the authors which is less of a problem with printed sources from well-established periodicals, daily newspapers etc. Due to the extremely unstandardized presentation of the projects it was necessary to make assumptions, i.e., to infer specific information that fit into the survey pattern by "reading between the lines". This was always done in a rather conservative fashion and seems legitimate particularly for factors such as the employment status, the tasks that were teleworked and also for the funding of the project. All these factors could often be deduced from the setup of the

---

[31] See Freudenreich, Klein & Wedde 1997, pp. 11-15.

project, the company involved and other information. The topicality of the projects – if not given – was often approximated by taking the "last change date" of the HTML-document as an estimate. For the projects obtained from printed media the publication date was used if no other date was given. This is, of course, a "best case"-estimator, yet the only available at all. (Most web-documents tend to be maintained rather infrequently so this seems justifiable.)

It is particularly a limitation with respect to the validity of the survey that no single definition of telework and related terms exists. It could almost never be known what the exact definition behind "telework" was when a project was described. An example where the three terms satellite office, telecenter and telecottage are used as synonyms (for stylistic reasons, it seems) is that of a Swiss satellite office[32]. Therefore, the results from the survey have to be looked at cautiously.

Another limitation are the language barriers that made surveying difficult for some countries. After all, not all information on the Internet is in English or German. That is why genuine research in Greece, Portugal, Italy and Eastern Europe was not possible. It is simply not true that telework is exclusively discussed in the major European languages. Much of the information targeting teleworkers themselves (as opposed to a big academic audience) is "customized to local markets", and, therefore, written in local languages. Furthermore, only *published* projects were accessible to this secondary source survey – and not all companies have an interest in publishing their experiences with telework.

4.3 Dissemination of Telework Projects throughout Europe

Let alone Germany[33], not surprisingly, most of the projects have been found in Sweden as it has very good conditions for telework. Its telecommunications market with very low costs for telephony is perhaps the most open one in Europe. Its population of close to 9 million residents is spread over a country of immense proportions with many residents looking for opportunities to combine high-quality work with staying in their rural areas. Sweden is the European country with the longest experience in telework. Second comes the UK which has a very high rate of telework in practice in Europe and has – like Sweden – extremely fertile ground for good telework-development. Both of them have in common that their good performance in launching telework projects can be traced down to their setting up of center-based telework. Nevertheless, a major difference was detected as most of the Swedish programs were started in 1995, a little less in 1996 and none in 1997,

---

[32] See Brueckenbauer 1997.
[33] Due to the better availability of (particularly printed) sources, Germany is certainly overrepresented in this survey. This is why it will be plaid down a bit.

whereas the UK established very few projects in 1995 and boosted telework in 1996 and even more in 1997.

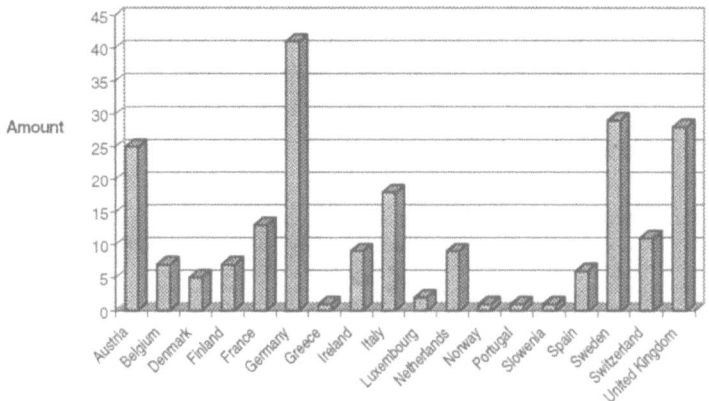

Figure 2: Telework-projects in the EU (n = 202)

However, the fair performance of Ireland as well as the good performance of Germany and Austria stand out. Ireland is a black box with regard to telework. 1.4% of the workforce is teleworking but it is not obviously determinable where this telework comes from. Neither too much general information is available, nor have many projects been found. Moreover, small scale initiatives prevailed. Germany and Austria, on the other hand, have been said to be definite late-comers but they apparently try to give the lie to latest forecast as they launched many projects in the mid 1990s (especially in 1996 and 1997). Italy surprises as well with quite a quantity of recent programs. It seemingly tends to catch up, although some legal and technological problems can be detected. The catching-up might be due to the high potential of interest in telework (with 20.1% the second highest in Europe).

France and the Netherlands are definitely under-performing. Both are said to be very open to telework and surely have a sound basis for its development (e.g. in France: manifold general telematic programs; in the Netherlands: good infrastructure and managerial and public interest in telework) but the amount of found programs does not back this up. Yet, although the total sum of projects is small, their launching has increased progressively in recent years (see figure 2)[34].

The rest of Europe is not exaggeratedly active in telework. They all seem to be close to the same stage of development. Yet, this is misleading as Luxembourg,

---

[34] Sometimes one project was carried out in different companies/countries.

Portugal, Greece and Norway really show very little action; Spain and Finland, on the other hand, are pressing on to catch up. Luxembourg did even only join in projects started by Belgium and France. Still, Spain, Finland, Portugal and Greece are even lacking the necessary technological premises and infrastructure. Denmark, Belgium and Switzerland are indifferent or hesitant to adopt telework completely. They have a good environment for telework and there are activities, but they are limited. Last but not least, there is Slowenia which co-operated in one French project. Apart from this exceptual telework project in Eastern Europe just one other project was found there. Unfortunately, it was a Swedish program which just affected a Czech worker and, therefore, was not included as Czech project.

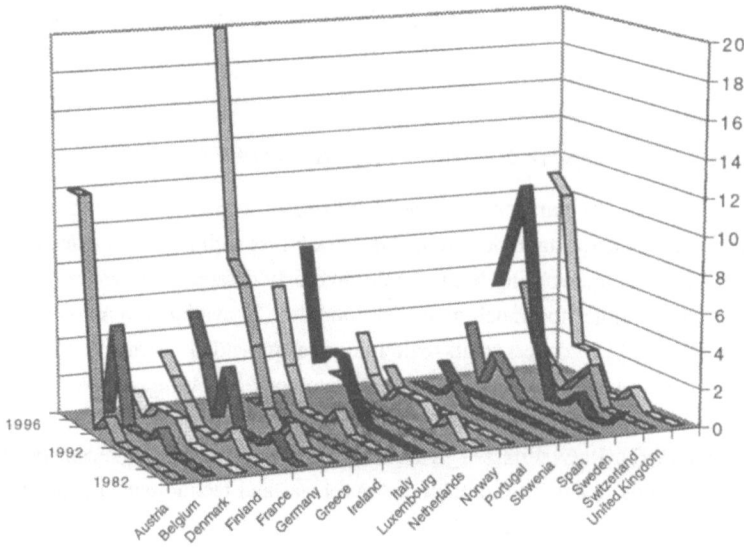

Figure 3: Telework-projects in the EU – annual quantity (n = 202)

In figure 3 we can see how the projects were spread over Europe and in which year they had been launched. The number of projects increased continuously in the 1990s whereas programs that originated in the 1980s are scarce. This happens to be the result of many institutionalized former programs that had been started in the 1980s but that were not continued or expanded as a project in 1997. In other words, although there might have been more projects in the 1980s they were not going on as projects in 1997.

Often institutionalization means a slow-down in telework activities, i.e., existing telework places are being maintained, but no further ones are about to be created.

Therefore, figures do not reflect the actual situation of telework in a country, but the amount of activities undertaken to increase the presence of telework during the last decade. It can just be seen which country is active in launching telework projects, but it cannot be deduced to what degree telework has penetrated a country's labor market.

Seemingly, there is a relation between the recognition of the potential of telework and its implementation. Most of the countries that have been in favor of telework for a long time boosted its development some years ago. Now that they have institutionalized several of the former projects they seem to pause, i.e., although the importance of telework is not decreasing there is little action and implementers seem to wait for new impetus or opportunities (or even new necessity) to establish projects. Other countries, on the other hand, had not detected telework as an option until recently and are now expanding massively their activities. Another group of countries is still hesitating to make more efforts to push the existing moderate development of telework. The last group contains those countries which have shown little interest in telework so far which means that their support of telework is meager. Table 4 shows which country is in which state of attitude towards telework.

Table 4: State of attitude towards telework				
State of Attitude	Massive Support	Pausing	Hesitating	Low Support
Country	• Sweden • Austria • Germany • Italy • Finland[35] • UK	• Netherlands • France • Ireland	• Belgium • Switzerland • Denmark • Spain[36]	• Greece • Portugal • Luxem-bourg[37]

Sweden is a special case: it was one of the first European countries – along with Denmark – that picked up on the idea of telework in the early 1980s. Unfortunately, there was little information available about how it had developed throughout the 1980s and the early 1990s. It was largely known for telecottages that time. However, according to Internet sources which provide especially data from the 1990s on Sweden is a major player in telework. The results were astonishing: if the figures are

---

[35] Finland strongly supports telework, but it has not been obviously visible since Finland is supporting telework in rural rather than in urban areas. The projects are often on a telematic level but, in contrary to other European telematic programs, their main aim is setting up teleworkplaces.

[36] Spain is a difficult case. It has a relatively high percentage of tele-workforce, but few projects have been found. It is also possible to put it in the group of the pausing countries. Yet, Spain has recently started the introduction of information technology. Therefore, Spain might enter the massive support category soon if it leaves its blurred position behind.

true, Sweden's tele-workforce in percentage of the total workforce is higher than that of the USA (S: about 7%, USA: about 4.45%. Though, other sources mention 3.77 or even 0.77% for Sweden).[38] Aside from this it could be derived from the oscillation in telework support that Sweden passed through a "telework-drought" in the late 1980s. Many telecottages had been established in the early 1980s. From then on there was little information available and just recently Sweden is pushing telework again with many projects which started especially in the mid 1990s. Further countries seem to go through a similar evolution. France, the UK and Ireland showed little movement in the field of telework in the late 1980s and early 1990s although they maintained their leading position in Europe. Since the late mid 1990s all of them are expanding their activities anew.

4.3.1 Criterion 1: Organizational Forms of Telework in Europe

Over many years alternating telework has been preferred by the majority of teleworkers as it combines the opportunities of the new form of organizing work with maintaining the advantages of working in an office. Especially the loss of social contacts was thought to be avoided by doing alternating telework. Center-based telework is another concept that maintains social contact while working remotely. Although promoted strongly by trade unions, it was neglected in practice. Now it seems, though, that Unions succeeded in making center-based telework the prevailing organizational form. 80 projects included center-based telework, whereas alternating telework was mentioned 64 times and home-based telework was 63 times part of a program (see figure 4). From a general point of view the advantages of teleworking center-based are obvious as it is very similar to office-based work: coworkers might not be colleagues from the company, but there is no loss of social contact. Nevertheless, the workplace is close to the home of the remote worker. Home-based telework also has a strong position which might come from the better work-agreement-based protection of the teleworker which is being enabled by increasing flexibility in the legal framework. The line between home-based and alternating telework was not always drawn very clearly. Supposedly, employers establishing telework wanted to leave their employees the option to back out of pure isolated tele-homework. This might be a further reason for the high number of projects including alternating telework.

---

[37] Luxembourg seems not to be present in the telework world at all. Apart from one telecottage project that did not suit our criteria and a French as well as a Belgium project in which Luxembourg joined in no data has been found. Not even its telework-homepage gives much information.
[38] See Telework 97 Conference 1997, Dacom 1997 and Bertin & O'Neill 1997.

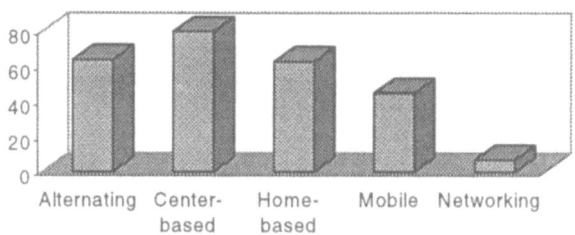

Figure 4: Organizational forms of telework in Europe (n = 193)

Networking was sometimes used to enter the first stage of telework within a company, i.e., the network was established and work was done remotely via information technology but the worker did not necessarily leave his office. Furthermore, it was occasionally used in a broader sense so that the work still was telework and not teleco-operation, but it was not explicitly mentioned what kind of telework it was. Intranet application as well as outsourcing, virtual offices, work formerly done without information technology-use (e.g. mobile- or project work) and teamwork via information technology were mentioned. Last but not least, mobile telework was encountered 45 times. It is still the favorite of managers and outdoor staff. If the trend towards highly skilled tele-workforce persists, mobile telework is likely to gain momentum.

4.3.2 Criterion 2: Task Structure

New concepts (like business reengineering, etc.) might yet be too new for telework. Only very few projects contained information about what kind of task or process structure had been transformed into telework. Neither it was mentioned too often if there was planned a transformation of existing jobs in order to make them teleworkable. Only in some projects (e.g. Daimler Benz, Saritel, A Workplace in DK, The Show Project, Process Reengineering and Telework, Telecom Italia, ITALTEL) co-operative business processes were mentioned. Unfortunately, it was not classified what structure the business processes had.

Isolated tasks seem to dominate telework but it is not certain (see figure 5). They merely are easy to identify and therefore have been mentioned more often than business processes or project management. In other words, supporters or agents were related to their tasks, whereas for professionals, marketers, etc. it was just mentioned what category their work was part of, but it was never explained what the work exactly was about.

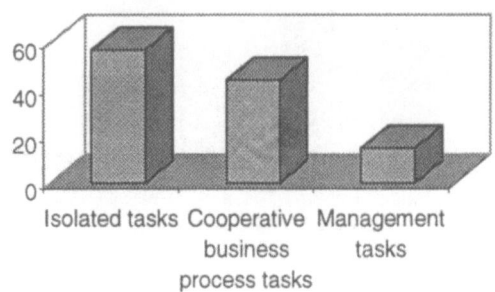

Figure 5: Concepts of business-reengineering in European telework (n = 195)

Moreover, most of the teleworkplaces were given to professionals and marketers which seldom fulfil exclusively routine work or isolated tasks so that highly and semi-structured processes, and isolated tasks and co-operative business processes should at least be in an equilibrium (see figure 6). Consequently, it is neither possible to relate job and task structure nor task and process structure.

Nevertheless, should the investigation turn out a true proportion, isolated tasks would be predominating telework (66%), business processes would be gaining momentum and project management would still be considered inappropriate for telework.

4.3.3 Criterion 3: Occupational Groups Taking Part in European Projects

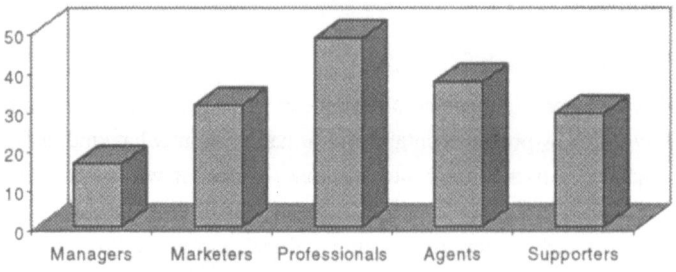

Figure 6: Occupational classification (n = 107)

Telework is not restricted to supporting tasks (see figure 6). It becomes more and more apparent that not only highly structured tasks can be carried out in telework. Although there are still many teleworking supporters doing mainly easy work and isolated tasks, the majority of remote workers are highly qualified professionals. Position 4 is occupied by marketers, who also fulfil demanding tasks, followed by managers. The marketers have to communicate a lot of information and figures prove that technology makes it feasible to convey it via information technology, otherwise there would be no teleworking marketers or managers. It can be deduced that the majority of teleworkers (professionals and marketers) are doing semi-structured work as it is typical for that kind of work.

The second position is occupied by the group consisting of agents and supporters. They, presumably, are mainly carrying out isolated[39], highly structured tasks in highly structured processes. Managers are still far away from being typical teleworkers. Unfortunately, sources did not provide data about whether and how task and process structure were related with the type of job. Thus, the above-mentioned relations are merely a conjecture.

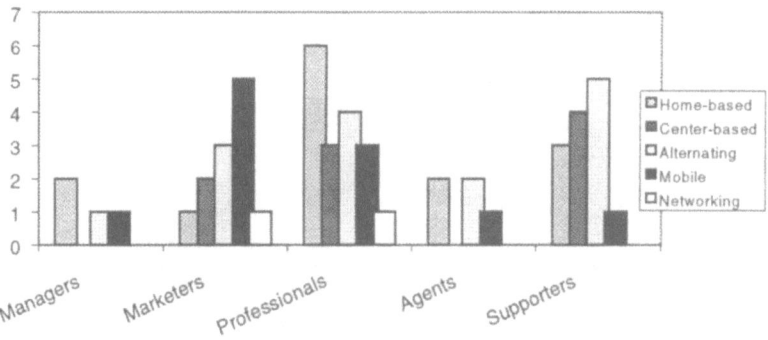

Figure 7: Relation between organizational form of telework and occupational classification (n= 107)

However, figure 7 charts the scarcely found information about how organizational form of telework and occupational classification were related whenever they were mentioned in a project's description. Managers prefer either to work completely at home or to be independent from a specific location. Most marketers opt for mobile or alternating telework and the majority of professionals work at home. The latter can be found as well in alternating, home-based and mobile telework. It is not immediately apparent whether or how job and organizational form of telework are linked as different extremes coincide in almost all categories. Professional's work is fulfilled in any kind of telework. Looking at figure 7 a more logical explanation seems to be that it depends upon the employee's or employer's likes or dislikes as to which organizational form is chosen for which type of telework rather than considering criteria like work structure or interoperability.[40]

---

[39] Especially supporters.
[40] Note: Figure 7 shows a predominance of alternating before home-based and center-based telework. As we can see in figure 4, the number of alternating teleworkers should almost equal the number of mobile teleworkers. There have just been mentioned more relations of alternating telework and occupational

4.3.4 Criterion 4: Employment Status of European Teleworkers

Although there are only a few special telework contracts (see figure 8), most teleworkers stayed in their previous employment status (i.e. direct employment). The problem persists that the special demands of telework have been included very seldom in agreements. Companies try to avoid the difficulties that occur when transforming a traditional job into telework, as they found out that maintaining the previous employment status protects the employee according to ancient standards but it does not cover problems that exist when teleworking. Therefore, a special contract would be most appropriate. The latter, however, are often not ratified due to opposing trade unions.

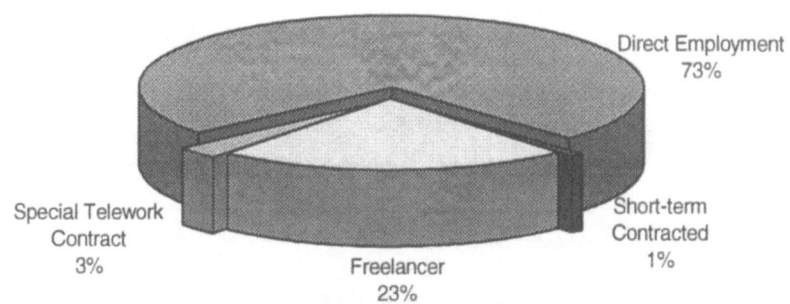

Figure 8: Employment status[41] (n = 125)

Another problem for teleworking from the legal point of view is that there is no distinct legal framework addressing teleworking in any EU member state. The legal status of a teleworker is unclear and so are the laws to be applied.[42] Especially telework that crosses a country's border is not sufficiently protected by law.

Cross or trans-border teleworking is employing people working not only non-office-based, but in a different country. The main difficulty which organizations may experience is determining which legal jurisdiction is to be applied to disputes about terms and conditions of cross-border employment, rather than how to cope with national legal regimentation. Although harmonization is proceeding, European lawmaking is not conform yet. Besides Portugal, in all EU countries the law to be applied is

---

class than others. Figure 7 aims at showing which teleworker prefers which kind of telework rather than repeating figure 4. The general picture counts here rather than the absolute (coinciding) number.
[41] Nominally self-employed subcontracted employment status was not mentioned in none of the sources.
[42] See EC 1994, p. 16.

that of the place where the contract is implemented, i.e., where the work is performed or services are delivered.[43]

Barriers to cross-border teleworking place significant impediments on businesses that want to expand their activities across Europe. Firms might concentrate their teleworking activities in those countries where local and national laws are the most favorable to flexible working practices and where information technology is the most advanced.[44] A recommendation for the proceeding of telework would be a harmonized European legal system concerning telework that enables every country to create good conditions for a flourishing telework society, although the country itself might not be convinced by the potential of telework.

4.3.5 Criterion 5: Monetary Sponsorship

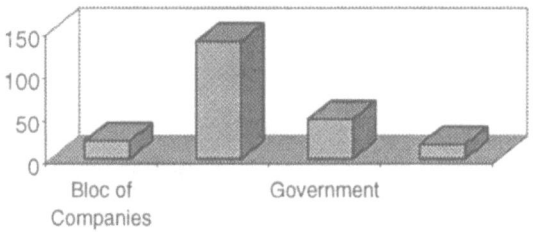

Figure 9: Sponsors of telework-projects (n = 195)

Most of the projects are financed by the company that launches the project (see figure 9).[45] Some have additional financial back-up by the EU or by national, local or regional government or have been included in existing EU or governmental programs.

The histogram illustrates that most companies cover the costs for telework implementation themselves. Surely they can count on EU or government-financed infrastructure but EU or government presence in the actual project is not too high. Many public financed projects are furthermore just partially supported by public means, i.e., there are often costs left over to be paid by the enterprise. However, there is a huge amount of governmental and EU effort to provide the necessary information technology infrastructure. These projects are often of telematic nature and could seldom be included.

---

[43] See EC 1994, p. 47.
[44] See EC 1994, p. 16.
[45] 'One Company' refers to the company which implements telework. The Attribute "private sponsoring by a different 'third party' company" has not been found.

4.3.6 Criterion 6: Project-Life-Cycle

Figure 10 shows that most projects are already at the stage of implementation. Many companies are busy implementing telework and do not yet think about new programs. Moreover, some countries have reached a certain stage of 'initiation-stagnation' meaning that they have already institutionalized their ancient projects and do not initiate new ones. The reason for this is not apparent, but it is either possible that telework has already been incorporated in a company's hierarchy and regenerates itself, so that no further stimulus is necessary or that some companies are not keen on implementing further projects.

The actual evolution should be decreasing in time: there could be far more initiatives than adopted telework projects, and even less implemented and institutionalized projects. That it is not like this might come from continuing ancient programs which are still being implemented or institutionalized. This means that projects are still going on although they could already have been institutionalized.

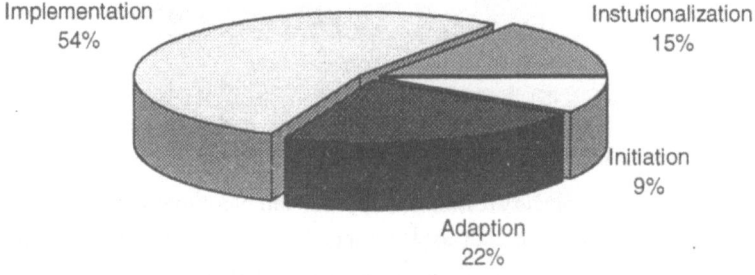

Figure 10: European projects according to their life-cycle (n = 193)

5 Future Prospects of Telework

5.1 Development Trends in the Different European Countries

Telework encounters different conditions in different countries. Since Europe is recently being bound together there exist huge discrepancies between the various member countries because of their distinct stages of development and attitudes towards information technology. Considering Europe as a continent the result of an investigation would be even less homogeneous, as telework is not very common in Eastern-European states. The inconsistency among the countries of the European Union, on the other hand, is smoother because of their converging high economic standard encouraging telework. Notwithstanding, the deviation from the average EU telework situation is big enough to recognize that the situation of each country should to be looked at separately, too. Aside from EU programs Norwegian and Swiss telework projects could be found and were included in the survey.

Table 5: Stages of growth of European countries	
Conception	Greece, Norway, Portugal
Initiation	Denmark, Finland, Luxembourg
Contagion	Austria, Belgium, Germany, Italy, Spain, Switzerland
Consolidation	France, Ireland, Netherlands, Sweden, UK

The descriptions of the telework-friendly or telework-adverse environmental conditions in particular European countries lead to the results listed in table 5. Several inconsistencies have been detected, but it will be tried to draw a picture that reflects a European situation.

Hence, the average European country has just passed the threshold to contagion. It, apparently, turns out to be difficult to make a general statement about the European telework situation. The gap between poorly and well performing countries is too wide. Even within the stages, huge discrepancies have been detected. Finland and Denmark, for example, are located at the same stage, but whereas Finland is eager pressing on telework Denmark has better conditions. The same happens when comparing France and Sweden, Belgium and Austria, Switzerland and Germany. It might be useful to make a further distinction besides the stage of growth which just depicts the actual stage of evolution. It is more important to see whether the countries are in an upward trend or in a stalemate. The entire survey provides the necessary information so that we can draw a further picture (see table 6).

Table 6: Development trends	
Upward Trend	Austria, Finland, Spain, UK, Germany, Italy, Sweden
Stagnating Trend	Greece, Luxembourg, Portugal, Switzerland, Belgium, France, Ireland, Netherlands, Denmark, Norway

Although Coulan and Murphy seem convinced that telework will always be a minority preference, it cannot be condemned to be it.[46] It is true that there is still a long way to go to realize the full potential, but should it really be reached, telework will no longer be a minority preference. As other sources put it: "2/3 of Fortune 1000 companies currently have telecommuting programs, half of which were instituted in the past two years. A majority of those with telecommuting programs expect them to continue to grow while nearly 60% of executives from companies without programs expect to

---

[46] See Coulan & Murphy 1997.

institute [some] within the next two years. [...] Nearly 2/3 of the Fortune 1000 executives view telecommuting as not only good for employers, but also advantageous to
employees".[47] This scenario is a more adequate description of what has to be expected
from telework in the future.

5.2 Development Trends for Europe as a Whole

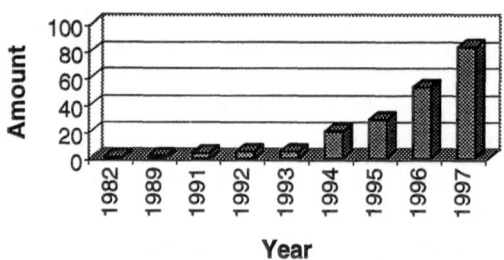

*Figure 11: Accumulated number of projects (of the random test referring to the
starting date of the project) (n = 199)*

The accumulated sum of the randomly detected and selected projects is charted
in figure 11 for Europe in total. There is an obvious upward trend and the amount of
projects grew especially in the mid 1990s. The 1980s' figures have not been used for
the following future forecast as the quantity of data is insufficient and this would cause
a strong deviation. Figure 12, therefore, is only a scatterplot of the 1990s projects.

The tremendous increase of project launching since 1993 is very likely to be
due to the better availability of data about recent projects. Older programs that had
been institutionalized or had been finished were often not considered worth naming
(especially in the Internet). Moreover, the starting date was not always mentioned explicitly so that it is possible that the date referred to and the starting date do not coincide. Different estimation methods such as logarithmic, linear and polynomial regression have been considered. A polynomial trend-line would show a progressive development that would reach about 450 projects by 2004. But with a look at the years before 1994 it can be seen that an estimate like that would be exaggerated. That is why a
linear trend-line was chosen. Since no 1990 projects have been found the graph starts
in 1991 and ends in 1997. Figure 12 shows the scattered data, the actual correlation r^2,
the formula of the trend-line and the trend-line itself. In continuation the slope of the
linear graph will be determined in order to explain the future prediction of how many
projects will probably be launched in the coming years.

---

[47] See Teleworker 1997.

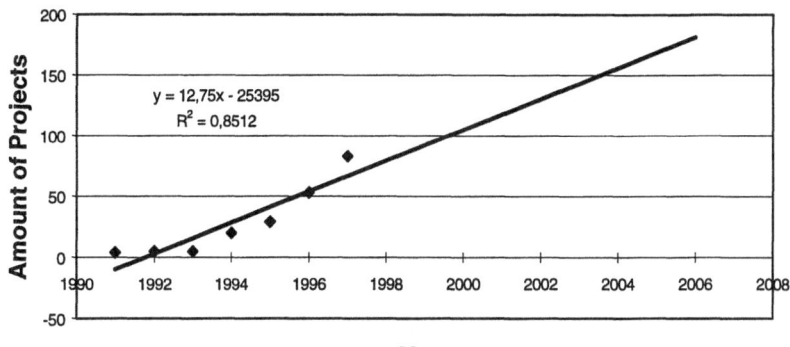

Year

Figure 12: Scatterplot and estimated projection (n = 199)

$Y = bx + a$ is the formula for the trend-line, b (= 12,75) is the slope of the linear graph and -25395 is the value of the predicted y when $x = 0$.[48] Since we look at years, the value of predicted y is pretty high, but it allows making a future forecast about the increase in the amount of projects that will be undertaken.

Of course, it is not possible to predict whether those projects will succeed or be abandoned, nor what exactly they will be about, but at least the quantity of existing telework will probably increase as the slope (12,75) of the trendline of our random sample is positive (see figure 12). Moreover, considering every project creates about the same average amount of telework places, the total number of teleworkers would increase from 2.5 million 1996 to about 8 million in Europe in 2005. This is a fairly smooth prediction when compared with other scientific estimations. It is possible that the amount of teleworking people increases progressively to the amount of projects. Contemplating the fact that between 1994 and 1996 the amount of remote workers has doubled, i.e., doubling within a two years time (from 1.25 million to 2.5 million), there would be far more than 8 million teleworkers in 2005.[49]

The 1998 – 2005 figures are based on estimation. The amount of telework projects will grow steadily assuming that the good correlation r^2 (= 0.85) excludes extremely progressive or regressive growth. This corresponds also to latest predictions since a steady but not progressive evolution has been foreseen. Taking into account the restrictions the survey was faced with, it seems realistic that the 10 million telework places – estimated by the EU – will be established by the year 2000.

---

[48] See Moore 1997, p. 338.
[49] See Bertin & O'Neill 1997.

6 Conclusion: Trends of Telework Development in Europe

Trends in telework development that became visible when examining the projects of the survey[50]:

*   A trend towards more co-operative process structures in telework tasks compared to the "early days" of telework

*   An increasing general acceptance of telework in all economic sectors due to the many experiments that have mostly been successful – if not very successful – in almost every field of the European economy. Knowledge of telework is also being spread increasingly due to many national and European-wide telework promotion programs. However, as of 1997, telework is still a minority work practice and clearly visible regional differences prevail.

*   Organizations are still experimenting with different forms of telework and new variations come up continuously. On the other hand, alternating telework and center-based telework are established now and mobile telework is on the increase. Experiences with home-based telework were in some cases dubious. Consequently, (isolated) home-based telework seems to be on the decline.

*   Telework is technically facilitated by the rapid development of information technology and economically by the decreasing costs of telecommunication, partly caused by the liberalization of telecommunication markets in many EU states.

*   A legal framework concerning the status of teleworkers and their rights and duties has been established in many states, generally in a joint process among employers, trade unions and policy makers. Still, this frameworks can be improved and should be updated as permanently as telework is changing.

*   Taking into account the restrictions the survey was faced with, it seems realistic that the 10 million teleworkplaces – estimated by the EU – will be established by the year 2000.

References

Attica (1997). *Quotes.* Available:
<http://www.teleworker.com/quotes.html> (1997, November 27).[51]
Bertin, I. & O'Neill, G. (1997).*Telefutures*. Available:
<http://www.forbairt.ie/telefutures/ch1-7.htm> (1997, November 27).
Blake, M. (1994): Teleworking in the '90s: A Look at Current Views. *Managing Information*, 1(4), pp. 24-26.

---

[50] A thorough discussion on the future of telework in the EU can be found in EC 1997.

[51] Note: Internet Sources sometimes did not mention document date or author. When there was no document date stated, it was assumed that it coincided with the access date. The authors of this thesis have no influence on removing of Internet-pages.

Bmbf (1996). *Elektronischer Leitfaden zur Telearbeit*. Bonn: Bundesministerium für Bildung und Forschung. Available: <http://www.iid.de/telearbeit/leitfaden>
BMWi (1996). *Bericht der Bundesregierung: Info 2000*. Bonn: Bundesministerium für Wirtschaft, Referat Öffentlichkeitsarbeit.
BMWi, BMAS (1996/97). *Telearbeit – Chancen für neue Arbeitsformen, mehr Beschäftigung, flexible Arbeitszeiten*. Bonn: Bundesministerium für Wirtschaft (BMWi) and Bundesministerium für Arbeit und Sozialordnung (BMAS).
British Telecom (1994). *A glimpse of the future*. Available: <http://www.bt.com/library/online/telework.index.htm> (1997, December 14).
Brückenbauer (1997). *Die Arbeit kommt nach Hause*. Available: <http://brueckenbauer.ch/INHALT/9632/32report.htm> (1997, November 28).
Coulan, A. & Murphy, C. (1997). *Telefutures*. Available: <http://www.forbairt.ie/telefutures/foreword.htm> (1997, November 27).
DACOM (1997). Available: <http://www.dacom.co.at/Studie2/default.htm> (1997, November 27).
Die Welt (1994, October 4). Im Jahr 2000 will EU 10 Millionen Tele-Arbeitsplätze. *Die Welt*, pp. 13.
Dostal, W. (1985). Anmerkungen zur Arbeitsmarktrelevanz dezentraler Informationastätigkeit. *Mitteilungen aus Arbeitsmarkt und Berufsforschung*, 4, pp. 467-480.
Elola, J. (1997, March 23). La oficina virtual. *El País Semanal*, 1,069, pp. 52-59
Empirica (1994a). *Paneuropäische Befragung zur Telearbeit, Bericht 4*. Bonn: Empirica.
Empirica (1994b). *Paneuropäische Befragung zur Telearbeit, Bericht 5*. Bonn: Empirica.
Empirica (1994c). *Paneuropäische Befragung zur Telearbeit, Bericht 6*. Bonn: Empirica.
ETO (1996). *Hjemmerarbeydspladser og det mobile kontor*. <http://www.fsk.dk/fsk/publ./1996/it-i-tal/kap24.html> (1997, November 27).
EC (1994). *Legal, Organizational and Management Issues in Telework*. Brussels: European Commission DG XIII.
EC (1997). *Status Report on European Telework in 1997*. Brussels: European Commission.
Freese, E. (1992). *Organisationstheorie*. Wiesbaden: Gabler.
Freudenreich, H., Klein, B. & Wedde, P. (1997). *Entwicklung der Telearbeit – Rechtliche Rahmenbedingungen – Abschlußbericht*. Stuttgart: Fraunhofer Institut im Auftrag des Bundesministerium für Arbeit und Sozialordnung.
Geenen, J. (1992). *Eine Analyse von Teleheimarbeit unter besonderer Berücksichtigung von Büroaufgaben*. Diplomarbeit zur Erlangung des akademischen Grades Dipl. Kfm. Universität Trier (Prof. Dr. Wächter).
Heilmann, W. & Mikosch I. (1989). Telearbeit – Der ungeplante Wandel. *Information Management*, 2, pp. 46-52.
Huber, J. (1987). *Telearbeit: Ein Zukunftsbild als Politikum*. Opladen: Westdeutscher Verlag.
Huws, U. (1994). Teleworking in Britain. *Employment Gazette*, 102(2), pp. 51-59.
Jablonski, K. (1997). *Case Study SNI*. Available <http://www.iess.ae.it/mirti/handbook2framebe.htm> (1997, November 26).
Kirchmair, G. (1996). *Telearbeit: Realität und Zukunft*. Wien: V. d. ÖGB.
Korte, W. B. & Wynne, R. (1996). *Telework: Penetration, Potential and Practice in Europe*. Amsterdam: IOS Press.
Lukinnen, C. (1997). *Teleworkers in Close-up*. <http://tkk.utu.fi/telework/raportit/rl.html> (Dec. 06, 1997)
Moore, D. S. (1997). *Statistics – Concepts and Controversies*. New York: Freeman and Company.
Nilles, J. M. (1994). *Making Telecommuting Happen*. New York: Van Nostrand Reinhold.
PA Consulting (1994). *Study on Sweden's Information Technology Infrastructure*. PA Consulting for the Swedish Ministry of Telecommunication.
Picot, A., Reichwald, P. & Wigand, R. (1996). *Die grenzenlose Unternehmung*. Wiesbaden: Gabler.
Rieker, J. (1995). Telearbeit: In weiter Ferne. *Manager-Magazin*, 25(11), pp. 199-209.
Stanworth, J. & Stanworth, C. (1991a). *Telework: The human resource implications*. Exeter: Short Run Press.

Stanworth, J. & Stanworth, C. (1991b). *Work 2000*. Liverpool: PCP.

Telework 97 Conference (1997, September 26). *Newsletter*. Available: <http://www.nutek.se/telework_97conference/ld2ww.htm> (1997, November 28).

Teleworker (1997). *Quotes*. Available: <http://www.teleworker.com/quotes.html> (1998, September 25).

Telework Homepage (1997). Available: <http://www.eto.org.uk/nat/ch/index.htm> (1997 November 28).

Telework Ireland (1997). <http://www.cwee.ie./navtelew.htm#2> (1997, November 27).

VDI Nachrichten (97/98). Sonderteil Ingenieurkarriere, WS 97/98, p. 5.

Wedde, P. (1994). *Telearbeit: Handbuch für Arbeitnehmer, Betriebsräte und Anwender*. Köln: bund.

Worldwide Learning with Java[1] and New Information and Communication Technologies[2,3]

Winfried Reiss

1 Introduction

In many discussions on the 'electronic classroom' participants usually criticize heavily the custom of adding only a diskette to a standard textbook and instead ask for building new computer-based courses from scratch.

This is what I want to do with the program I am presenting here. It is aimed for presentation and not fully completed. Nevertheless, I hope that the essential features can be recognized.

The program is demonstrated by the example of a course on microeconomic theory. It is, however, obvious that the employed concepts and ideas can also be used in other areas of economics as well as in other fields of science.

2 CAL, HTML and Java

2.1 Interactive Computer-aided Learning

When students work with an interactive computer-based training program, they should be able to perform the following tasks:

1. They should read statements on a special problem. These texts can be printed texts but should preferably be texts shown on the screen.
2. They should solve problems, decide on solutions with the answers evaluated by the program.
3. If they have problems with some tasks, they should be able to ask for context-sensitive help.
4. They should input points into a diagram, draw curves on that chart, decide on the position of curves and interpret those diagrams.
5. They should watch developments in charts. Such developments can depend on time, price changes, information progress, and on others.

---

[1] Java is an object-oriented and platform-independent programming language, designed by Sun Microsystems.
[2] The author is grateful to Jane Fadden, Ralf Menkhoff, and Wolfgang Rothfritz for valuable comments.
[3] An Internet-version of this article can be found at Reiss 1998.

2.2 CAL and SuperCAL

Kevin Macken and Ken Randall (1995) coined the term SuperCAL to describe the form of Computer-Aided Learning which they believe should dominate the late 1990s, and which will, as they believe, be appropriate to the information SuperHighway. This new form of learning will be familiar to the rapidly growing community of Internet users. The authors justify the need for such an approach by

• the costs to produce high-quality software materials,
• the coordination and communication problems for the CAL-software producing teams,
• the high costs of adopting CAL materials to contribute a significant part of the students' learning.

"What has impressed the authors about Web servers in general and MOSAIC as a browser is its elegance, simplicity and power as a solution to almost all the problems which currently face CAL developers. We see the separation of the core HTML document from any of the other applications to which it can transfer the user as the key to productivity. Most CAL applications are extremely sophisticated and their structure is not obvious to the user. It is the simplicity of the Internet structure which could be used to create a new kind of CAL (which we have termed SuperCAL) which would be as easy to authors to use as an HTML file. By separating text from interactions we get advantages in each problem area" (Macken & Randall 1995, p. 14).

The authors do not propose specific software packages for the programming of the interactions but instead write that "the software the author's University finds most efficient is the obvious choice for the interactions". I, however, think that the new programming language Java should be the first choice for that purpose.

2.3 Java in Computer-Aided Learning

Java is very suitable to be used as a basis for interactive teaching.

1. Java has an Abstract Windowing Toolkit (AWT). This platform-independent library contains classes for basic interface components such as events, colors, fonts, and controls such as buttons and scrollbars.
2. It has a quite powerful platform-independent event handler which enables the user not only to do calculations but also to
   a) make logical decisions,
   b) communicate with other applications,
   c) evaluate keyboard actions and mouse events.
3. It has fairly good graphic facilities. It is possible to construct and change graphs dependent on user decisions.

4. It can handle objects. Macros can be assigned to those objects (buttons, simple charts and so on). This enables the user to perform certain actions by choosing that object.

5. Java applications can be embedded into an HTML-file and executed anywhere on the network (– these embedded applications are called 'applets'). Because compiled Java code is architecture-neutral, Java applications are ideal for a diverse environment like the Internet.

6. Java provides multilingual support. Therefore, it is possible to write multilingual CAL-Software.

In the following I will show the usefulness of these features (for a more thorough description see The Java Language – An Overview) for interactive learning.

3 The Structure of "Jewel"

3.1 The General Layout

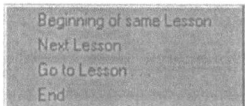

Figure 1: Menu bar with 'Go to'-menu

The program is composed of a series of lessons which are technically very much alike: each lesson has a menu, a set of buttons, and a status-bar for messages and help topics. Moreover, each lesson has a similar layout: a third of the frame in the left serves for formulating and explaining the exercises and also for input and output of parameters. The remaining part of the screen shows the graphics and figures.

This uniform structure is enabled by the fact that all lessons are coded as objects which extend a common parent object. This parent object defines the layout and the basic methods (like 'showing help', 'changing parameters', 'redrawing' etc.). The parent object itself extends an object which supplies the menu system, the set of buttons and the status-bar.

3.2 The General Structure

The Jewel-system shall contain different 'books'. A 'book' corresponds, in a way, to what is traditionally regarded as a book, i. e. a self-contained presentation of a certain topic. The following list shows titles which could fit perfectly into the program.

```
Jewel
  |
  +------------Book1 (e.g. Macroeconomics)
  |
  +------------Book2 (e.g. Chaos-Theory)
  |
  +------------Book3 (e.g. Analysis)
  |
  +------------Book4 (e.g. Polynomials)
  |
  +------------Book5 Microeconomics
  |
  +------------Book6 (e.g. CES-Functions)
```

Each book is subdivided into different chapters. Thus, 'Microeconomics' is structured as follows:

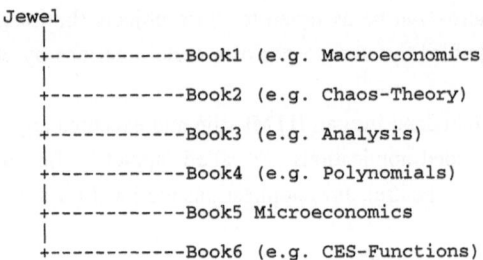

```
Jewel
  |
  +-----Book1 (e.g. Macroeconomics)
  .
  .
  +------Book5 Microeconomics
           |
           +-------Chapter1 A. Smith: Division of Labour
           |
           +-------Chapter2 D. Ricardo: Distribution of Income
           |
           +-------Chapter3 K. Marx: Exploitation
           |
           +-------Chapter4 H.H. Gossen: The Marginal Revolution
           |
           +-------Chapter5 V. Pareto: Preference Theory
           |
           +-------Chapter6 Consumer's Theory
```

Each chapter is subdivided into different lessons. A lesson is a unit which normally should be finished in one go. I, for example, have the following list of lessons for the chapter 'Consumer's theory':

```
Jewel
   +-----Book5  Microeconomics
           .
           +----Chapter6:  Consumer's Theory
                   |
                   +----Lesson1: Utility Function
                   |
                   +----Lesson2: Indifference Curve
                   |
                   +----Lesson3: Offer Curve
                   |
                   +----Lesson4: Edgeworth Box
                   |
                   +----Lesson5: Contract Curve and Pareto-optimality
                   |
                   +----Lesson6: Price and Equilibrium
                   |
                   +----Lesson7: Tâtonnement
```

3.3 The Package Structure

I use the package-structure of the Java language to structure the Jewel-system.

- Jewel itself is a package which contains all the classes, which are important and useful for all books and chapters in that system (e.g. the starting routine, the general layout, the graphic routines, and so on).
- Each book is a package with those classes relevant for that book and all its chapters.
- Each chapter is a package, containing all the lessons of that chapter.
- A lesson is a descendent of the AWT-class Frame and hence an independent window with a menu.

This lesson frame is characterized by a special layout and event handling routines. Such a lesson can be regarded as a program unit which provides tasks for the user, handles the user's responses and reacts appropriately.

I therefore arrive at the following structure:

```
Jewel (package)
 |
 +---Mikro (package)
      .
      +----Chapter6 (Consumer's Theory) (package)
            |
            +----Lesson1 (Utility Function)(frame Lesson1)
            |
            +----Lesson2 (Indifference Curve)(frame Lesson2)
            |
            +----Lesson3 (Offer Curve)(frame Lesson3)
            |
            +----Lesson4 (Edgeworth Box)(frame Lesson4)
            |
            +----Lesson5 (Contract Curve) (frame Lesson5)
            |
            +----Lesson6 (Price and Equilibrium) (frame Lesson6)
            |
            +----Lesson7 (Tâtonnement)(frame Lesson7)
```

3.4 The Lesson Structure

Each lesson indirectly descends from Frame. The inheritance is as follows:

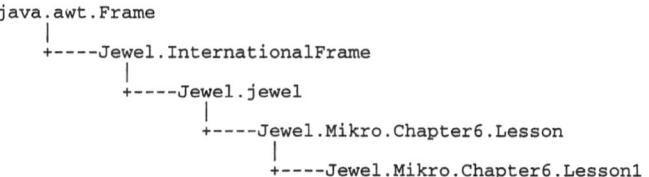

```
java.awt.Frame
    |
    +----Jewel.InternationalFrame
         |
         +----Jewel.jewel
              |
              +----Jewel.Mikro.Chapter6.Lesson
                   |
                   +----Jewel.Mikro.Chapter6.Lesson1
```

Class InternationalFrame constructs a menu system and defines the layout. Dependent on the constructor we get one of the structures shown in figure 2.

To construct a menu system the class InternationalFrame uses the string arrays in an interface MenuText, which is implemented by the class. Besides the menu system, it adds a BasePanel in the 'South' of a BorderLayout. The panel BasePanel serves only as a container with one or two lines (depending on the constructor). Its lower (or only) line contains the messageLabel and the helpinfoLabel. The BUT-

`TONPanel` with the buttons and the `datumLabel` (the clock) is placed either (a.) in the upper line of `BasePanel` or (b.) as a separate panel in the 'East'.

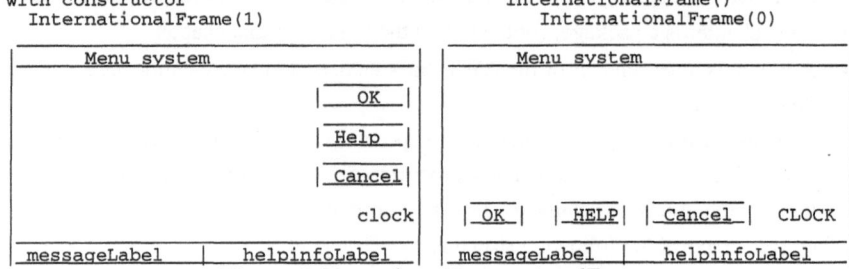

Figure: 2 The outlay of InternationalFrame

The class `InternationalFrame` is parent to the class `jewel` which for constructor `jewel()` has the following appearance:

```
                 Menu system
        (inherited from InternationalFrame)
  explain   S
   Canvas   e
            p
  DOPanel   e        GraphicCanvas
            r
  task      .
  Canvas
  basePanel (with buttons,clock,messages)
       (inherited from InternationalFrame)
```
Figure 3: The outlay of Jewel

As `jewel` extends `InternationalFrame` it inherits in addition to the menu system a `BorderLayout` and a `BasePanel` in the 'South' of that BorderLayout (and eventually for `InternationalFrame(1)` a `buttonPanel` in the 'East'). The class `jewel` adds to this in the 'West' the panel `left` and in the 'Center' the panel `GraphicCanvas`. The panel `left` (BorderLayout) serves only as a container. It contains the `explainCanvas` in 'North', `DOPanel` in 'Center', `taskCanvas` in South, and `Seperator` in 'East'.

With this, the structure of the lessons is explained insofar, as it is determined by the package Jewel.

Inside a book and/or inside a chapter the structure can be specified even further. In the case of the book 'Microeconomics' I use the given structure in the class `JEcon`. This class is parent to different lessons, which formulate tasks, draw figures, evaluate user inputs, and react on these inputs.

4 The Demonstration of "Jewel"

In the following I will give a short description of some of the contents of one (and to this day – to be honest – the only in existence) of the books within the program. Evidently it is impossible to show all the steps and methods used; therefore users should test the program themselves to discover the excellent opportunities for computer-based economics teaching provided by Java. Instead, I will go into the particulars of the structure and especially the usefulness of the concepts in other fields of education.

4.1 Examples

Example 1: The Cobb-Douglas Utility Function

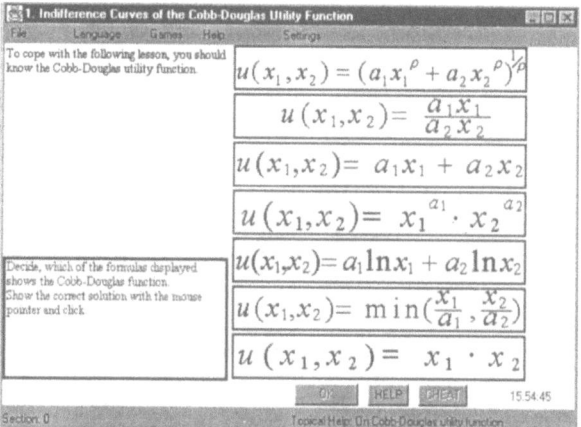

Figure 4: The Cobb-Douglas utility function

This lesson asks the user to do some derivatives and decide on the right solution.

The composition of this unit is simple. It merely consists of a number of objects with small bitmap-pictures (formulas) and text-fields containing correct, incomplete, and wrong solutions.

The topics are utility functions, methods to determine indifference curves, and the formula of the indifference curve. All answers given are evaluated. Dependent on these answers new questions are asked. There are context-sensitive help items for all problems; after a number of failed attempts the user can ask for the solution.

This unit is more or less an interactive form of a multiple-choice lesson as it is (and should used sparingly) in many parts of computer-based learning.

This procedure is very common in scientific teaching, be it the calculation of an integral in mathematics, the verification of a formula in physics, the estimation of a probability in statistics or the ciphering of a cost function in economics.

Example 2: Indifference Curves of a Cobb-Douglas Function

Starting from the results of lesson 1, the user should now calculate points of indifference curves and enter these into a diagram. Just as in that lesson these actions are standard in teaching.

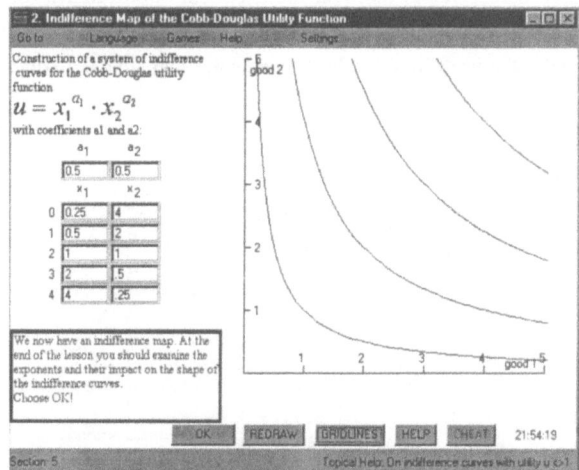

Figure 5: Indifference curves of a Cobb-Douglas function

If the users enter the wrong values they are informed about the incorrect inputs and asked to correct them.

If the inputs of the table are all correct, the users are asked to enter the points into the diagram. To assist them in finding the right positions they can ask for gridlines. After clicking, the answer is evaluated. If all five points are inserted the users can ask for the connecting indifference curve. They then have to show indifference curves with different levels of utility and will finally get a complete indifference map.

Tasks such as these in this unit are standard in many parts of science: polynomials and trigonometric functions in mathematics, trajectories in physics etc. These methods can therefore be employed in other fields of education.

Example 3: Construction of an Offer Curve

In this unit, the construction of an important tool of equilibrium theory – the offer curve – is introduced. This demonstrates the possibility of guiding the users step by step through a procedure by which they will learn essential parts of the theory.

These steps are accompanied by changing HELP options. During the first steps it is HELP ON BUDGET LINES, later on HELP ON OPTIMA and thereafter HELP ON OFFER CURVE.

Similar applications could be employed, e.g., in the introduction of IS-LM-curves in macroeconomics or in envelopes in mathematics and physics.

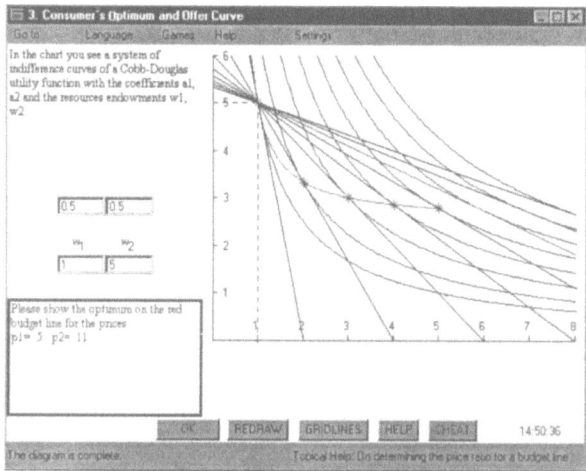

Figure 6: Construction of an offer curve

Example 4: Edgeworth Box

This unit shows the construction of an Edgeworth box. The turning around and shifting together of two indifference maps, always difficult on the board, becomes some-what a little motion picture (at least if the speed of the processor is high enough).

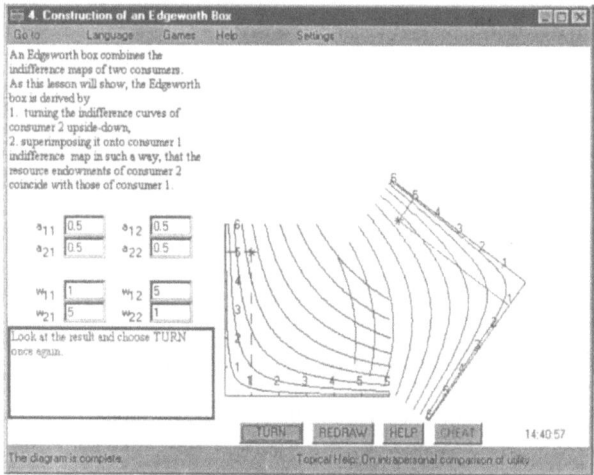

Figure 7: Edgeworth box

In equilibrium theory, the Edgeworth box is used to show the interdependency of exchange transactions of economic agents. With the aid of this tool important concepts like Pareto optimum, exchange, disequilibrium, equilibrium and price adjustment processes can be visualized. Therefore, this box is the most important graphical tool in equilibrium theory.

As there are often examples in scientific teaching where charts are composed of different parts in some clever manner by rotating, mirroring, sliding and so on, such a unit can aid teaching.

The technical realization uses the fact that Java can draw images in an offscreen buffer and draw to the applet window when it is time to update.

Example 5: Edgeworth Box and Pareto-optimality

In this unit users are introduced step by step to the concept of Pareto-optimality. For this they have to decide, whether allocations exist where both consumers can improve upon a given allocation. This is done with the help of the Edgeworth box (the construction of which was shown in lesson 4).

In this way the users are directed towards the concept of the contract curve. Finally, the users are asked to examine the dependency of this curve on the parameters of the utility function.

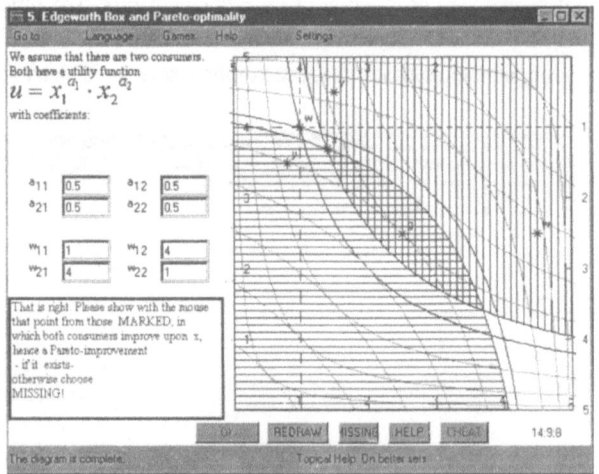

Figure 8: Edgeworth box and Pareto-optimality

Technically, this unit uses the fact that Java can evaluate mouse events anywhere on the screen. Therefore, parts of the Edgeworth box are characterized as "better-sets", "indifference-sets", "Pareto-superior-points" and "Pareto-optima". By pointing and clicking the user can make statements about areas, curves, and points of charts. Techniques by which parts of pictures, charts, maps, and drawings have to be shown, are of value in any part of science (e.g. geography, geometry, medicine, etc.).

Example 6: Edgeworth Box, Equilibrium Prices and Pareto-optimality

In this unit the users should use the Edgeworth box to acquire knowledge about the connection of prices, disequilibrium, and equilibrium.

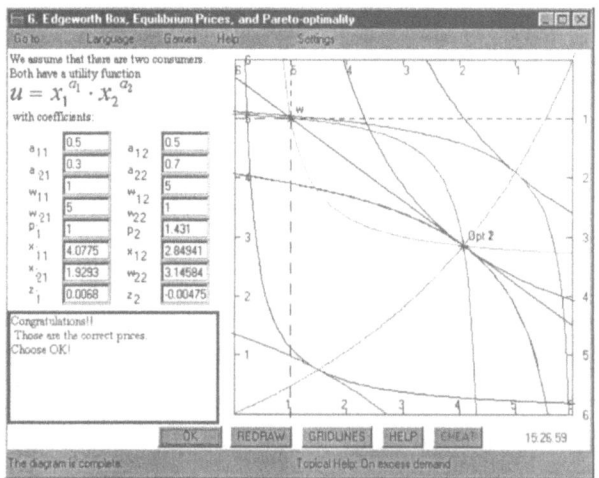

Figure 9: Edgeworth box, equilibrium prices and Pareto-optimality

First, they are asked to read the excess demands for goods 1 and 2 from the Edgeworth box displayed. Second, they have to answer in which way prices have to be altered to approach equilibrium. Third, they have to find equilibrium prices by purposely altering prices.

Procedures like these are often required in science and scientific simulations to achieve a "feeling" about the effect of certain parameters. Other examples are the importance of temperature in thermodynamic systems or advertising efforts in business simulations.

Example 7: Tâtonnement in an Exchange Economy

This unit shows a tâtonnement process. The users can watch the calculations and the adjustments in an Edgeworth box. The underlying model of the process is explained and the structure is shown in the help topics.

The users can watch the tâtonnement process in the Edgeworth box as well as in a table, which displays the formal model.

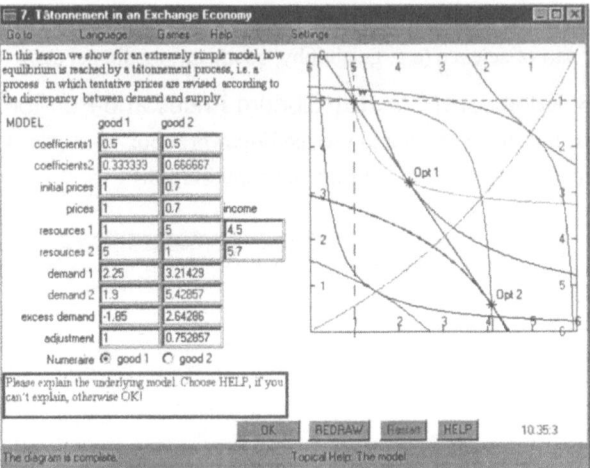

Figure 10: Tâtonnement in an exchange economy

Technically I employ the fact that Java can fairly easily work with 'threads'. One thread is employed for the calculation of the model, the other for updating the graphics. Dynamic processes like this one can be used in every part of computer-based learning.

Example 8: Interrelated Figures

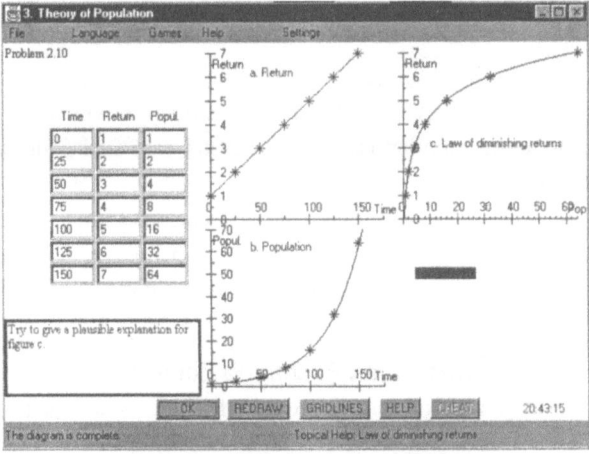

Figure 11: Interrelated figures

This example demonstrates the possibility of using a set of interrelated figures. Changes in one figure are accompanied by changes in other figures. In the example displayed, the 'law of diminishing returns' depends on the propagation of returns as well as the propagation of population. Similar interrelated figures can be helpful in displaying IS-LM-diagrams in Macroeconomics, the connections between factor markets, production-possibility curves and consumption in equilibrium analysis (see Reiss 1992a or Reiss & Lorenz 1993) or the Harberger model in Public Economics.

Example 9: Three-dimensional graphics

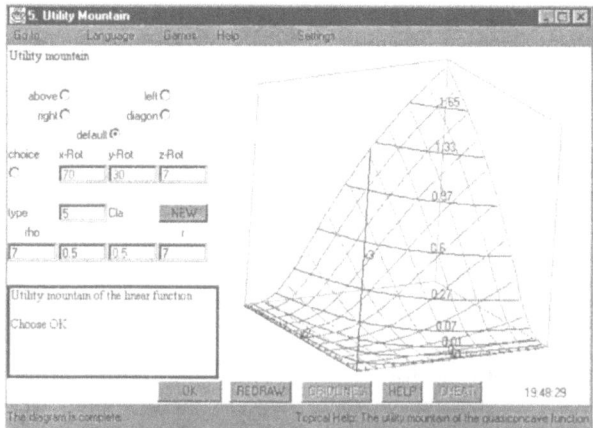

Figure 12: Three-dimensional graphics

In all parts of science there are many examples of how to use three-dimensional graphics. It is, e.g., used in microeconomics to display utility-mountains and production mountains (see e.g. Reiss 1994). Figure 12 shows an example for utility mountains. The users can rotate the mountain and by doing so display an indifference map (bird's eye view), curves of proportional factor variation, and curves of partial factor variation. For this he can use predefined views or select his own angles of rotation (by entering values or by using the mouse).

4.2 The Help System

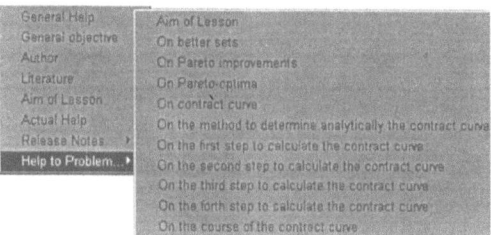

Figure 13: Menu bar with 'Help'-menu

There is an extensive help system within the program. The help topics range from 'General Help' over 'Help on special topics' to 'Help for the actual task'. The user can reach the different help topics through the menu system. The title of the actual help topic is shown in the status bar. This topic is displayed if the user clicks the button 'Help'.

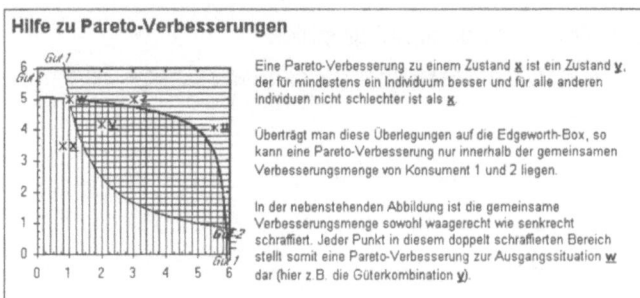

Figure 14: A (German) help page on Pareto-improvements

4.3 The Multilingual Feature

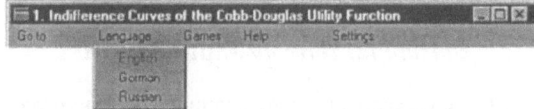

Figure 15: Menu bar with 'Language'-menu

It is always possible within the program to switch from one language to another. On the one hand this improves the acceptance of the program, on the other hand it opens the possibility for the user, to acquire basic knowledge of, e.g., economics in other languages.

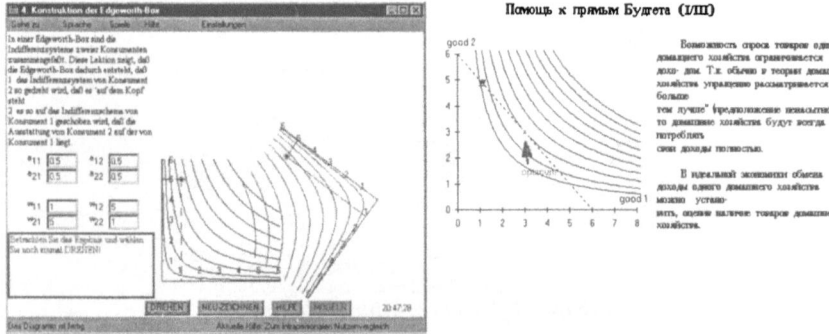

Figure 16: Lesson 4 in German   *Figure 17: Help on budget line (I/III) in Russian*

Technically this switching of languages is realized by gathering all texts in 'interfaces' which are implemented to the classes. At the moment English and German are supported; Russian is in preparation.

4.4 Motivation by Games

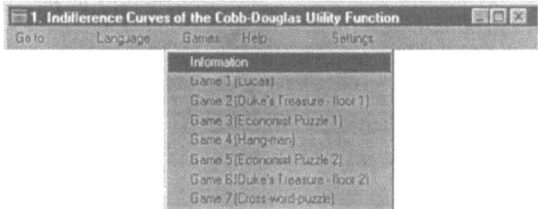

Figure 18: Menu bar with 'Games'-menu

During the evaluation of a precursory version of this program I observed, with some surprise, how the users can be motivated by 'rewards' in the form of computer games. This is why this version implements games as well. After each completed lesson the user is granted the possibility of playing a game. These games are Java-versions of well-known games. Some games have an economic background (e. g. crossword-puzzles).

Figure 19: Economists puzzle

4.5 The Class Documentation

The structure of the classes for this program is fairly simple. A documentation was generated with the help of the 'javadoc'-tool and is available online (see Jewel 1998).

5 Summary

It was shown by this paper (together with the underlying set of classes) that it is possible to use Java as a basis for interactive teaching in economics. The program used for this demonstration has the following features:

5.1 Features of "Equilibrium in a Cobb-Douglas World"

5.1.1 Contents

1. A series of lessons with rising difficulty.
2. An extensive help system with context-sensitive help (realized as HTML-files).
3. Multilingual implementation (until now English and German).
4. Interactive realization.
5. Menu structure.
6. Contains sound and games, to motivate the user.

5.1.2 Software Structure

The program is written with Java (see The Java Language – An Overview) and is therefore:

1. Architecture neutral: the same version of the application runs on many platforms–on a PC with Windows95, NT and OS/2 as well as on an Apple Macintosh and a Unix workstation.
2. Object-oriented: the components can be reused in other courses.
3. Multi-threaded: while the user reflects over his solution the program prepares the next step in advance (drawings etc.).
4. Internet-based: can easily be used with nearly every Internet-connected computer.

5.1.3 Weak Points of the Program

1. It covers only a small section of microeconomics.
2. Most of the texts and help topics are rather short.
3. The interactivity of the course is not really complex.
4. The English texts should be corrected and polished by a native speaker.
5. More languages should be implemented.

5.2 Future Proceedings

I will extend this work in at least three directions:

1. In cooperation with others the program will be enlarged from a 'book' on "Microeconomics" to a complete set of books for different topics and tested with students of different graduations.
2. A set of objects will be structured and documented for serving as a starting point for computer based training programs in economics as well as in other parts of science.

3. The existing program will be employed in education. As the program produces a log-file, examination of the log-files of each user will demonstrate the possibilities of interactive education in general and of this program in particular.
4. I will use the concept of JavaBeans. A JavaBean is a reusable software component that can be visually manipulated in builder tools. This enables the visual construction of applications (as in Visual Basic) and facilitates the production of CAL applications.
5. I will change from the Abstract Window Toolkit of Java 1.0 with its limited capabilities to the more powerful set of 'Java Foundation Classes' (see "Swing Short Course", Part I & Part II). This allows developers to build more easily full-featured applications.

References

CAL-References

Boucher A. (1995). Systems Modelling in Economics: Use of Object-Oriented Software. *CHEER*, 9(2). Available:
<http://www.ilrt.bris.ac.uk/ctiecon/cheer/ch9_2/ch9_2p03.htm> (1998, September 16).
Dinwiddy, C. L. & Teal, F. J. (1988). *The Two-Sector General Equilibrium Model – A new Approach*. New York: St. Martin's Press.
Jewel (1998). *Online-Documentation*. Available:
<http://econscience.uni-paderborn.de/Java/Jewel/Documentation/Documentation-0.html> (1998, September 16).
Katz, A. (1996). Upping the Ante for Instructional Software: Learning How Students Learn. *CHEER*, 10(1). Available:
<http://www.ilrt.bris.ac.uk/ctiecon/cheer/ch10_1/ch101p02.htm> (1998, September 16).
Lawler, R.W. & Yazdani, M. (Eds.) (1987). *Artificial Intelligence and Education*, Vol. 1. Norwood, NJ: Ablex.
Macken, K. & Randall, K. (1995). CAL and SuperCAL. *CHEER*, 9(2). Available:
<http://www.ilrt.bris.ac.uk/ctiecon/cheer/ch9_2/ch9_2p13.htm> (1998, September 16).
Matsumura, M. (1998, January). The real future of Java – Where are we going with Java, and who is going to take us there? *JavaWorld*, 1. Available:
<http://www.javaworld.com/jw-01-1998/jw-01-miko.html> (1998, September 16).
Reiss, W. (1992). Introduction into Equilibrium Theory using the Spreadsheet EXCEL. In: S. J. Varghese & H. Pirkul (Eds.), *The Impact of Information Technology on Business Schools: Research, Teaching, and Administration, Proceedings of the 20th North American Conference of the International Business School Computer Users Group*. Ohio.
Reiss, W. & Lorenz, W. (1993). Allgemeine Gleichgewichtstheorie mit Spreadsheets [General Equilibrium Theory with Spreadsheets]. *Wirtschaftswissenschaftliches Studium*, April, pp. 189–194.
Reiss, W. (1992). The Two Sector General Equilibrium Model in a Spreadsheet (Paper presented at the Conference of Computer Applications in Social Sciences and Business, Portsmouth 1992). *CHEER* 7(20).
Reiss, W (1993). Moving and rotating symbols and diagrams in an EXCEL Chart, demonstrated by parameter dependent arrows. *CHEER*, 8(18), pp. 7-14.
Reiss, W. (1994). Produktionsgebirge [Production mountains]. *Wirtschaftswissenschaftliches Studium*, February, pp. 91-98.
Reiss, W. (1998). *Computer-based Economic Teaching using Java*. Available:
< http://econscience.uni-paderborn.de/vwl/Mikro/java/Combet/Documentation/Expose-0.html> (1998, September 30).

Riley, F. (1995). *Understanding IT: Developing Multimedia Courseware.* University of Hull. Available: <http://www.hull.ac.uk/itti/bk_dnld.html> (1998, September 16).

van Loo, J. & Maks, H. (1996). Dynamizing Micro-economics: MicroSim. *CHEER,* 10(2). Available: <http://www.ilrt.bris.ac.uk/ctiecon/cheer/ch102/ch102p10.htm> (1998, September 16).

Java-References

The Java Language™ – *An Overview.* Available: <http://www.javasoft.com/doc/Overviews/java/java-overview-1.html> (1998, September 16).

Swing Short Course, Part I. MageLang Institute. Available: <http://developer.javasoft.com/developer/onlineTraining/swing/> (1998, September 16).

Swing Short Course, Part II. MageLang Institute. Available: <http://developer.javasoft.com/developer/onlineTraining/swing2/> (1998, September 16).

Sands, J. (1998, January). *JFC: An in-depth look at Sun's successor to AWT–Swing into great UI development.* JavaWorld. Available: <http://www.javaworld.com/jw-01-1998/jw-01-jfc.html> (1998, September 16).

Voss, G. *JavaBeans Tutorial.* JavaSoft. Available: <http://developer.javasoft.com/developer/onlineTraining/Beans/TOC.html> (1998, September 16).

Java[1] for the Web – Economic Implications[2]

Ralf Menkhoff

1 Introduction

According to many recent analyses all types of electronic commerce[3] (e-commerce or EC) over the Internet will dramatically gain importance in the next few years (see e.g. Henry et al. 1998). It is a well-known fact, however, that this development is only realistic if the infrastructure of the net can cope with the sharply increasing demand. The legal and security issues arising with e-commerce have to be solved, and cheap and secure payment systems have to be developed. In numerous articles, economists address these and related topics.[4] Nevertheless, most economists do not explicitly take into account that proper software is needed, too. Indeed, the literature about the "economics of software" as a whole is relatively rare. This is a surprising fact: the software industry is, e.g., a leading sector in the U.S. economy and it is growing rapidly. "From 1984 to 1993, employment in the [U.S.] computer and data processing industry grew at a hefty 7 percent annual rate, well above the one and three-fourths percent growth in total nonagricultural employment over this period" (Sichel 1997, pp. 51-52).

In the following article I would like to provide some basic insights into the economics of web-based programming, because web-based software applications are necessary to fully utilize the economic potential of the Internet. The analysis is carried out as follows: first I will investigate what types of software applications are needed for the web as an economic environment. Following that I will describe some important characteristics of an economically "ideal" programming language for the web.[5] Moreover, I will investigate whether Java meets these characteristics. Therefore, I will describe some important technological aspects of Java and closely related technologies. In section 4 I will try to work out fundamental economic implications of using Java as a web-based programming language. In order to derive the inferences I will

---

[1] Java is an object-oriented and platform-independent programming language, designed by Sun Microsystems.
[2] The author is grateful to Anja Bunte, Winfried Reiss, and Wolfgang Rothfritz for valuable comments.
[3] "Electronic Commerce stands for the interactive, online transaction of business processes incl. marketing, sales, payment, distribution and after-sales [services]" (Altgeld 1998, p. 3). Sometimes the term "electronic commerce" is used only for transactions with end users. In this analysis a broader definition of electronic commerce – including business-to-business transactions – is used.
[4] For an overview see e.g. Varian 1998.
[5] Programming languages are used to develop software like, e.g., operating systems, device drivers, office applications, etc. Nevertheless, a programming language itself is a piece of software.

choose three different outlooks: the perspectives of producers, users, and intermediaries of software. Finally, I will summarize the main results of the investigation.

2 Software Applications for the Web

After the emergence of the World Wide Web (WWW)[6] at the beginning of the 90s and the introduction of comfortable and multimedia-capable web browsers[7] such as NCSA Mosaic many companies realized that the web has great potentials for advertisement, for buying and selling goods and services, etc. Today, almost every important enterprise has its own homepage. The same applies to many small and medium-sized businesses. Nevertheless, e-commerce is still in its beginning: while product information is widely available, transaction-oriented e-commerce solutions are – at least in Germany – not ubiquitous. However, these transaction-oriented solutions are necessary to fully utilize the economic potential of the web.

Figure 1 illustrates the development of electronic commerce over the Internet, or rather the WWW. Especially the more sophisticated e-commerce solutions enable productivity enhancements by lowering costs. In addition, this new distribution channel should allow for quicker penetration of new markets, higher revenues, better customer understanding, and higher customer satisfaction. The customers may profit through greater choices (including new products and services), lower prices, better service, and more fun.[8] Of course, many of these advantages are also true for non-commercial undertakings like public schools, universities, etc. (See Altgeld 1998, pp. 14-15.)

From the technical point of view, web-based systems are software applications. These applications have in common that they all operate over the Internet.[9] Accessing the Internet is possible with a variety of different devices, e.g. Personal Computers, Apple Macintoshes, PowerPCs, Laptops, Set-Top-Boxes, Handhelds, etc. All these devices may operate with many distinct operating systems, equipped with varying browsers. This heterogeneous environment makes application development a serious challenge.[10]

---

[6] A brief description of the Internet (inclusive WWW) and its basic technologies such as HTML (HyperText Markup Language) and TCP/IP (Transmission Control Protocol/Internet Protocol) can be found in Barron et al. 1996.
[7] A web browser is a tool for viewing documents of the web (so-called HTML pages) and for navigating through the web. The navigation is accomplished by hypertext links.
[8] For more details see section 4.
[9] In the business-to-business environment Extranets (privately-owned networks) and Virtual Private Networks (VPN; "privatized" parts of the Internet) also play an important role. In the following these networks are not treated separately since they both use Internet technology.
[10] Usually software programs are designed for a specific environment only (see also sections 3 and 4).

This is true because HTML, the basic language of the web, is not suited for the development of interactive[11] applications.[12] Hence, other solutions have to be used.

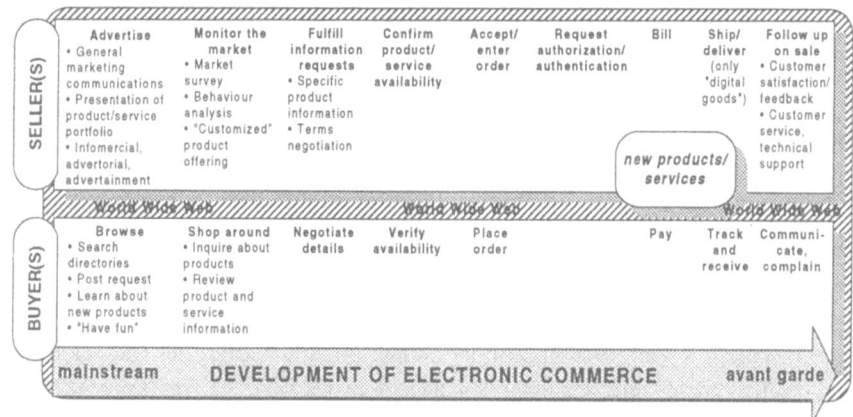

Figure 1: Development of Electronic Commerce (See Altgeld 1998, p. 6.)

In many cases it is sufficient to use a database server as the back-end in conjunction with a web server as a special front-end and a ready to use e-commerce application[13] (see Kossel & Wronski 1998, p. 148). Usually, it is possible to access such a web-based application with common web browsers without modifications. In this case, the standard e-commerce application provides the necessary interactivity. Different e-commerce applications use various technologies to achieve interactivity.

The common gateway interface (CGI) often serves as a way to access programs which are located on the web server.[14] It is, e.g., imaginable to provide a program which allows to initiate a query to a product database. Through CGI it is possible to access this program with the web browser using forms[15]. Launching the program with

---

[11] "The common thread that runs among all these applications [stock trading, home shopping, home banking, etc.] is that, they require a sequence of interactions between the user and a server (or servers)" (Shah 1996, 19.2).

[12] The development of ordinary, i.e., static, web pages is a relatively simple task: on the one hand HTML is a standardized language, on the other hand most modern office applications allow files to be saved as HTML without manual intervention.

[13] Many different vendors offer such standard applications. Sometimes these applications already contain a special database server (see e.g. Kossel & Wronski 1998).

[14] "The Common Gateway Interface (CGI) is a standard for interfacing external applications with information servers, such as HTTP or Web servers. A plain HTML document that the Web daemon *retrieves* is *static*, which means it exists in a constant state: a text file that doesn't change. A CGI program, on the other hand, is *executed* in real-time, so that it can output *dynamic* information" (NCSA 1998).

[15] "Perhaps the biggest advance that the HTML 2.0 specification made over its predecessors was the inclusion of elements that allowed for users to input information. These elements are the *Form* elements. They provide for the inclusion of objects like text boxes, choice lists, etc., and have proved

the web browser will start a new task of the program; it is important to note that this task is actually running on the web server. The results of the query are transmitted back to the web client. Here, CGI is the key to "solve" the problem of heterogeneity.[16] Obviously, this solution is well-suited for many standard web applications as well as for individual web-based programs.[17]

Nevertheless, CGI is not the all-embracing solution for web-based programming[18]: while the server has to run the program which provides the necessary functions, the web client is used as a simple access tool. In many cases this is – at least from an economic point of view – dissatisfying. Think about the execution of more complex applications. If, e.g., thousands of users try to access such a program simultaneously, the load of the server is rising dramatically.[19] At the same time the numerous web clients are more or less idle.

The following section describes some important characteristics of an economically "ideal" programming language for the web, i.e., a language which, among other things, allows to create programs which use the infrastructure of the web in a more flexible way.

3   Java – An Economically "Ideal" Programming Language for the Web?

In his article "Economic Incentives in Software Design" Varian distinguishes between "...two sorts of costs involved when one uses software: the fixed cost of learning to use a piece of software and the variable cost of operating the software" (Varian 1993, "Abstract").

Adopting this distinction to programming languages makes it necessary to further subdivide the user costs, since there are two types of users: on the one hand there are the software developers (in the following called "developers" or "programmers"). They use the programming languages in order to create "new" programs. On the other hand there are the users of the "new" programs which were written with the programming languages (in the following called "users"; see footnote 5). At first glance, one

---

invaluable for recent HTML applications, particularly search engines, database query entry and the like" (Le Hunte 1998, "The HTML Language Reference\Form Elements\An Introduction").
[16] For further information about CGI visit CGI 1998.
[17] Very often scripting languages like JavaScript (from Netscape Communications) and Visual Basic Script (from Microsoft) are used to access events such as startups, exits, and user mouse clicks.
[18] It is beyond the scope of this paper to describe all possible solutions for web-based programming. For a more complete overview see e.g. Thiemann 1998.
[19] "There really is no limit as to what you can hook up to the Web [via CGI]. The only thing you need to remember is that whatever your CGI program does, it should not take too long to process. Otherwise, the user will just be staring at their browser waiting for something to happen." (NCSA 1998.)

could imagine that it is sufficient to concentrate on the cost which programmers have to bear. The further investigation, however, reveals that this is insufficient.[20]

Let us first concentrate on the fixed cost of learning how to use a piece of software.[21] Before the developer is able to create the first program he has to invest a substantial amount of time in order to understand the basics of the language. Therefore, he has to read the documentation, work through tutorials, investigate examples, and practice for some time. This cost is a fixed cost, because it is more or less independent from the frequency of use. The amount of this fixed cost depends on the "ease of learning".[22] Usually it is, e.g., easier to learn a visual language than a textual language. Likewise, the textual languages can be more or less cryptic and complex. The available development environments (if provided) can have different types of menus, icon bars, help screens, etc. Moreover, the quality of the accompanying documentation, including tutorials and examples, matters. (See Varian 1993, pp. 1-2.)

Users incur a comparable cost of learning, but regularly on a lower level, since most application programs are not as complex as programming languages.[23] Nevertheless, items such as menus, icon bars, (interactive) help screens, user prompts, error messages, (interactive) assistants, and the integration in the overall system do remarkably affect this type of cost. Hence, a programming language which, e.g., does not allow to create applications which are tightly integrated into the overall system, incurs – via the developed applications – higher costs to the users than necessary.

The variable costs users incur each time they use an application are time costs and – for a web-based application – eventually transmission costs. These costs depend in part on the "ease of operation". This again depends, among other things, on the performance of the application: "how quickly and how well the software does the job it is supposed to do" (Varian 1993, p. 2). This in turn is not independent from the programming language used to create the application.

User can only profit from the performance of an application, if they are able to invoke the appropriate commands. Thus, the variable cost of using the software is also

---

[20] Note that this is not the only feasible approach: it would also be possible to take utility into account. As a result the "further subdivision" should be unnecessary.

[21] While the cost of learning how to use a piece of software is fixed with respect to the frequency of use, it is variable with respect to already existing experiences: an experienced programmer (software user) only has to learn the differences between the programming languages (programs) he already knows and the new one.

[22] "Reviews of software often talk about "ease of use". The above distinction suggests that there are two dimensions to ease of use: ease of learning and ease of operation" (Varian 1993, p. 1).

[23] Sometimes application programs have integrated programming languages (e.g. Microsoft Visual Basic for Word, Excel, Access). Thus, one has to distinguish between the "pure" application and the programming language.

determined by the time it takes to invoke the commands. "If one has to wade through an elaborate menu structure to perform a simple task, then this is a cost that must be born every time the task is undertaken" (Varian 1993, p. 1).

The transmission cost of a web-based application usually varies with the size of the application, which again depends on the programming language used to create it.[24] This seems to be true whether the application is actually executed on the web client or on the web server.[25]

The programmers also have to bear a variable cost which, in part, depends on the performance of the language. For a compiler the "compilation time" is – from the programmer's point of view – the most important performance characteristic. Likewise, for an interpreter the "interpretation time" is most crucial.[26]

Besides, the "efficiency" of the syntax (textual languages only) and of the graphical expressions (visual languages only) affects these variable development costs, respectively. These are also related to points such as fault detection, reusability[27], predefined elements, integration with CASE tools (computer-aided software engineering tools), and so forth[28].

Although the explanations about usage costs given above are by no means complete, it can be concluded that an "ideal" programming language generally has to minimize fixed and variable cost of usage for programmers as well as for users. It remains to be determined which special features a web-based programming language should have.

In the previous section it was already mentioned that a web-based programming language should be flexible with respect to the utilization of the whole infrastructure. To be more concrete: in order to fully utilize the given infrastructure of the web, the programming language should allow to develop applications that can be executed – without modifications[29] – on every server and on each client. As a result

---

[24] It is possible that the user does not have to bear this cost. This is true, e.g., if the user's provider and telephone company only charge flat fees.

[25] This may be incorrect, if the user has to bear volume-oriented fees only.

[26] "Computer programs written in any language other than machine language must be either interpreted or compiled. An interpreter is software that examines a user program one instruction at a time and calls on code to execute the operations required by that instruction. This is a rather slow process. A compiler is software that translates a user program as a whole into machine code that is saved for subsequent execution whenever desired" (Encyclopædia Britannica 1997, "Computer Science, Programming Languages"). Obviously, with an interpreter users and developers have to bear the same variable cost due to "performance".

[27] Reusability means that it possible to use parts of already existing work.

[28] It depends on the particular project whether these characteristics really alter the variable cost of programming.

[29] If modifications are necessary, matters are more complicated: the costs of modification have to be compared with the advantages of distribution.

it would be possible to distribute the applications in order to optimize the usage of the scarce resources of the web (especially CPU power and bandwidth of the underlying communication infrastructure).

Since the Internet is an open network without central authority, there is no overruling access control system. Under these circumstances, the distribution of applications results in serious security problems.[30] An "ideal" programming language has to solve these problems.

During the Industrial Revolution great productivity enhancements could be achieved through division of labor. It is one of the characteristic features of the software industry that division of labor is relatively limited (see e.g. Baetjer 1997). If one keeps in mind that the web is a space without borders, it becomes clear that it could serve as an "enabler" for a specific form of labor division: it is in principle possible to split the production process between workgroups located in different countries, e.g. in order to reduce development times. A programming language which does not facilitate this process cannot be treated as economically "ideal".

Of course, an "ideal" programming language for the web also has to support

- common Internet standards (especially the TCP/IP-protocol HTTP[31]),
- the creation of multimedia-rich applications,
- persistence[32],
- an appropriate messaging model (see below),
- the smooth integration into existing IT infrastructure.

The "special features" described up to now[33] and the more general characteristics of an economically "ideal" programming language are taken to examine the qualities of Java as a web-based language. Note, however, that it is not intended to derive quantitative findings.

In 1994, Sun Microsystems (respectively SunSoft[34]) released the first (pre-) version of Java[35]. According to Sun's Java White Paper (see Sun 1994), the language is – among other things – object-oriented, simple, distributed, secure, architecture neutral, and high-performance:[36]

---

[30] All types of computer viruses may lead to the most critical problems (e.g. sabotage, espionage, etc.).
[31] HTTP = HyperText Transfer Protocol; for computer oriented abbreviations and acronyms see e.g. Kind & Kind 1998.
[32] "Persistence implies that memory management involves both in-memory and on-disk objects" (Weiner 1996b).
[33] This list does not claim to be complete. Further details can be found in, e.g., Shah 1996.
[34] SunSoft is a wholly-owned subsidiary of Sun Microsystems.
[35] Information concerning the programming language Java can be found at Sun 1994.
[36] Sun describes Java with a list of buzzwords (see Sun 1994, p. 1). The remaining characteristics are outlined in Huang 1996.

(1) Java is object-oriented

Java is a derivative of C++, a very popular object-oriented programming language: object-oriented programming is a "...technique in which a program is written with discrete objects that are self-contained collections of computational procedures and data structures. New programs can be written by assembling a set of these predefined, self-contained objects in far shorter time than by writing complete programs from scratch" (Encyclopædia Britannica 1997, "Computers, Programming Languages").

Object-orientation assures reusability which in turn reduces the variable programming cost. The amount of the potential cost reduction depends on (a) the degree of object-orientation and (b) the quality and quantity of predefined objects. Java is strongly object-oriented[37] and has sophisticated and standardized supporting libraries (see Huang 1996, 21.3.2). Moreover, the component model JavaBeans[38] allows to develop reusable objects which further simplifies the production of Java applications (see Weyerhäuser 1997).[39]

Much of the popularity of object-oriented programming is due to expected cost reductions. But the concept of object-oriented programming itself puts the developers to expense. They have to bear the fixed cost of learning: "Certain aspects of Java are easier to learn than C++ [see below], but the difficulties most people have in learning to program in both C++ and Java have little to do with the language itself" (Huang 1996, 21.3.3). Instead, most of these difficulties are caused by the basic concept of object-oriented programming.[40]

(2) Java is simple

One of the design goals of Sun was "...to build a system that could be programmed easily without a lot of esoteric training..." (Sun 1994, p. 1). Thus, Sun decided (a) to omit some more complicated features like pointer arithmetic and multiple inheritance and (b) to ad auto garbage collection (simplifies memory management).[41] In comparison with C++, this reduces the cost of learning. In many cases this "simplicity" should reduce variable development cost, too. Especially the easy memory management prevents common mistakes. However, pointer arithmetic and multiple

---

[37] "As compared to C++, Java is more strict in terms of its object-oriented nature. In Java, everything must be done via method invocation for a Java object. You must view your whole application as an object; an object of a particular class" (Huang 1996, 21.3.1).
[38] See Sun 1997.
[39] A component "is not a complete application, but can be used to build cheap, personalized applications. Components reduce the cost and complexity of software development" (Shah 1996, 19.1.2).
[40] Information about the concept of object-oriented programming in, e.g., Büttgenbach 1992 and Varhol 1993.
[41] For more details see Sun 1994, p. 1-2.

inheritance could be powerful programming features. From this point of view, the absence of these features may sometimes raise cost (see Weiner 1996b).

While the new Java software component JavaBeans can be manipulated visually in a builder tool Java itself is a textual programming language without an integrated development environment. Textual languages have the disadvantage that they do not use the 2D and 3D visual pattern recognition of human beings (see Weiner 1996a). Furthermore, Java's syntax is very compact (or cryptic). Thus, for a "newbie" (someone without any programming experience) Java is not easy to learn. Today, however, many visual development environments are available. These software packages could lower the fixed cost of learning.[42] Nevertheless, in every serious Java programming project source code modifications are unavoidable.

All in all, Sun's notion of "simple to learn" is rather "familiar to C++ programmers": somebody who is able to master C++ is able to learn Java without much training (see Huang 1996, 21.3.1). But "simple" also means "small", a substantial condition for web-based programming. Java programs are, indeed, relatively small so that they can be executed even on less powerful devices.[43] This is a prerequisite for the flexible utilization of the network (lines and computers). The "live" distribution of applications over the Internet is, e.g., only practical with small programs. Besides, the size of the programs usually influences any transmission cost of web-based applications. Moreover, smaller programs should execute faster in a network environment than bigger ones. Faster execution, in turn, means lower variable cost of usage.

(3) Java is distributed and secure

Java is a language which is intended to be used for network-oriented programming. Therefore, it supports TCP/IP-protocols like HTTP and FTP[44]. Hence, Java programs are able to easily access objects across the Internet via URLs[45]. In addition, Java provides several security mechanisms to protect systems from being damaged. This is, in part, reached through the exclusion of pointer arithmetic (see above). Moreover, Java uses a code verifier: before execution an instant virus scan is performed. After that a RSA data signature is generated. This signature verifies the source of the code and assures that it has not been corrupted or altered. "These security provisions make Java programs the first certifiable citizens of the Net" (Gilder 1995).

---

[42] Do not confuse: Java is a pure textual programming language; any graphical representations are missing. The visual development environments for Java try to deliver appropriate graphical representations. Such an approach is inevitably limited in some respect.

[43] "One of the goals of Java is to enable the construction of software that can run stand-alone in small machines. The size of the basic interpreter and class support is about 40K bytes; adding the basic standard libraries and thread support ... adds an additional 175K" (Sun 1994, p. 2). See also section 4.

[44] FTP = File Transfer Protocol.

[45] URLs = Uniform Resource Locators; a common addressing system for the Internet.

Nevertheless, in 1996 Weiner comes to the result that Java's security mechanisms are simplistic. "If some part of a system needs to be protected, Java removes access to it. Java disallows pointers to direct memory addresses and thereby forces one to use another language to write operating system-level or embedded system methods that read and write to specific addresses. [...] Unfortunately, the price of such protection in Java is a set of odious restrictions that limit the types of professional development projects to which it can be applied" (Weiner 1996a). According to Weiner, Java lacks programmable firewalls.[46]

(4) Java is architecture neutral

The Java compiler generates bytecode instructions which have nothing to do with a particular computer architecture. This bytecode is directly executable on any system that implements a so-called Java Virtual Machine (JVM/VM). This is possible through the Java interpreter. Today, Java Virtual Machines are ubiquitous. As a result, it is – at least in theory – possible to execute Java programs nearly anywhere on the network (more details in section 4). This is a key feature for web-based programming; without this feature it would seem to be difficult to use the web as a distributed computing system[47].

Sun claims that the basic design of Java – compilation and interpretation of architecture neutral bytecode – makes the development process much more rapid and exploratory (see Sun 1994, p. 5). However, Java does not provide a mechanism for an interactive development: "...syntax errors remain in the code until compile time. Semantic errors often aren't caught until run-time, potentially, even at customer sites." (Weiner 1996a).

(5) Java is high-performance

In comparison to other interpreted languages, Java is – through bytecode interpretation – high-performance. According to Sun, "...the performance of interpreted bytecodes is usually more than adequate..." (Sun 1994, p. 5). To further boost performance Java allows for just-in-time compilation[48]. Nevertheless, insufficient performance is one of the biggest problems of Java: "Performance remains a problem for Java applications. Since Java is a semi-interpreted language (the VM must interpret the byte code for your machine), Java applications run slower than those compiled into native code for a specific platform" (Coffee 1998). Even with just-in-time compilation,

---

[46] The article cited "Java Development Weaknesses" was written for Cubicon Corporation, a company which tries to develop a competing programming language. In a way the paper is a little bit outdated. See also section 4.

[47] Today, "the Web is essentially a huge distributed system, but more like a distributed file system rather than a distributed computing system" (Shah 1996, 19.1).

[48] "The bytecodes can be translated on the fly (at runtime) into machine code for the particular CPU the application is running on" (Sun 1994, p. 5).

native C++ code has clearly a performance edge over Java. Today, many Java applications still give a leisurely performance.[49] (See PC Magazine Online 1998.)

While the recent performance improvements of Java will go on, it is unlikely that Java can completely close the gap to, e.g. C++. This is due to fundamental technological reasons (see Huang 1996, 21.3.3).

None of the characteristics – object-oriented, simple, distributed, secure, architecture neutral[50], high-performance (as described above) – is unique to Java. But it is for the first time that a programming language combines all these properties. This is one of the reasons why Java is a strong competitor in the market for web-based programming solutions.

The explanations given so far, however, show that Java is, at least from an economic perspective, by no means perfect: with respect to the "ease of programming" it has to be realized that there seems to be a trade-off between "ease of learning" and "ease of operation" with a clear focus on minimizing the variable cost of programming. This is not surprising. Programming, especially in a heterogeneous environment, is a complicated undertaking which requires a certain level of abstraction. This, in turn, causes a fixed cost of learning. Compare this to mathematics: most people have to bear a relatively high fixed cost of learning in order to understand the foundations. Nevertheless, mathematics is a very powerful tool for every-day problem solving. Therefore, it is highly questionable, whether it is possible to create an "ideal" programming language as described before. That is why research has to concentrate on minimizing the tradeoff.

In this context it is interesting to see, whether the market provides the right incentives to minimize both types of costs. Unfortunately, this requires a separate analysis (see e.g. Varian 1993)[51].

With respect to the "cost of usage" (user's point of view) it is already clear that Java – by being small – reduces any transmission costs. The security mechanisms protect the user's system from being damaged and, thus, avoid recovery costs. However, Java also entails some negative aspects: a slow performance means a high variable cost of usage. Moreover, the integration of Java programs into the overall system is often weak. In the earlier versions of Java there was, e.g., no support of "drag and drop" and "cut and paste", commands familiar to every Windows user.[52] This raises cost, too.

---

[49] Of course, performance depends also on the architecture of the application developed. See e.g. Roulo 1998.

[50] "Historically, the UCSD p-code system was the best that used a binary-code interpreter to achieve platform-independent portability" (Huang 1996, 21.1).

[51] "I show that a monopoly provider of software ["applications"] generally invests the right amount of resources in making the software easy to learn, but to little in making it easy to operate" (Varian 1993, "Abstract").

[52] JDK (Java Development Kit) 1.1 supports the clipboard. JDK 1.2 also supports "drag and drop".

With regard to the demanded "special features" of an "ideal" web-based language it was clarified above that Java supports some of the most important characteristics: Java is architecture neutral and small which allows for a flexible utilization of the web's infrastructure. In addition, the security problems arising with web-based computing have been principally solved by Java. As a language designed for computing over the web, Java naturally supports common Internet standards. It is closely integrated into the World Wide Web infrastructure. Through its strong object-orientation it enables a problem-free division of labor in the software industry. Its internationalization provides the means to create programs with country-specific properties. Moreover, Java facilitates the development of multimedia-rich applications. Therefore, it provides special Java Media APIs[53] (Java 2D, Java 3D, Java Advanced Imaging, Java Media Framework, Java Sound, Java Speech)[54].

Without going to much into details it can be said that persistence in Java is currently restricted to selected data objects only (see Liberman et al. 1997, pp. 29-30).[55] A programming language supports persistence when the created objects and variables of the developed programs continue to exist and retain their values between runs of the programs (see FOLDOC, "persistence"). This is an important factor in many programming projects. In order to achieve persistence with Java, it is usually necessary to utilize a separate database. This is, e.g., possible through JDBC (Java database connectivity, a standard SQL database access interface.).

On the whole it can be stated that Java is not an economically "ideal" programming language (for the web). This is not surprising: it is highly questionable whether it is possible to create such a language. Nevertheless, the concept was used to derive – without "hype" – the qualities of Java from an economic point of view. This derivation suggests that Java is not really a revolutionary language. But it is an interesting programming language with a clear focus on network-centric computing. Today, Java is without doubt a key technology for web-based computing. Despite this fact, Java's early success was clearly influenced by perfect timing (Java arrived right on the time of the explosive growth of the Internet) and a brilliant marketing strategy on the part of Sun (see Huang 1996, 21.1).

Of course, Java is not sufficient for turning the web into a huge distributed computer system. Shah identifies two basic technologies for overcoming the current

---

[53] API = Application Programming Interface. "The interface (calling conventions) by which an application program accesses operating system and other services. An API is defined at source code level and provides a level of abstraction between the application and the kernel (or other privileged utilities) to ensure the portability of the code" (FOLDOC, "API").
[54] Not all of these APIs are currently available. More information at the Java Technology Homepage at Sun 1998d.
[55] With JDK 1.1 Sun introduced the Object Serialization API which added basic support for persistence.

shortcomings of the web: *"Distributed Object Architectures* and *Compound Document Frameworks.* Distributed object architectures help in building client/server applications using 'distributed objects' and provide services such as security, transactions, state management, licensing, etc. Compound document frameworks act as containers in which heterogeneous 'components' can be placed to build customized applications" (Shah 1996, 19.1.2.).

Java itself is – through Remote Method Invocation (RMI) – in part a distributed object architecture: it is possible to create Java objects whose methods can be invoked from a different Java Virtual Machine. This virtual machine may be running in the same physical machine or on a remote server (see Shah 1996, 19.2.2). Moreover, Java supports another important and more complete distributed object architecture, namely CORBA (Common Object Request Broker Architecture, by the Object Management Group).[56] With CORBA it is possible to integrate Java programs into the existing IT infrastructure.[57]

Although the component model JavaBeans is not a complete compound document framework such as OpenDoc (a standard proposed by Component Integration Labs) and OLE (Object Linking and Embedding, by Microsoft), it holds a lot of promise in this field. Furthermore, IBM and Apple are working with Sun to ensure interoperability between OpenDoc and JavaBeans applications (see Shah 1996, 19.3.3/19.3.4).

So far, the analysis was – more or less – focused on the programming language Java. "But just as Windows is more than just a graphical user interface, Java is more than just another way to write code. [...] Java and the Java VM together provide a set of services that Java programs can rely on, regardless of the underlying hardware and OS [operating system]. In this respect, Java has become positioned as a new platform– a target environment for applications" (Clyman 1998, "Java as a New Platform"). In the following it is investigated how this platform can influence the economics of software production, software utilization, and software intermediation. Connections to e-commerce are made where appropriate.

---

[56] "Java is trying to cobble together support like this [Internet-wide object-to-object communication] through CORBA and other mechanisms, but has no architectural backbone to support it" (Weiner 1996b, "Cubicon's design focuses on network-wide messaging").

[57] CORBA makes it possible to integrate objects programmed in different computer languages to one application (see Middendorf & Singer n. d.): "The ability to reuse and extend existing legacy code using CORBA allows developers to protect their existing investment, while taking advantage of the Java programming language" (Morgan, 1997).

4   The Utilization of Java – Some Inferences[58]

Software production, software utilization, and software intermediation are, of course, closely related. Nevertheless, for the sake of simplicity these outlooks are separated. Note, however, that in real life a "player" can be, e.g., a producer and a user in one.

4.1   The economics of software production

Nearly all the costs involved in the development of software are fixed with respect to the number of units sold: designing, writing source code, compiling, debugging, testing, documenting (source code and the final product), and marketing, to mention the most important (see Varian 1993, p. 3). The pure costs of reproduction are almost negligible: with the overwhelming success of the CD-ROM and the Internet it is very cheap to "produce" an additional unit of the software[59]; even the accompanying documentation of the product is – more or less – on the CD-ROM or on the web. Moreover, support is in many cases separated from the license to use the software. Packaging (if necessary) and distributing seem to be the most important variable costs. Thus, producers of software usually face a downward sloping average-cost curve. This is especially true for web-based applications because in this case the distribution costs are usually more or less transferred to the user. The producer has only to run a web server.

Under these circumstances a for-profit software company will only develop a piece of software if (a) there is a potential customer base (PCB)[60] which is big enough and/or (b) the willingness to pay on the part of the potential customer(s) is high enough so that a successful exploitation of the investment seems to be possible.

This is depicted in a very simple manner in figure 2, assuming a constant willingness to pay (all potential customers are actually willing to buy the product for a certain amount of money)[61], and negligible variable costs.

Under these circumstances a producer would definitively incur a loss in the initial situation Y_0^{PCB} / MR_0: with a constant willingness to pay, marginal revenue (MR) equals average revenue. Thus, the total revenue ($MR_0 \times Y_0^{PCB}$) would be substantially

---

[58] Parts of this section are taken from Menkhoff 1998.

[59] Software itself is a public good; you only produce it once a time because there is no rivalry. Up to now only the required media (CD-ROM, booklets, etc.) are private goods bringing about variable costs.

[60] Let us define the potential customer base as the sum of people who are possibly interested in buying the product.

[61] Obviously, this is a rather unrealistic assumption.

lower than total cost ($MR_1 \times Y_0^{PCB}$)[62]. The software would not be supplied. However, with a bigger potential customer base and/or a higher willingness to pay, it may be possible to supply the product successfully (see e.g. situation Y_1^{PCB} / MR_1).

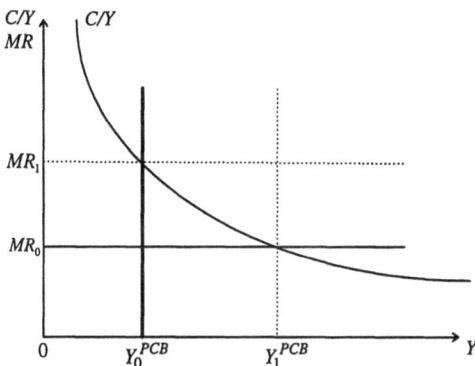

Figure 2: Downward sloping average-cost curve

At least for standard applications, such as word processors, spreadsheet programs, and so on, factor (a) seems to be more important, because for this type of software, the willingness to pay appears to be relatively low. In the software industry, the potential customer base mainly depends on the type of software (office applications, graphic programs, DTP tools, communication programs, games, etc.), the hardware requirements, and the software requirements. While the first aspect is important for all products available in different types or forms (clothing, food, etc.) the remaining aspects are due to strong complementarities.

The meaningful utilization of a computer is only possible with an appropriate combination of hardware, operating system, and application software: while the application software provides the functionality demanded, the operating system manages and controls the operation of the hardware. Obviously, each operating system (or version of it) is developed for a specific type of computer (e.g. IBM-compatible PC, Apple-Macintosh, PowerPC, etc.)[63]. Whereas this is an expected result, it is – at least at first glance – surprising that application software is usually designed to work with a specific operating system (platform) only. Thus, one speaks of platform-dependency: it is, for example, not possible to use a Microsoft

---

[62] In order to further simplify figure 2, MR_1 was chosen to be equal with the average cost in the initial situation.
[63] For an operating system the CPU (in an IBM-compatible PC this may be a 80586 microprocessor) is most important.

Win 95-program on a computer running IBM OS/2. This is one of the major problems in network-oriented programming.

The compatibility decides whether an operating system and application software can be combined to a useful unit. "Product compatibility is not synonymous with product *standardization*. Compatibility is a relational attribute between products, that is, they 'go together'. Standardization is a *particular way* of making products go together. Standardized products go together because they have been designed in conformance with a common technical specification – the standard" (Gabel 1991). With platform-dependent software this standard is the operating system. Hence, the installed base of the operating system is – from a technical point of view – also the potential customer base of the application software. With Java, this changes dramatically: neither a specific operating system nor a certain type of computer directly influences the potential customer base. Rather, all computers equipped with a Java Virtual Machine constitute the relevant installed base, i.e., the Java platform.

The differences between (ordinary) platform-dependent software and Java programs are illustrated by figures 3 and 4a/b (OS = Operating System).

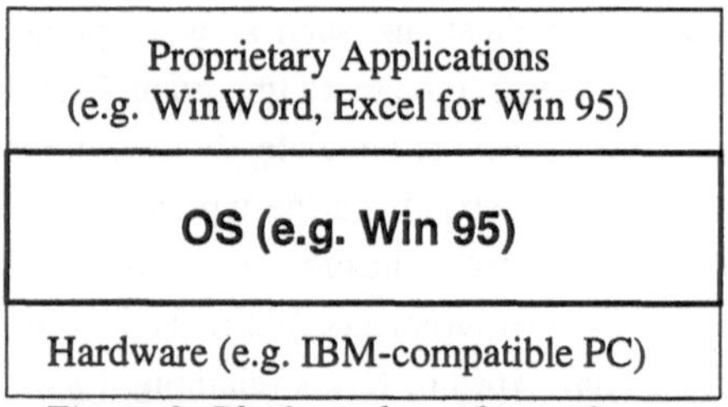

Proprietary Applications (e.g. WinWord, Excel for Win 95)
OS (e.g. Win 95)
Hardware (e.g. IBM-compatible PC)

Figure 3: Platform-dependent software

According to figures 4a/b there are three different types of Java programs: Java applets, Java servlets and Java applications. The main difference between applets and applications is that applets cannot run without a Java-enabled browser (browser with a JVM). Usually, Java applets are directly loaded from the web and executed on the client (see below). They "...are suitable for a nomadic existence on the Net, rather than a mere settled life on the desktop" (Gilder 1995). Java applications, however, have to be installed on the target system. Therefore, they do not have to fulfill the strong security restrictions of applets. Without a "signature", applets are, e.g., not able to access the local disks of the client.[64] Java servlets are essentially an alternative to CGI scripts.[65]

---

[64] At the beginning of the Java development process, applets were not able to access the local disks of the client ("sandbox principle"). It was impossible to assign this right to the applet, which was a major drawback. With JDK 1.1 an "all or nothing" strategy is possible through "signing". A more precise security handling is available with JDK 1.2 (see Menge 1998, pp. 38-39).

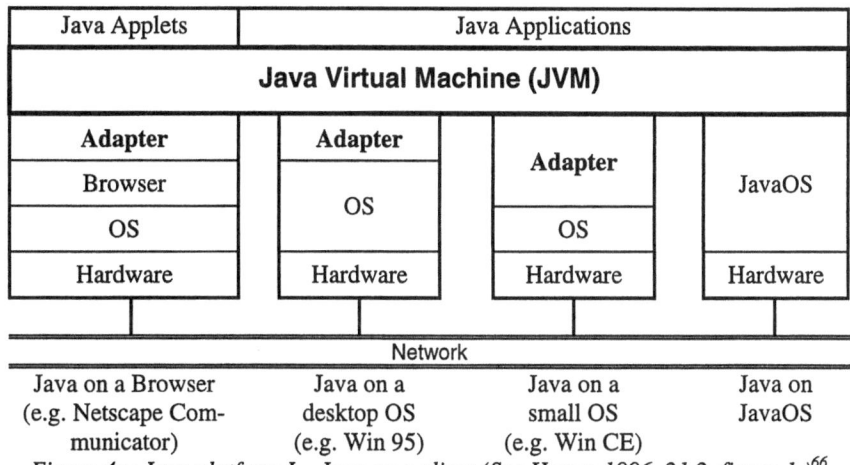

Java Applets	Java Applications

Java Virtual Machine (JVM)

Adapter	**Adapter**		**Adapter**	JavaOS
Browser	OS		OS	
OS				
Hardware	Hardware		Hardware	Hardware

Network

Java on a Browser (e.g. Netscape Communicator)	Java on a desktop OS (e.g. Win 95)	Java on a small OS (e.g. Win CE)	Java on JavaOS

Figure 4a: Java platform I – Java on a client (See Huang 1996, 21.2, figure 1.)[66]

Java Servlets and Java Applications

Java Virtual Machine (JVM)

Adapter
Server OS (e.g. Win NT)
Hardware (e.g. IBM-compatible PC)

Figure 4b: Java platform II – Java on a server[67]

Today, Java-enabled browsers are available for every major operating system. The fact that these browsers are usually obtainable as freeware has led to their wide dissemination (often these browsers are already integrated into the operating system). Moreover, some operating systems (e.g. OS/2) provide an integrated Java Virtual Machine for the direct support of Java applications. On the server side, the support of Java is constantly rising. Thus, the Java platform is a giant target for application development. This holds particularly true for Java applets, which are obviously well-suited for many kinds of web-based programs.

---

[65] "Servlets are to servers what applets are to browsers. Unlike applets, however, servlets have no graphical user interface" (Bloch 1998).
[66] Win CE = Windows CE by Microsoft (see Microsoft 1998a); JavaOS by Sun (see Sun 1998e).
[67] Win NT = Windows NT by Microsoft (see Microsoft 1998b).

Other things being equal (performance, reliability, feature sets, etc.), a profitable application development should be easier with Java, since the customer base "Internet" is huge and still growing at an astonishing rate. Furthermore, as already known, Java programs (applets and applications) are normally relatively small so that they can be executed also on less powerful computer systems (clients). Nevertheless, they (servlets and applications) are also suitable on the server side. This further widens the potential customer base.

As stated in section 2 e-commerce over the Internet should allow for a quicker penetration of (new) markets. For Java applets, it is evident that the natural distribution channel is the web (see below). This should also simplify an economically successful application development.

Up to now we have taken costs for granted in this section. How does the Java platform then influence development cost?

The production costs of software applications are clearly affected by their complexity. It is usually relatively cheap to develop a simple (i.e., not complex) program which provides only some functions. Today, however, the overwhelming majority of software applications in the commercial sector are very complex systems providing a variety of different functions. Buying the text editor WinWord, for example, means also purchasing a (simple) drawing program, a spell-checker, a (small) database program, and a (simple) spreadsheet program. The resulting complexity of such programs is an important "cost driver". One way to reduce complexity – i.e. costs – without losing functionality is modularization.

Modularization means that a complex system is separated into several more or less closed subsystems which communicate only via a few exactly defined mechanisms (see Kraemer 1996). The strong object orientation of Java and the possibility of distributed programming (different parts of a program can be located on different servers) through RMI and CORBA facilitate this modularization. While this is not unique to Java, one (dis-)advantage only applies to applets: Internet-based applications which are designed to run on the client (in a browser) must have a modular design[68] in order to ensure an acceptable transmission speed.

Software production based on modules and/or components (JavaBeans) also lowers the barriers of market entrance. The lively activities in the field of Java seem to confirm this estimation. Suddenly, there are beside the well-established manufacturers new vendors of, e.g., office applications such as Applix Inc. New competitors also emerge from other market segments (see Computerwoche 96).

---

[68] "Java developers are finding that Java applications work better when they are put together as bits and pieces, as in Lotus's eSuite" (Clyman 1998, "Java as a New Platform").

Another potential source of cost reduction lies again – as already revealed in section 3 – in Java's strong object-orientation: "...unlike C++, Java is object-oriented from the ground up. This helps programmers enforce good object-oriented practices, which leads to more maintainable code" (Clyman 1998, "What Is Java, Really?").

At first glance, one would also expect that Java's cross-platform capability clearly reduces the development costs of products that are available for different platforms, such as Lotus Notes, a groupware product available for UNIX, Windows 3.x, Windows 95/NT, OS/2, and Macintosh. But this is not necessarily true, because of tremendous implementation problems with the Java Virtual Machine. The basic idea to use a virtual machine on top of the existing platforms in order to reach cross-platform compatibility is both simple and elegant. It is also an economic attempt: instead of porting[69] a mass of programs to different platforms it is sufficient to create a Java Virtual Machine for every target platform. In reality, however, the problem is that the Java Virtual Machines[70] are often not compatible with each other. Improperly implemented and outdated Java Virtual Machines are serious obstacles to Java. "Write once run everywhere", as proclaimed by Sun, is – at least up to now – still a dream. Without intensive testing on different platforms, cross-platform compatibility is currently not possible with Java. (See PC Magazine Online 1998.)

Sun tries to address this problem through standardization: Java is going to be standardized by the ISO (International Standards Organization) with Sun being the Publicly Available Specification (PAS) submitter[71] (see Sun 1998a)[72]. Moreover, Sun has launched a 100% pure Java program: "Some products that use Java technology may run on some platforms but not on others. The 100% Pure Java logo lets potential customers and end-users know that the product bearing the logo is portable across all Java compatible systems [i.e., the product does not use any platform-specific functions]" (Sun 1998b).

If Sun is able to solve the implementation problems and to encourage vendors of Java Virtual Machines to faster adopt new Java versions, a substantial cost saving in software development may be possible. In this case, not only "write once

---

[69] Of course, it is also possible to develop a program which is running on different platforms using "traditional" programming languages. The main difference is that porting is necessary with these languages (e.g. C++): adaptation of the source code and re-compilation.
[70] Note that Java Virtual Machines are supplied by many different vendors (licensees). Often these virtual machines are "optimized".
[71] "The new PAS process was designed by JTC1 [ISO's Joint Technical Committee] to speed the conversion of de facto industry standards like the Java Platform into ISO International Standards" (Sun, 1998).
[72] For further information concerning Java standardization see e.g. McMillan 1997, Day 1997, and McKay 1997. ·

run anywhere" but also "learn once program anywhere"[73] may be feasible. "According to a Zona survey of 279 IT professionals who are planning to use Java in the next year: Java has value to developers in terms of time savings of up to 80 percent..." (Krochmal 1997).

With Java the decision for which type of computer and operating system a specific program should be developed is in principle obsolete. Nevertheless, this is a very crucial decision with "traditional" software, because most of the fixed costs are sunk costs, i.e., they are not recoverable, if the firm exits the market (see Varian 1993, p. 3). In an industry, as dynamic as the software industry, this is an important aspect.

All in all, it seems to be conceivable that software projects which are not profitable with "traditional" programming languages may be profitable with Java due to (a) a huge potential customer base, (b) an efficient distribution channel, and (c) cost reductions in the development process. But another aspect may be more important: with web-based Java applets it is possible to develop a completely new type of programs. These programs are potentially available to every computer owner. Rather than being restricted to the set of programs one has locally installed, one can use any applet on the web, just as one can tap any information on the web (see Gilder 1995).

4.2 The economics of software utilization (user's point of view)

Obviously, this new type of software, called applets, also enables a new way of software utilization, the so-called "programs at your fingertips": starting a Java-enabled browser, entering an appropriate URL[74] and pressing the return key or just clicking a link is sufficient to get things working (see Gilder 1995). The applet loads transparently and runs within the browser without any installation. There is no need for plug-ins[75] or anything else.[76] This offers, among others, a tremendous potential for e-commerce.

For example, with Java applets an electronic brokering company is in the position to provide its customers with a full-featured program for account management (possible features may be placing and canceling of orders, modifying limits, calculat-

---

[73] "IMHO, cross-platform PER SE is not as important to me as stability and or PROFESSIONAL portability ... to be able to migrate between machines in a relatively painless manner. This has tremendous potential to allow programmers to catch up with the technology curve: how about "LEARN once, WRITE anywhere"? Having been a SMALLTALK and heavy LISP user in the past, I can see how the JAVA infrastructure (JVM being but one example) can be portable, stable, and still have built-in capabilities for extension which does not necessarily break everything that went before..." (Lindahl 1997).

[74] Try http://econscience.uni-paderborn.de/vwl/Mikro/java/Combet/games/Puzzle/Puzzle1E.html.

[75] "A file containing data used to alter, enhance, or extend the operation of a parent application program. [...] Plug-ins ... are stored locally. Plug-ins come in different versions specific to particular operating systems..." (FOLDOC, "plug-in").

[76] "Whether a film, a graph, an animation, a real-time bit stream on the Nasdaq ticker or the Reuter wire, a virtual reality visualization, or a game, it can be downloaded to your machine with its program in tow" (Gilder 1995).

ing of depot value, etc.). The customers can use this program from all over the world. The only thing necessary is a Java-enabled browser connected to the Internet. Without applets only data (in this case information about the account) can be transferred, but with applets the data have their own program in tow.

In the same way, the company can provide the most recent charts of any stocks of interest. The user has only to select the desired assets. The data and an applet are transferred to the browser; within the browser (maybe in a separate window) the applet then draws "live-charts" using the most recent data. New data, thus, lead to an instant redraw of charts. Such an applet can also supply additional interactivity. It is, e.g., imaginable that the applet allows modifying items such as type of chart, level of details displayed, amount of supporting information, relevant time-period, time-interval, etc.

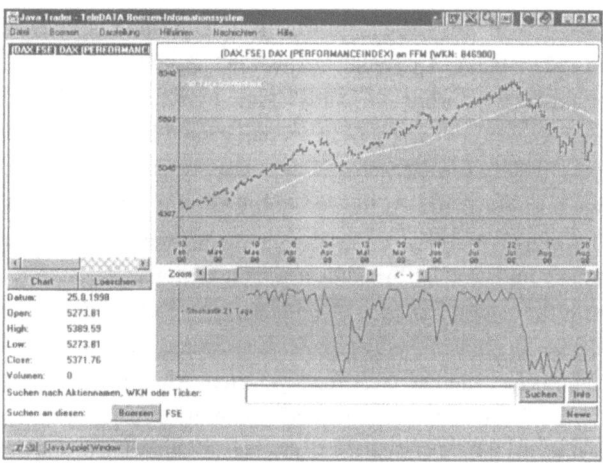

Figure 5: Java-Trader

Figure 5 is a screen shot of an interesting applet called Java-Trader[77], developed by the German company TeleDATA (see Teledata 1997b). It is a Java-based chart analyzer with a variety of features. The screen shot shows the performance of the DAX (Deutscher Aktienindex) between 02/13/98 and 08/25/98.

Another example may be a company of the automobile industry which uses Java applets to present its products interactively. Thus, it is feasible to generate fully customized (model, engine, equipment, etc.) 2D and 3D illustrations of the cars which can be manipulated by the user. The user may be able to freely choose the line of vision, the resolution (zoom in/out) the state of the car's body (open/closed), the environment

---

[77] More information at Teledata 1997. Unfortunately the information is currently only available in German.

(highway/off-road/...) and so forth. Certainly, the customer would be able to perform all these manipulations with his browser. No additional tool is required. The applet may also support the calculation of the price of the currently selected and customized car. Furthermore, the applet may allow to request information about delivery time, currently available demonstrators (same model with comparable equipment), the next local dealer, etc. In addition, it may permit a direct ordering of the already customized car.

Saab is currently experimenting with Java applets in its interactive showroom which is reachable at Saab (n. d.). Other automobile manufacturers like Rover are also using Java applets to display their products.

A design studio which is specialized in business cards, greeting cards, CD-labels, etc. may serve as an additional example. With Java applets a similar studio could offer a new type of service: on the one hand it may be possible to place a Java applet at the user's disposal which is intended for the simple creation of business cards (and/or greeting cards/CD-labels). An applet of this kind should guide the user through the development process by using "wizards" (step-by-step dialogs). It should support "drag and drop" and "cut and paste". A toolbar should be available as well as an extensive template gallery (on the web). With this applet customers would be able to design their own business cards. At the end of the development process the finished design would be transferred back to the design studio by simply clicking a button. Finally, the studio could produce the cards using the customer's design.[78]

On the other hand it may also be possible to reverse the process described above. In this case the customer would only provide the necessary information (credit card number for payment, name, address, preferred style, etc.). After that, the design studio would create a blueprint. Finally, the customer could print the cards at home (special paper required) by loading the prepared design – with a suitable applet in tow – into his browser.

The fictitious and real examples given so far in conjunction with figure 1 elucidate that Java applets may play a major role in future e-commerce solutions. This is especially true in two areas: "new products and services" and "follow up on sale".

While there seem to be many interesting fields for applet-based e-commerce solutions it is worthwhile noting that in practice it is still difficult to find good examples.[79] There are at least five reasons why this may be the case:

1. A lack of compatibility between different Java Virtual Machines and a slow adoption[80] of new Java versions by the licensees (see above).

---

[78] Payment and delivery have to be fulfilled in a traditional manner.

[79] However, EarthWeb's Java Review Service is a good starting point (see EarthWeb 1998).

[80] "Java Plug-in ... software enables enterprise customers to direct Java applets or JavaBeans™ components on their intranet web pages to run using Sun's Java Runtime Environment (JRE), instead of the browser's default Java runtime. This enables an enterprise to deploy Java applets that take full

2. An insufficient performance of Java programs (see above).
3. Slow transmission speeds, particularly with private users (non-commercial).
4. A lack of Java programmers.
5. Insufficient knowledge at the part of management.

The technological progress should be able to eliminate reason 3 within the next months (take ADSL[81] as an example). Compared with this, it is likely that the remaining reason continue to exist for a longer time. However, they affect Java applets much more than Java servlets and applications. On the server-side, Java's flexibility (Java is architecture neutral and small) and efficiency (Java is object-oriented and simple) seem to predominate these difficulties in many cases: "...Java's productivity as a language and its hooks to multiple back-end platforms make it a natural for middle-tier application servers, users report. Brad Albers, director of IS at The Home Depot in Atlanta, said Java's importance to his company lies in its ability to tap into their mixed mainframe and Unix back-end systems. Java lets some 100 Java-trained developers use one language to write an application layer on top of what the retailer already has. That is much more efficient than ripping out existing systems or working in multiple languages" (Bowen & Radosevich 1998).

It seems to be that Java is already a viable option on the server-side. Client-side Java computing becomes a viable option as soon as items 1.-3. are solved. Then the utilization of software applications may become easier and more flexible on a broad basis: Java applets are usable without installation[82] (they only have to be "installed" on the server) and they are always up to date (it is sufficient to keep a current version of the applet on the server). Instead of buying software it also seems to be possible to rent applets. This may be interesting for software which is not often used. Moreover, Java programs are executable on many different devices. In comparison to "traditional" software they enhance the freedom of choice.[83] The strong complementarities between platform-dependent applications and the corresponding platform are replaced by Java's cross-platform capability. It is important to note that this prevents a "lock-in"

---

advantage of the latest capabilit[i]es and features of the Java platform and be assured that they will run reliably and consistently" (Sun 1998c).

[81] Asymmetric Digital Subscriber Line: "A form of Digital Subscriber Line in which the bandwidth available for downstream connection is significantly larger than for upstream. Although designed to minimize the effect of crosstalk between the upstream and downstream channels this setup is well suited for web browsing and client-server applications as well as for some emerging applications such as video on demand" (FOLDOC, "ADSL", spelling corrected by the author).

[82] This has at least two advantages: the first advantage are time savings, the second an unchanged system (e.g. no dll-conflicts, no need for de-installation, no unused or outdated entries in system files, etc.).

[83] "Most consumers value the ability to choose among a wide variety of competing products and brands that differ in various ways" (Pindyck & Rubinfeld 1992, p. 428).

effect[84] on the underlying platforms. This in turn may alter competition and technological progress in the computer industry (see e.g. Menkhoff 1998).

It remains to be seen if/how Java influences the need for software intermediation. In this context it seems to be adequate to concentrate on Java applets because
they differ most compared to "traditional" software. Nevertheless, some of the aspects
discussed do – on a smaller scale – also apply to other software. These aspects are
closely related to a problem-free electronic delivery of software.

4.3 The economics of software intermediation

According to the explanations given above Java applets can easily be distributed via the web. This is possible since it is unnecessary to deliver media such as CD-
ROMs. This is one reason why applets are well-suited for many e-commerce applications. Applets of this kind are normally free of charge for the end user (customer service). Nevertheless, applets – even those mentioned before – are often commercial
products intended for sale (maybe also intended for renting out)[85]. With a growing
popularity of Java on the client this market will gain importance.

With an online payment system there is no substantial difference between buying an applet in, e.g. Russia, Japan, Great Britain, Israel, or Germany. The costs of
distribution are usually negligible and vary only with the quality of the connection
between buyer and seller. If it is possible to complete the whole transaction over the
web, an often cited function of intermediaries (wholesaler, retailer) becomes obsolete:
the reduction of delivery cost. At first glance, one could conclude that, under these
circumstances, a direct transaction between software user and software producer
makes good economic sense and that there is no need for intermediaries. However, this
only seems to be true at first glance.

Delivery costs are only a special type of costs resulting from the completion
of a business transaction. The completion of a business transaction, in turn, is only
one part of the whole process that is necessary in order to reach an exchange of
goods and services over markets. This process can be subdivided into three parts:
search, evaluation, and completion. Search and evaluation costs are mainly time
costs but also include costs for the technologies used during the contact with suppliers. The costs for the financial transactions are the remaining "completion
costs". (See Buxmann et al. 1996, "Transactions on Markets".)

---

[84] "The installed base of an established technology generates a "lock-in" effect. All else equal, consumers prefer to remain with the established technology and enjoy its larger network benefits [externalities]"
(Gilbert 1992, p. 4). The basic concept of network externalities is explained below (see page 153).
[85] The analysis focuses on applets which are intended for sale. However, the explanations given below
are also valid for applets which are intended for renting out.

From an economic point of view intermediaries make good economic sense when they are able to reduce the overall costs of the process described in the preceding paragraph (overall transaction-costs).[86] It was stated above that an intermediary is not able to reduce delivery costs of Java applets. But this does not mean that the utilization of intermediaries raises delivery costs. In fact, each intermediary in the value chain profits in the same way from the efficient distribution channel Internet as the manufacturer itself (see Sarkar et al. 1995, "Critiquing the Threatened Intermediaries Hypothesis"). Furthermore, there is no reason to believe that a direct sale could reduce the costs of payment. Thus, it is sufficient to concentrate on the costs of search and evaluation. These costs clearly depend on the type of software. If one concentrates on standard applications[87] one has to differentiate between universal software such as office applications (word processor, spreadsheet program, etc.), business applications, groupware applications, etc. and specific software (e.g. address manager, CD-labeler, etc.). This is necessary because network externalities are much more important for universal software than for specific software.

The basic concept of network externalities[88] could easily be illustrated by using the example of natural languages. Each language (English, French, etc.) constitutes a separate linguistic network. Communication is possible within such a network. The larger a linguistic net is, the better are the communication possibilities and with this the higher its value[89] (see Gabel 1991, pp. 1). From this follows: the decision of individual X to learn language Y favors not only X (the individual is able to communicate with all members of network Y) but also all individuals already belonging to network Y (there is one new potential communication partner in the net). Since these individuals gain from the decision of individual X, one speaks of (positive[90]) external effects or externalities (the cause for the effect – the improved communication possibilities – is outside of the decision field of the affected individuals).

From the "language" example, it already becomes clear that network externalities are not limited to physical nets – such as telephone networks. Software user also

---

[86] "Already in the 19th century Ricardo and Edgeworth pointed out that intermediation can increase a national economy's wealth without raising the amount of production..." (Buxmann et al. 1996, "Intermediary Performance and Services").

[87] Standard software is predefined software which is programmed "for the market". Individual software is programmed for a specific task of a specific user.

[88] The concept of network externalities is based on the theory of externalities (see e.g. Cornes & Sandler 1996).

[89] Here value has to be interpreted as stock of human capital which determines the communication possibilities.

[90] In this article – as usually in the literature – network externalities are only positive. Especially in physical networks "negative network externalities" play a role. These can be neglected here.

constitute (virtual) networks. Within these networks externalities play an important role. They arise, e.g., from the possibility to exchange files and information. These network externalities lead to a natural tendency towards quasi-standardization, which means everyone is using the same application (see Katz & Shapiro 1994, p. 105). Therefore, in the relatively mature markets for universal software, search and evaluation costs do not play an important role. Other things being equal, it should be possible to reduce the overall transaction-costs by cutting the value chain.[91]

In the case of specific software, search and evaluation costs are much more important because the tendency towards quasi-standardization is much weaker. Thus, users benefit (cost reduction) from an assistance in search and evaluation. Intermediaries could assist the users in many forms, e.g. by choosing the product mix and focus, categorizing the available software, gathering information, etc. Under these circumstances intermediaries should be able to reduce the overall transaction-costs (see Sarkar et al. 1995, "Towards a Broader View of Intermediary Functions").

Summarizing the preceding explanations it is evident that there may well be a continuing role for intermediaries in the markets for Java applets. The crucial question is, how strong network externalities will be. Currently, markets for Java applets are slowly evolving. Hence, network externalities are – at least today – negligible in these markets. This in turn should allow for a successful intermediation. Note, however, that this time the intermediary is an electronic one. "Electronic intermediaries support all... [kinds of intermediary services (see above)] with their underlying information infrastructure. Especially for intermediaries trading and handling information there are technologies available, that support these transaction phases: database connected web servers, search engines and electronic payment systems to name only a few" (Buxmann et al. 1996, "Electronic Intermediaries", spelling corrected). The Java Repository[92] may serve as an example for an electronic intermediary.[93]

5 Conclusion

Global electronic commerce over the web requires the development of sophisticated software which is able to operate via the net. It is necessary to transform the web from a huge distributed file system to a distributed computing system.

---

[91] In reality, institutional and social reasons may also play an important role.

[92] "To allow Java developers and users an easy reuse of classes and sources there is a need for evaluation of all those resources available on the Internet. The Java Repository has the aim to support this need by collecting and presenting documented Java resources to make the ideas available to others" (The Java Repository 1998).

[93] Intelligent software agents may also appear as a new intermediary service that buyers "hire" when in need of a particular good or service (see Sarkar et al. 1995, "Cybermediaries: New Network-Based Intermediaries"). More information about intelligent software agents at The Agent Society 1998.

In this article I have demonstrated that Java is a key technology for web-based programming. It was revealed that Java may be able to reduce software development costs in heterogeneous environments. Thus, Java may be a "cost reducer". It is, however, more important that Java may also be an "enabler". "What makes Java significant is what makes the transistor significant: a shift in the direction of technology and how we use it. It's not about rewriting old applications in Java or moving from C++ to Java. It's about a new class of functionality that just wasn't considered practical before" (Siddalingaiah 1997). This functionality offers an enormous potential for new products and services which can be offered in the global market Internet.

In order to take full advantage of this new technology, the compatibility and performance problems have to be solved. A fast adoption of the technology and its improvements has to be ensured. It has to be guaranteed that no for-profit company is – at least in the longer run – able to take one-sided advantage of Java. Therefore, the whole language[94] has to be standardized by an official committee.

In spite of Java's interesting features, the language is in no way a solution for all problems in the field of programming. It is, e.g., very unlikely that Java can significantly reduce the backlog of business-critical application development needs (see Weiner 1996a). For the majority of business people Java is too complicated to encode their own knowledge bases into executable systems. There seem to be two solutions for this problem: (a) creating a comparable programming language which is easier to learn or (b) "reducing" the fixed cost of learning the programmer has to bear. Teaching the basic concept of object-oriented programming at the school and/or at university level as a compulsory subject may be practicable to reach solution (b). This, however, would only lead to a redistribution of a part of the fixed cost of learning.

References

Altgeld, J. (1998). *Vom Sinn (und Unsinn?) des Electronic Commerce* [Sense and nonsense of electronic commerce]. Available:
<http://www.commercenet.de/cnveroeff.htm> (1998, August 15).
Baetjer, H. (1997): *Software As Capital – An Economic Perspective on Software Engineering.* Los Alamitos, Califfornia: IEEE Computer Society.
Barron, B., Ellsworth, J. H. & Savetz, K. M.(1996). *Internet für Insider,* authorized translation of "Internet unleashed". Haar bei München: SAMS Publishing.
Bloch, C. (1998). *Servlets,* in: The Java Tutorial. Available:
<http://www.java.sun.com/docs/books/tutorial/trailmap.html> (1998, August 25).
Bowen, T.S. & Radosevich, L. (1998). *Java on server is tasting good – But release of JDK 1.2 won't solve client incompatibilities,* in: Infoworld, Top News Stories. Available:
<http://www.infoworld.com/> (1998 July 28).

---

[94] The Java language, the virtual machine specification, the core platform APIs, and the extension APIs.

Büttgenbach, B. (1992). Eine Einführung in die OOP-Grundbegriffe – Paradigmenwechsel erfordert die Kenntnis der neuen Terminologie [An introduction to the basic terms of OOP – change of paradigm requires knowledge of new terminology]. *Computerwoche*, 45.

Buxmann, P., König, W. & Rose, F. (1996). *The Java Repository – An Electronic Intermediary for Java Resources.* Available:
<http://java.wiwi.uni-frankfurt.de/papers/JavaRepository_eng.html> (1998 August 15).

CGI (1998). *The Common Gateway Interface.* Available:
<http://hoohoo.ncsa.uiuc.edu/cgi/> (1998, September 25).

Clyman, J. (1998). Your Guide to Java for 1998. *Java for 1998, PC Magazine Online*, 04/9/98. Available:
<http://www.zdnet.com/pcmag/features/java98/index.html> (1998, June 4).

Coffee, P. (1998). Why Java? *Java for 1998, PC Magazine Online*, 04/9/98. Available:
<http://www.zdnet.com/pcmag/features/java98/index.html> (1998, June 4).

Computerwoche (1996): Preiskampf bei monolithischen Büroanwendungen – Modularisierung bringt Office-Markt in Bewegung [Price war in the market for monolithic office applications – modularization shakes up the office market]. *Computerwoche*, 46, pp. 17-18.

Cornes, R. & Sandler, T. (1996). *The theory of externalities, public goods, and club goods.* Cambridge: Cambridge University Press.

Day, B. (1997). The impact of Java standardization. *JavaWorld*, 12. Available:
<http://www.javaworld.com> (1997, November 17).

EarthWeb (1998). *The Java Review Service.* EarthWeb, Inc. Available:
<http://www.jars.com/> (1998, September 25).

Encyclopædia Britannica (1997) Britannica CD 97.

FOLDOC. *Free On-Line Dictionary of Computing.*
<http://wombat.doc.ic.ac.uk/foldoc/index.html> (1998, August 19).

Gabel, H. L. (1991). *Competitive Strategies for Product Standards – The strategic use of compatibility standards for competitive advantage.* London, New York: McGraw-Hill.

Gilbert, R. J. (1992). Symposium on Compatibility: Incentives and Market Structure. *The Journal of Industrial Economics*, XL(1), pp. 1-35.

Gilder, G. (1995). *The Coming Software Shift*, first published in Forbes ASAP, August 28. Available:
<http://homepage.seas.upenn.edu/~gaj1/shiftgg.html> (1998, August 17).

Henry, D., Cooke, S. & Montes, S. (1998). *The Emerging Digital Economy.* Available:
<http://www.ecommerce.gov/emerging.htm> (1998, July 25).

Huang, G. (1996). *Java*, in: World-Wide Web: Beyond the Basics, Virginia Polytechnic Institute & State University. Available:
<http://ei.cs.vt.edu/~wwwbtb/book/> (1998, August 19).

Katz, M. L. & Shapiro, C. (1993). Systems Competition and Network Effects. *Journal of Economic Perspectives*, 8(2), pp. 93-115.

Kind, I. & Kind, R. (1998). *BABEL: A Glossary of Computer Oriented Abbreviations and Acronyms.* <http://www.access.digex.net/~ikind/babel.html> (1998, September 25).

Kossel, A., Wronski, H.-J. (1998). Web-Warenhäuser – Erfolgreich verkaufen im Internet [Web department stores – successfully selling in the Internet]. *c't – magazin für computer technik*, 11, pp. 146-150.

Kraemer, P. (1996). *Die Grundidee der Modularisierung* [The basic idea of modularization]. Available:
<http://www.uni-wuppertal.de/hrz/kurse/fortran/node69.html> (1997 September 16).

Krochmal, M. (1997). *Java Delivering For Developers: Zona Study Says*, in: TechWeb News. Available:
<http://www.techweb.com/wire/news/1997/10/1014jva.html> (1997, October 19).

Le Hunte, S. (1998). *The HTML Reference Library, Version 4.0 (build: 175).* Available:
<http://hot.virtual-pc.com/htmlib/> (1998, September 18).

Liberman, B., Griffel, F., Merz, M. & Lamersdorf, W. (1997). Java-Based Mobile Agents – How to Migrate, Persist, and Interact on Electronic Service Markets. *Mobile agents: proceedings of the first international workshop* (pp. 27-38) (Berlin, April 7-8, 1997). Berlin: Springer.

Lindahl, C. (1997). *JavaWorld Internet Poll, Comments from Readers.* Available: <http://www.javaworld.com/jw-10-1997/jwpoll.10-03-97.results.html> (1998, September 25).

McKay, N. (1997). Java to be standardized by ISO. *JavaWorld,* 12. Available: <http://www.javaworld.com> (17 Nov. 1997).

McMillan, R. (1997). Sun's plan B for Java standardization: change nothing. *JavaWorld,* 10. Available: <http://www.javaworld.com> (17 Sep. 1997).

Menge, R. (1998). Suns neues Java Development Kit 1.2 – Sicherer, schöner, besser integriert [Sun's new JDK 1.2 – securer, nicer, better integrated]. *Byte* (German edition), 5, pp. 38-42.

Menkhoff, R. Java and object standardization in the Internet – A way to more competition in the software industry? *NETNOMICS* (Economic research and electronic networking), forthcoming journal. Available: <http://www.baltzer.nl/netnomics/> (1998, September 18).

Middendorf, St. & Singer, R. *Java-Applets – Programmierung und Einsatz im Intra- und Internet* [Java applets – programming and application in the Intra-, and Internet]. Available: <http://www.garos.de/dik/vortraege/Middendorf.html> (1997, September 16).

Morgan, B. (1997). Corba meets Java. *JavaWorld,* 10. Available: <http://www.javaworld.com> (1997, September 17).

Microsoft (1998). *Microsoft Windows CE.* Available: <http://www.microsoft.com/products/prodref/120_ov.htm> (1998, September 25).

Microsoft (1998). *Microsoft Windows NT Server 4.0.* Available: <http://www.microsoft.com/products/prodref/427_ov.htm> (1998, September 25).

NCSA (National Center for Supercomputing Applications) **(1998).** *Common Gateway Interface – Overview.* <http://hoohoo.ncsa.uiuc.edu/cgi/intro.html> (1998 August 16).

PC Magazine Online (1998). Java for 1998, 04/9/98. Available: <http://www.zdnet.com/pcmag/features/java98/> (1998, June 4).

Pindyck, R.S. & Rubinfeld, D.L. (1992). *Microeconomics.* New York et al.:Macmillan.

Roulo, M. (1998). Accelerate your Java apps! *JavaWorld,* 9. Available: <http://www.javaworld.com> (1998, August 22).

Saab. *Saab Java Page.* Available. <http://www.saabusa.com/models/showroom/java/> (1998, September 25).

Sarkar, M. B., Butler, B. & Steinfield, C. (1995). Intermediaries and Cybermediaries: A Continuing Role for Mediating Players in the Electronic Marketplace. *Journal of Computer-Mediated Communication,* 1(3). Available: <http://jcmc.huji.ac.il/vol1/issue3/vol1no3.html> (1998, September 18).

Shah, A. B. (1996). *World Wide Web and Object Technology,* in: World-Wide Web: Beyond the Basics, Virginia Polytechnic Institute & State University. Available: <http://ei.cs.vt.edu/~wwwbtb/book/> (1998, August 19).

Sichel, D. E. (1997). *The Computer Revolution – An Economic Perspective.* Washington, D.C.: Brookings Institution Press.

Siddalingaiah, M. (1997). The future of Java – rhetoric or reality? *JavaWorld,* 12. Available: <http://www.javaworld.com> (1997, November 19).

Sun Microsystems (1994). *The Java Language: An Overview.* Available: <http://java.sun.com/> (1997, September 16).

Sun Microsystems (1997). *JavaBeans – API specification, Version 1.01.* Available: <http://java.sun.com/beans> (1997, September 16).

Sun Microsystems (1998a). *Java Standardization.* Available: <http://java.sun.com/aboutJava/standardization/index.html> (1998 January 25).

Sun Microsystems (1998b). *100% Pure Java Program Home Page.* Available: <http://java.sun.com/aboutJava/standardization/index.html> (1998, August 24).

Sun Microsystems (1998c). *Java™ Plug-in Overview.* Available: <http://www.java.sun.com/products/plugin/> (1998, August 26).

Sun Microsystems (1998d). *Products and APIs.* Available: < http://www.java.sun.com/products/index.html> (1998, September 25).

Sun Microsystems (1998e). *JAVAOS™: The Standalone Java™ Application Platform.* Available: <http://www.java.sun.com/products/javaos/index.html> (1998, September 25).

Teledata (1997a). *Java-Trader.* Teledata Börsen-Informations GmbH. Available: <http://www.teledata.de/html/body_java-trader.html> (1998, September 25).

Teledata (1997b). Homepage. Teledata Börsen-Informations GmbH. Available: <http://www.teledata.de/> (1998, September 25).

The Agent Society (1998). Homepage. Available: <http://www.agent.org/> (1998, September 25).

The Java Repository: *About the Java Repository.* Available: <http://java.wiwi.uni-frankfurt.de/jr/about.html> (1998 August 27). Also reachable at: <http://java.wiwi.uni-frankfurt.de/> (1998, September 25).

Thiemann, U. (1998). Web-Informationssysteme – Das Netzwerk ist der Computer [Web information systems – the network is the computer]. *Byte* (German edition), 5, pp. 65-69.

Varhol, P. D. (1993). *Object oriented programming: the software development revolution.* Computer Technology Research Corp.

Varian, H. R. (1993). *Economic Incentives in Software Design.* Available: <http://info.Berkeley.EDU/~hal/people/hal/papers.html> (1997, June 10).

Varian, H.R. (1998). *The Information Economy.* Available: http://www.sims.berkeley.edu/resources/infoecon/ (1998, September 29)

Weiner, B. (1996a). *Java Development Weaknesses.* Available: <http://www.cubicon.com/java-weak.html>, (1998, June 5).

Weiner, B. (1996b). *Java Virtual Machine Weaknesses.* Available: <http://www.cubicon.com/java-vm-bad.html> (1998, August 17).

Weyerhäuser, M. (1997). Echte Bohnen – Komponenten für Java: Beans [Genuine beans – components for Java: Beans]. in: *c't – magazin für computer technik*, 9, pp. 300-308.

Learning Management Science in Hyperspace

Astrid Blumstengel, Stephan Kassanke, and Leena Suhl

1 Introduction

In this paper, we discuss approaches of learning an interdisciplinary subject with many different facets. We consider the field called Management Science (MS) which is closely related to Operations Research (OR). As the essence of management science we understand the application of the modeling approach for managerial decision support. The models are usually built using quantitative methods, such as linear programming, mixed-integer programming, network models, decision analysis, discrete and continuous simulation, queuing models, and so on. The underlying problems arise in fields such as production, financial planning, and vehicle routing. Traditionally, the emphasis in teaching management science, at least in Germany and Finland, has been placed on teaching mathematical methods, such as the simplex algorithm for linear programming.

However, to support managerial decision making we need much more than internal knowledge of complex algorithms. Managers are often confronted with *mess management*: They first have to identify the right problem to be solved, rather then gather the needed information. If a modeling approach is used, the next step is to choose one or more quantitative models to represent the problem and put it into a computer-readable form. Furthermore, some solution technique must be employed to generate a solution which is normally to be approved by the responsible manager.

The use of management science techniques involves skills from different areas such as mathematics, information technologies, business administration, and even psychology. The methods used are often mathematical. Although the user does not need to know mathematical details of each method, an understanding of the basic ideas is advantageous in order to judge appropriateness. Solutions of complex practical problems cannot be found without computers; this means that the methods have to become part of an integrated information systems architecture of a firm. In order to be used, a decision support system has to fit into the organizational landscape of a company. Sometimes psychological skills are needed to win the final acceptance of the users.

According to our experience, teaching only algorithms is not enough to prepare students to face the messy, complex problems of real-life situations. Similar to learning a craft, the ability to apply a technique to a real-life problem has to be learned by training that is carried out by the learner himself/herself – no one can do the job for another person. Otherwise the algorithmic knowledge remains "inert knowledge" that cannot be really used (see CGTV 1990; Reinmann-Rothmeier 1994, p. 43).

The ability to apply mathematical modeling techniques can be trained with case studies. Then methods are bound to a situated context and students have to work out themselves which method should be applied and in which way. This requires far more elaboration than merely using a given algorithm. However, situated learning is more fun, thus increasing the motivation to learn because students can feel an immediate success after constructing a solution themselves.

The traditional, method focused way of teaching management science does not leave much time for case studies, discussions, and student presentations in classroom. Furthermore, because there are often more than one hundred students with different backgrounds and interests (majoring in business studies, business computing, industrial engineering, computer science, or business education) in a university class, it is not possible to adjust the pace so that each student can easily follow a teacher-centered lecture. These were the reasons why we wanted to provide students with a tool which helps them to learn quantitative methods also outside the classroom at their own pace, thus leaving more time for discussions and teamwork during the classes. We believed that an interactive, computer based tool would be better suited than providing the students merely a textbook. With the realization that there was no such tool available, we started the development of ORWelt (World of Operations Research) in 1996. ORWelt is a hypertext-multimedia oriented learning environment for Operations Research/Management Science. In the subsequent sections of this paper we report about the development of ORWelt and first experiences of using it at the University of Paderborn.

2 Initial Evaluation

The research project "A hypermedia learning environment for OR/MS" was launched in 1996. To collect information about the current use of computers in this area, we mailed a questionnaire to all professors of OR/MS at German universities. It included questions about the content of classes concerned, the use of software (especially educational software), the additional need for such software as well as instructors' expectations and concerns. The questionnaire revealed that there is a significant need for educational software. 76% of the instructors questioned considered a learning software to be at least partially useful for teaching purposes, but not one of them intended to develop a system on his/her own (see figure 1). The relatively high acceptance of computer based tools is not a surprise because of the key role of computers in OR/MS. Due to the complexity of algorithms, solutions to practical problems can only be obtained by using computers. Most instructors use professional optimization software, but only 10% of them use educational software. The massive gap between instructors' usage and demand for educational software is mostly caused by a lack of flexible educational tools covering their area of interest.

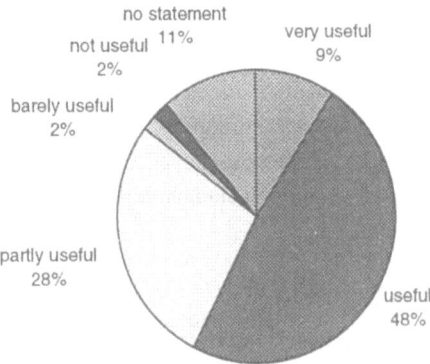

Figure 1: Questionnaire result: "Do you consider a computer based learning environment to be useful?"

Additionally, the study revealed that certain core areas of Operations Research, such as linear programming and discrete simulation, are taught by the majority of all instructors. Therefore, if we develop scalable and configurable educational software for these core areas, it can be used also in other faculties, even if they emphasize different aspects in their teaching. This would make such software usable for OR/MS faculties of other universities, too.

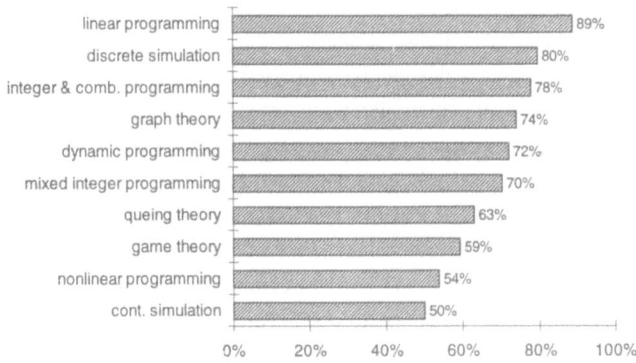

Figure 2: Questionnaire result: content of relevant classes

The results of the questionnaire finally convinced us to start the development of ORWelt. The enormous amount of work involved in developing hypermedia applications seemed justified by the huge potential in using it.

Besides professors, we also questioned students about their expectations and preferences considering hypermedia software. This study gave us also very encouraging feedback. This initial questionnaire is followed by a continuing evaluation process where new and experienced students are questioned on a regular basis about their computer literacy, frequency of computer use, available hardware equipment and attitudes towards computer based learning, including expected advantages and disadvantages as well as their own experiences.

3 Hypermedia as a Solution

By hypermedia we understand, loosely speaking, the combination of hypertext and multimedia. For a thorough discussion on how to define hypermedia, see Blumstengel 1998. The information scope covered by a hypermedia environment is also called hyperspace. Hyperspace is basically a network structure, in contrast to a book which always has a linear structure. This means that a hypermedia system consists of nodes being connected with various types of arcs. The nodes contain relevant information in form of text and multimedia items, such as graphics, pictures, video and audio sequences, and animations. The user can move in the network along the given arcs. The main navigation methods are hyperlinks, maps, guided tours, backtracking, history, and bookmarking (see Blumstengel 1998). Thus, there is no one and only way to move in hyperspace, but the user can freely choose his or her own preferences and sequences. Appropriate navigation methods help the user in the orientation to avoid the "lost in hyperspace" effect.

There are several reasons why OR/MS is a well suited area for using hypermedia learning software. First, as an interdisciplinary area it provides many different points of view on each subject area – this can be supported in a natural way by the network approach. A business student is more likely interested in specific applications of OR/MS in business while a student of computer science might like to know further details of general algorithms. In a hypermedia environment it is possible, on the one hand, to start with a case study based on a real-life application and proceed to the algorithms and software needed, and, on the other hand, start with a specific modeling technique and proceed to its applications. In the network structure it is possible to link together topics that are loosely, not linearly, connected (see Tergan 1997, p. 129). One topic can be linked to many other topics, since the restriction of linearity has been removed.

Second, many areas of OR/MS can profit from the interactivity and dynamics of hypermedia systems. Mathematical algorithms are characterized by a stepwise dynamic structure which cannot be fully expressed in a static book. An animated algorithm in hypermedia can illustrate the dynamics for various initial settings in a flexible way. In many areas such as network optimization, branch-and-bound, vehicle routing, random number generation, and discrete simulation, the advantages of animations are obvious.

Third, the basic contents of OR/MS are fairly stable over time. Basic techniques, such as linear programming or discrete simulation, were invented in the fifties and sixties, and they are also useful today. More recent approaches, such as neural networks or Tabu search are also there to stay. This justifies the high amount of developing effort necessary to create such systems. The stability of content makes it relatively easy to maintain the whole system. Developing multimedia is very expensive; changing major parts of the system on a regular basis would not be affordable.

To summarize, hypermedia provides various advantages over traditional forms of education, such as the following:

- Pace: Students control learning speed and number of repetitions. In contrast to a teacher centered lecture, a hypermedia learning environment gives students an individual choice of how long to spend on a topic and how often to repeat it.

- Sequence: In a hypermedia net there is no sequence at all. Although guided tours are offered, students control which way they progress through the net (guided tours are optional, not obligatory). This structure fits the manifold relations between different subject areas better than a linear one.

- Learner control: Students are in control, they decide which learning style they apply to the material. Some prefer a sequential approach with strong guidance, others tend to quickly glance over certain topic areas while studying other points down to the smallest detail. A learner centered hypermedia environment supports both types of learning while the traditional teacher centered lecture is restricted to only one (see Ravnborg 1998).

- Availability: Students control place and time of learning. Students can learn anywhere and at any time, at home or at the university, early in the morning or late at night.

- Interactivity: Students can become more engaged in the learning material, not just passively receiving. To achieve this goal, however, one has to use interactive elements, e.g., simulations, in the learning environment. It is not sufficient to transfer a book to a linear, electronic form. The degree of interactivity is a crucial factor for the success of a hypermedia learning environment (see Haack 1997, p. 152, Schulmeister 1996, p. 388ff.). Especially offering the possibility of "direct manipulation" of relevant objects plays a key role. Direct manipulation occurs throughout the whole learning environment, such as dragging objects, popping up additional information, etc.

There are also some possible disadvantages involved with the use of hypermedia learning systems:

- The well-known problem of disorientation describes the phenomenon that users navigating through hyperspace are often not sure about their actual "location" in relation to the whole net, thus "getting lost in hyperspace". Disorientation can be softened by providing additional navigational tools (see Tergan 1997 for further details on this issue).

- Students fear less personal contact between the teacher and themselves.

- Students fear that their learning behavior will be supervised by the system. This is a point that must be considered during development, since the success of the system depends entirely on user acceptance. If user actions are logged for evaluation purposes, you will have to dispel these objections by explicitly including the user and, e.g., using anonymous log files without any specific user references.

4 The Project ORWelt

4.1 Subject of the Project

The ORWelt project started in February 1996 with the intent of providing a hypermedia learning system that would cover all standard introductory material, supplemented by tests. Furthermore, case studies were provided in order to support different approaches to the same contents.

The purpose of ORWelt is not to replace the lecture but to give the lecturer more time to discuss real-life case studies with the students. We do not expect that computer based learning approaches will replace face-to-face communication in real-time between students and lecturer. The personal contact between teacher and student is still important because goals such as motivating students for the subject matter, i.e., providing input which affects the student in a positive manner, can hardly be achieved by a computer-based system alone.

Figure 3 shows a typical screenshot of ORWelt. Unfortunately, the paper medium is not suited to expressing the dynamics of the application. The learner views an animation showing the 2-opt algorithm, the corresponding matrix and a graphical representation simultaneously. The learner can run the algorithm step by step while the different representations are updated according to the algorithm step, e.g., new arcs are drawn in the graph representation and the corresponding coefficients in the matrix are marked. Moreover, the animation is interactive, i.e., the learner can move the nodes in the graph representation and thus create his or her own network. It is well-known that animations contain the risk of overloading the learner; he or she might not be able to process all information presented (Weidenmann 1997, p. 119). In ORWelt, users can slow down animations, step back and forth and repeat steps. They are supported by fading in text explanations for each step.

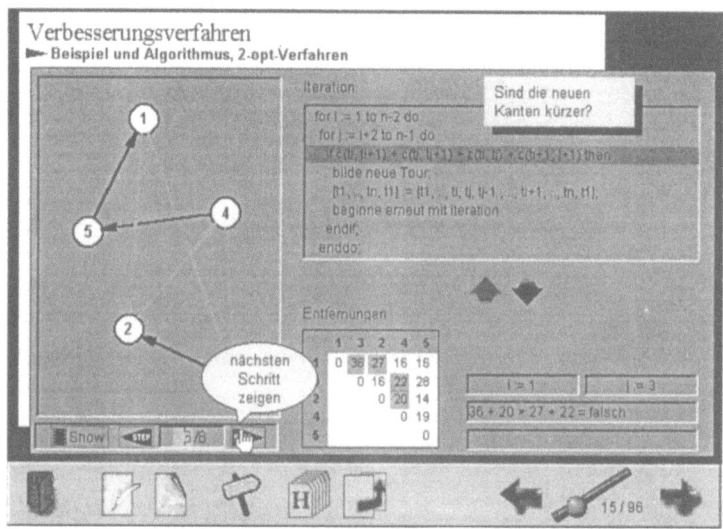

Figure 3: Page of subject module "vehicle routing and scheduling"

Currently, ORWelt comprises 19 subject and 15 test modules covering the main subjects of OR/MS on an introductory level. A graphic browser provides direct access to all modules and supports structural orientation. Footprints, bookmarks and history are implemented as standard navigational tools. Additionally, guided tours can be defined in order to avoid the "lost in hyperspace" effect. An assistant allows the tailoring of tours according to the needs of the individual user. Guided tours are designed to support especially less experienced students by providing sequences suggested by a teacher. The contents covered by ORWelt are shown in figure 4. Shadowed nodes labeled in italics denote subject modules supplemented with test modules. In addition to the subject modules, ORWelt includes test components to allow students a self-assessment of their comprehension. The tests are usually not multiple choice, but a wide range of interactive methods is used in order to allow the exploration of the test. Our goal is that students get engaged in learning instead of merely receiving information.

A key feature of ORWelt is the integration of the professional optimization code MOPS (Mathematical OPtimization System, Suhl 1994). MOPS allows the user to solve predefined optimization models while varying parameters of the model. The solver itself resides in the background, and the output does not necessarily have to be a tabular numerical report. It is left up to the developer as to how to visualize the results. Most MOPS models in ORWelt visualize the resulting solution graphically, for example using pie charts, indicating the way to interpret the solution. These "dynamic models" add a new quality of teaching that is not possible to achieve by means of a normal textbook. The dynamic representation allows the learner to interact with the model: he or she can alter parameters, compare solutions and explore the structure of the problem formulation.

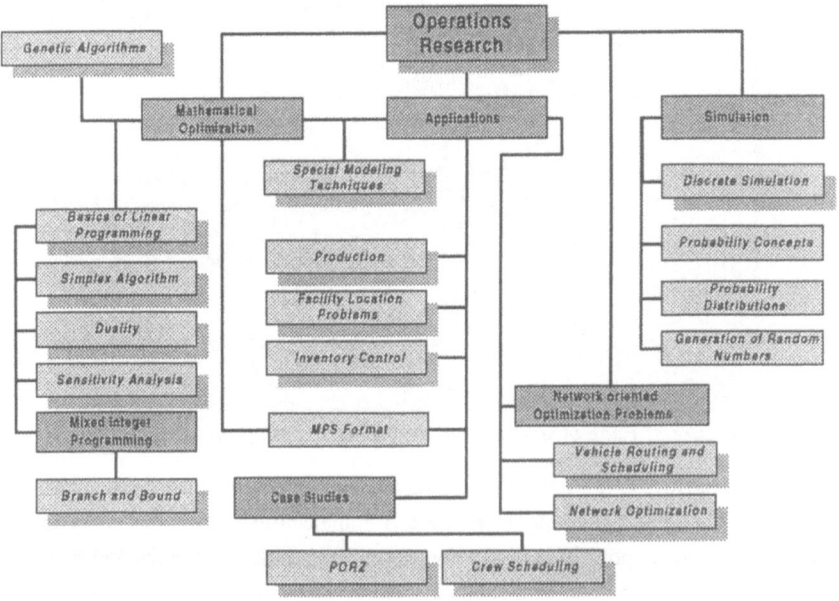

Figure 4: Content covered by ORWelt

4.2 The Development Model

The ORWelt project started with an experimental phase followed by iterative refinements of the development process. Students were participating in the development of ORWelt from the beginning. We use teams of typically 2-3 students attending a project seminar with a total of 2-6 groups per semester. The seminar is held by a group of two knowledge domain specialists and one or two programming specialists. The authoring environment we use is Asymetrix Toolbook®, currently version 6.1 (Instructor II).

Due to the lack of resources we choose a participative approach with the participation of students. Writing hypertext is not intuitive and requires certain skills in structuring information. "Unfortunately, even though you can easily get some ideas about hypertext authoring from your experience as a hypertext reader, we face the general problem that people have not learned how to structure information in hypertext networks the same way they have [sic] learnt to write linear reports through writing endless numbers of essays at school" (Nielsen 1995, p. 309). Furthermore it is quite demanding for students to develop educational material. Intensive coaching of students is necessary, but it is possible to achieve high quality software. See Blumstengel & Kassanke 1998 for a more detailed description of the development model.

4.3 Curricular Integration

At the moment, ORWelt is a supplementary offer for students, they can use it, but are not required to. The long-term goal of the ORWelt project is to alter teaching methods in the direction of application-orientated learning (Blumstengel, Kassanke & Suhl 1997). Lecture time should be used more efficiently to discuss real problems while teams of students learn part of the material, especially basic algorithms, supported by the learning environment. It can also be used as a reference and for exam preparation.

4.4 Evaluation

The development and introduction of an educational offer is outlined in figure 5 (see Alexander 1994 for further details). ORWelt has already passed the first three steps.

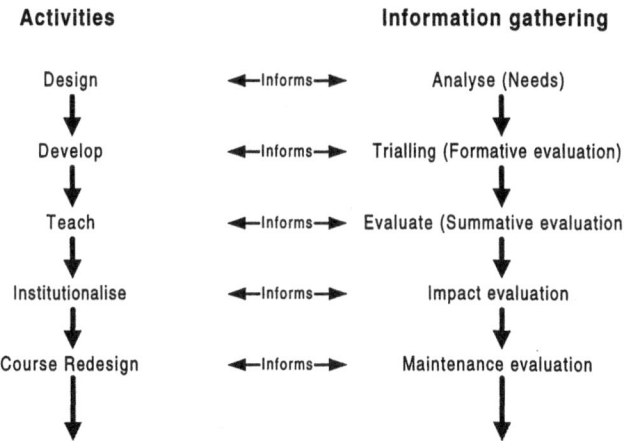

Figure 5: Activity and information gathering cycles (Alexander 1994)

At the end of each term students answer a questionnaire concerning questions about the usefulness of animations, usefulness of the navigational aids and questions about the user interface in general. Furthermore, the system protocols user actions in a separate log file. This log file is explicitly rendered anonymous and its content can be viewed to avoid resistance to ORWelt due to supervision issues.

It was interesting that some students assessed a certain feature (annotations) to be quite useful, but they never actually used this feature as the log file clearly revealed. This would indicate that evaluating a system can not solely rely on self-assessment by students. In order to obtain clear results, you have to keep automated log files.

As a preliminary result, students assessed the overall quality of ORWelt to be good, especially animations and tests were considered to be particularly helpful.

ORWelt is still under development, further modules are being added and existing ones improved. The current version of ORWelt can be downloaded at <http://dsor.uni-paderborn.de/downloads> (1998, September 30).

5   Extending the Learning Environment

In ORWelt, our students have the possibility to solve optimization models in MPS format. Students can use ORWelt as a cognitive tool to solve self-formulated models without having to worry about formulation syntax of other solvers, since the MPS format is an industry standard for optimization models. Although they can solve these models using MOPS, the model representation is not interactive in the sense of direct manipulation. Modifying a single coefficient requires altering the MPS file and reloading it. In ORWelt it was not possible to provide an interactive model representation due to technical restrictions of Toolbook. Optimization models can become very large and Toolbook does not properly handle large amounts of data.

This led us to the idea of combining ORWelt with other PC based systems and utilizing spreadsheets for educational purposes. Plain Spreadsheets already offer:

- a set of tools including graphical visualization capabilities,
- formulas,
- comfortable cell editing methods,

and last but not least:

- the user is – in most cases – already quite familiar in handling the spreadsheet program.

There is no need to learn another command language for formulating the optimization problem. The model is represented in an intuitive matrix form and the spreadsheet program facilitates data entry and modification. The first prototype of the spreadsheet solver "ClipMOPS" was developed for the Free University Berlin and is designed as an add-in extension for Microsoft Excel®. Although Excel already contains a solver module, the results generated are not necessarily reliable (see Thiriez 1998). ClipMOPS can be used as a stand-alone tool or in conjunction with ORWelt as well.

In the future, we intend to extend the learning environment by a platform independent component. At the time the ORWelt project was started, the technical possibilities of the World Wide Web lacked basic interaction mechanisms. This has changed dramatically since advanced JAVA technology became available. We are working on a customized framework for a learning environment based on common web standards (JAVA, HTML, etc.).

To summarize, the use of ORWelt and additional computer aided learning resources contributes essentially to a more efficient use of lecture time for discussion and case studies. ORWelt is the first step in the redesign of lectures toward a more learner-oriented approach.

References

Alexander, S. & Hedberg, J. G. (1994). Evaluating technology-based learning: Which model? In: K. Beattie, C. McNaught & S. Wills (Eds.), *IFIP Transactions: Interactive Multimedia in University Education: Designing for Change in Teaching and Learning.* 241, Amsterdam: North-Holland Elsevier.

Blumstengel, A. (1998). *Entwicklung hypermedialer Lernsysteme.* Ph.D. thesis, University of Paderborn.

Blumstengel, A., Kassanke, S. & Suhl, L. (1997). Praxisorientierte Lehre im Fachgebiet Operations Research unter Einsatz einer hypermedialen Lernumgebung, *Wirtschaftsinformatik,* 39(6), pp. 555-562.

Blumstengel, A. & Kassanke, S. (1998). A Hypermedia Learning Environment by Students for Students. *Proceedings of ED-MEDIA/ED-TELECOM 98,* Brussels.

CTGV (Cognition and Technology Group at Vanderbilt) (1990). Anchored instruction and ist relationship to situated cognition. *Educational Researcher,* 19(3), pp. 2-10.

Haack, J. (1997). Interaktivität als Kennzeichen von Multimedia und Hypermedia. In: L. Issing & P. Klimsa (Eds.), *Information und Lernen mit Multimedia,* 2nd Edition (pp. 151-165). Weinheim, Basel: Beltz Psychologie-Verlags-Union.

Nielsen, J. (1995). *Multimedia and Hypertext: The Internet and Beyond.* Boston, San Diego, New York: AP Professional.

Ravnborg, R. (1998). Multimediale Lernsoftware in der OR-Ausbildung. *OR News,* 2(3), pp. 22-23.

Reinmann-Rothmeier, G., Mandl, H. & Prenzel, M. (1994). Computerunterstützte Lernumgebungen: Planung, Gestaltung und Bewertung. In: H. Arzberger & K.H. Brehm (Eds.). Erlangen: Publicis-MCD.

Schulmeister, R. (1996). *Grundlagen hypermedialer Lernsysteme: Theorie – Didaktik – Design.* Wokingham, Reading, Menlo Park, New York: Addison-Wesley.

Suhl, U. H. (1994). MOPS – Mathematical Optimization System, Software Tools for Mathematical Programming. *European Journal of Operations Research,* 72, pp. 312-322.

Tergan, S.-O. (1997). Hypertext und Hypermedia: Konzeption, Lernmöglichkeiten, Lernprobleme. In: L. Issing & P. Klimsa (Eds.), *Information und Lernen mit Multimedia,* 2nd Edition (pp. 123-138). Weinheim, Basel: Beltz Psychologie-Verlags-Union.

Thiriez, H. (1998). Improved O.R. education through spreadsheet models, *Procedings of 16th European Conference on Operational Research,* Brussels.

Weidenmann, B. (1997). Abbilder in Multimedia-Anwendungen. In: L. Issing & P. Klimsa (Eds.), *Information und Lernen mit Multimedia,* 2nd Edition (pp. 104-121). Weinheim, Basel: Beltz Psychologie-Verlags-Union.

Semantic Integration of Emergent Online Communication

Wilfried Böhler

> *Only connect!* (E.M. Forster, Preface to *Howard's End*, 1912)
> *Nokia connecting people* (Advertisement, 1996)

1 Introduction

1.1 Conceptualizing Online Semantic Information

Theorists from many fields have developed models that help explain how semantic information is received, decoded, interpreted, stored, retrieved, encoded, and sent online in an interactive process. Our central theme expands this iterative model to include mechanisms for monitoring new information. On an instrumental level, our analysis indicates discursive strategies to increase the frequency of novel ideas considered worthy of being adopted by the communication partners. In this context, it is important to consider that before semantic selection can begin operating, novelty must be generated. There have to be new ideas to choose from. So we must consider the evolutionary process of variation, selection and retention, whereby the participants can reject those semantic data that are likely to be irrelevant and encourage alternatives that are more promising.

In spelling out the working principles that underlie our study, one plausible approach would be to analyze emergent online discourse from distinct perspectives, concentrating, for example, on technical, social, cultural, behavioral, legal, or economic aspects. However, a specialized focus is not always appropriate in studying an interactive process based on symbolic representation, as language output is the arbitrary outcome of a discursive process that combines all of the above-mentioned aspects. The crucial factor in online communication is maintaining flow. As in speech, where channel bottlenecks slow down the speed of transmission, online communication is compressed by leaving out any information that the recipient can mentally fill in from the context. Accordingly, semantic production orders physical objects in such ways that they can simultaneously carry information, *and* be integrated into a physical process. For example, online offerings may be decoded, read, interpreted, and then revised by subroutines, popularly called "agents", "demons", "executives", etc. It is important to recognize that semantic output – including metaphorical, probabilistic and ambiguous statements – is the outcome of coordinated patterns of concurrent interaction within a physical system, and do *not* constitute durable artifacts of history.[1]

We therefore propose a concept that defines emergent online discourse simply as *a state of immediate responsiveness to semantic communication in a networked system that supports the linking of information that usually is not thought of as related.*

This emergent state is realized, for example, in the collaborative structure of networked workflow systems. In such an interactive task environment the platform can generate audit trail data as part of the internal database architecture in such a way that live input will also run against the archived data. In a multi-server system, the participants may interact at different levels of capacity in each application environment, integrating, and synthesizing data both across and within domains. As long as the participants accept each other as communication partners, it is irrelevant whether the communication is generated by sophisticated software programs or by the human mind. Accordingly, the concept of online communication includes all channels of interactive communication via telephone, the Internet, automated teller machines, and user communities linked into other distinct electronic network families.

1.2 Emergent Semantic Quality

For the analysis of actual situations, semantic information can be thought of as any *data encoded in words* – such as perceptions, sensations, emotions, fragments memory, thoughts – which produce changes in consciousness, and behavior. To become meaningful, this data must stimulate and focus the psychological awareness of participants, an ability which is limited relative to the speed of information creation and transfer. This awareness must also be selective, as no participant could process all the meanings produced without dissolving into chaos. As a result, most of the semantic data produced is eliminated by diverse filters of cultural and individual interpretation. The mind remembers and recognizes only a portion of the information addressed to it. Therefore, in order o realize their aims in a social environment, participants must first convince others that their propositions are making a valuable contribution.

We assume further that on a cultural level, it is the collective opinions of experts from specific domains which pass judgment on the relationships between words and the concepts they stand for. Through repeated cycles of word selection, new branches of semantic canon are being created continuously and, further, deflected in pinball-like patterns through online media.[2]

---

[1] See Pinker 1997, p. 79.
[2] For example, the highly competitive selection of information transfer in the field of economics is characterized by George Stigler, as follows: "I keep telling my colleagues at the *Journal of Political*

But the emergent semantic canon is not stored and retrieved in form of facsimile images. Memory is essentially reconstructive, so that retrieval does not give an exact reproduction, but an interpretative reconstruction of the original image. Schematically, the mind may be viewed as representing narrative knowledge in five modes[3]: (a) the visual image, which, if it represents a thought, is necessarily ambiguous and must be accompanied by a caption; (b) the olfactory image, which is closely associated with emotional response; (c) phonological representation which is mainly stored in short-term memory; (d) syntactical representation of words and their components (e.g. roots, stems, morphemes, phonemes and syllables); and, finally, (e) mentalese, the language of thought, in which conceptual knowledge is framed, consisting of imagined scenarios, anticipated outcomes of actions, formulated future plans, and the design of new goals. These modes of knowledge representation may have evolved because they allow simple algorithms to compute meaningful combinations. In addition – important for our analysis – language enables a second order narrative that creates and recreates narratives out of nonverbal sensory and motor cortices, operating through the body state levers of pain and pleasure.

It is this second-order verbal construction that enables participants to form a subjective perspective of their own and others' mindsets, that is, to reach vastly beyond themselves from inside.[4] In contrast to the content-neutral form of digitalized information that constitutes the object of formal information theory, semantic information is meaningful, and functions as a vehicle of content. Relations exists not only to other words and sets of words, but also between words, the life and minds of the participants, and, in a holistic view, to their origins.[5]

1.3 Propositions

In analyzing the possibilities of semantic integration of emergent online communication, we argue that online networks can substitute for face-to-face communication in this domain if:

- Proposition 1: online networks maintain referential opacity and tacit information (chap. 2)
- Proposition 2: symbols selectively nest into larger structures of meanings (chap. 3)
- Proposition 3: semantic networks are based on symbolic connections (chap. 4)

Economy that anytime we get an article that fifteen of our profession, of the seven thousand subscribers, read carefully, that must be a major article of the year." Quoted in: Csikszentmihalyi 1996, p. 41.
[3] See Pinker 1997, p. 89f.
[4] The philosopher Nagel likens this recursive feat of reasoning with "stepping into what looks like a windowless hut and finding oneself suddenly in the middle of a vast landscape stretching endlessly out to the horizon" (Nagel 1997, p. 72).
[5] See Damasio 1994, p. 105f.

- Proposition 4: online interaction is embedded in role-defined business transactions (chap. 5)
- Proposition 5: external scaffolding is provided by sparsely connected semantic networks (chap. 6)

2 Semanticity in and around Organizations

2.1 Fluidity of Mental Representations

As stated above, the information concept in formal information theory is content-neutral and, therefore, does not fit the qualitative dimensions of semantic information. Moreover, in a major confusion of concepts that has its origin in the ambiguous usage of the term, semantic information is also often used as a mass noun, representing information as a substance that could be divided, condensed, moved, and stored on a computational level. However, it is important to consider that there are no real, natural, universal units of semantic information. Words can only be discussed in terms of an intended usage.[6]

Applied to a business language context, semantic or lexical constructs might describe business processes as a composition of activities, material, and information flow. In a concurrent process of decomposition, the components of this information might be broken down into document fragments or information objects of a particular document type that are classified and linked via semantic relationships within a database.

For example, the different representations associated with the concept "consultant" may be schematically depicted in a single *semantic network* (which may be conceptualized as a *dynamic schema, knowledge representation model*, or *propositional database*, too). Figure 1 shows an idealized model of the depicted network, and represents merely a fragment of the immense inventory of lexical layers in the human mind. Its aim is to connect visual images, phonological representation, syntactical representation, and mentalese in a schematic representation. Of course, within this network the associative combination of mentalese and other representations can generate a vast number of representations expanding exponentially with their size.[7]

Connecting the multidimensional semantic network in online databases requires a huge stock of movable, memorable semantic signposts that can be judged, shared, or

---

[6] See Pinker 1994, pp. 127ff. Thus, in one sense, a "word" may be regarded as a syntactic atom, constructed according to the rules of morphology (with phonemes, or units of sound, strung together to form morphemes which represent the smallest meaningful pieces into which words can be cut, as in "cor-por-ate"). In a different sense, "word" refers to a rote-memorized chunk, or listeme which must be memorized because it does not conform to a general rule, as is the case with word roots or irregular verbs.
[7] The semantic relationships listed in the diagram are based on Cruse (1995, p. 112) and Pinker (1997, p. 87).

criticized, from different perspectives. Most discussions about the knowledge-expanding possibilities of language assume a written language of thought. But, considering that writing and speaking are two entirely different evolutionary innovations, a discourse on the possibilities of online communication may provide a better perspective on how semanticity – the meaningful understanding of language – might expand our cognition if we compare it with face-to-face communication, a pragmatic category derived from our natural, public language.[8]

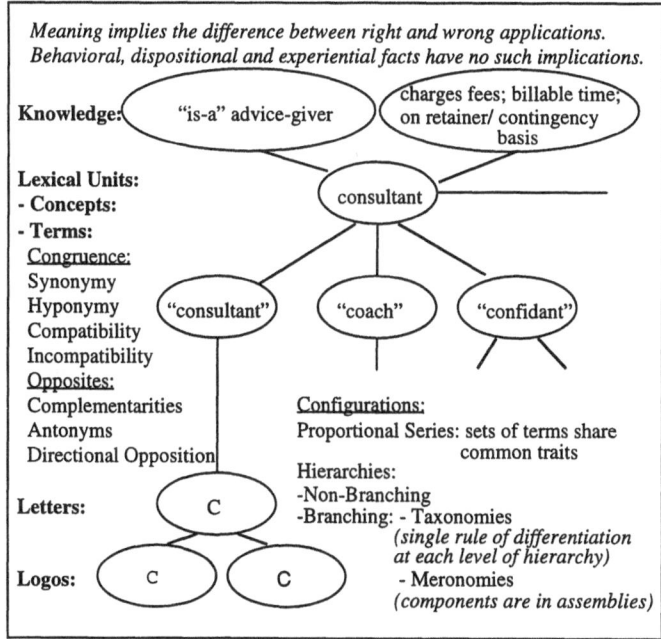

Figure 1: Schematic depiction of semantic networks with lexical relationships

2.2 Creating Stable Patterns of Shared Meanings

Whenever individuals, groups, and organizations communicate, they act on the basis of a particular perception (or misperception) of a particular situation. As explanations, judgments, and predictions rely on framing that unique historical perception, it is a key function of discursive communities to establish and maintain complex communication channels. To illustrate the potential information gains, a survey by Butler et al. demonstrates that by a realistic improvement in the use of the presently available online interaction capacity, the economic capacity to access information could actually

---

[8] See Dennett 1996, p. 147.

increase by a factor of ten, and the capacity to coordinate and monitor certain processes could increase between two- and tenfold.[9] One of the central questions in the field of online communication is, therefore, how the information-handling competence of users can deal with the quantity and quality of information.

From a decision-making perspective, participants are faced with two ideal types of information-processing situations. In the first type, the problem being addressed may either be well-defined – irrespective of the fact that certain pieces of information may be missing, and several possible solutions may exist. In a managerial context, such a well-defined problem would be the re-engineering of the order activity in a production planning process for a car company. In this situation, workflow-based applications may provide the appropriate solutions. In the second type, the situation may be so novel that various mutually exclusive interpretations are brought forward, making it necessary to build a shared understanding of a situation before action can be taken. An example would be designing a negotiation strategy for reducing supplier costs. This task would require the use of a rich interactive medium to fit the complexity of the language flow, and a flexible use of knowledge representation to fit the situation.

This form of problem solving includes communication for building an understanding of and for applying solutions to ambiguous problems.[10] The empirical studies of Sproull and Kiesler show that online interaction facilitates information flows that are useful for mobilizing collective action. Thus, participants discuss problems more frankly and more equally than in many face-to-face groups, and generate more proposals for action than other groups do. These findings also demonstrate that email is a way to preserve creative subcultures, particularly the invisible college of relationships among research workers who may not even work for the organization.[11]

In addition, administrative tasks involve routine managerial communication, for example, communicating priorities, coordinating activities, monitoring performance, and taking appropriate action for which workflow management systems, such as Cyber-InBaskets, have been developed.[12] Thus, in creating user interfaces, it is important to consider that online communication is unconsciously associated with face-to-face communication rather than with electronic or print media. From the subjective experience of a user, the high speed and background character of the operations, the perceived user-friendliness and the real-time capability of computer-

---

[9] See Butler et al. 1997, p. 13.
[10] The term "ambiguous" is used to describe a situation that is either so unclear as to defy interpretation, or that lends itself to multiple interpretations.
[11] See Sproull & Kiesler 1992, p. 68.
[12] See McLellan 1996. "Your InBasket, once the private domain of your workflow manager, will now contain your daily electronic newspaper (tailored to your requirements), junk mail from companies trying to sell you things, an email from your grandmother ... all mixed in with several overdue tasks" (p. 311).

aided interaction, may conceal the programmed nature of the operations, and even support the assumption of an intentional stance.[13]

2.3 Intentional Drift of Semantic Fit

In general, human-machine interactions are not singular events, but part of a sequence of repeated interactions, to which the participants bring their repertoire of roles, and derive the motivation and experience for future communication. Moreover, the interactions can take various forms between the formal or informal, public or private mode, and provide the setting for various types of interaction, such as work, socializing, or power games (for instance, by leveraging expert knowledge). Also, uncertainty is inherently present in expressing and interpreting roles and identities, meanings and action, feelings and emotions. Thus, while online communication frees participants from the constraints of time, space, material surroundings, and physical traits, the lack of co-presence means that many important pieces of sensual information – such as physical features, social signals, pragmatic cues – are filtered out. Furthermore, while online communication is largely sequential, real face-to-face interaction enables instantaneous feedback, and response through parallel channels. Moreover, it is difficult to detect opportunistic behavior in online communication.[14] In general, the electronically networked virtual organization is no less dependent on a network of relationships forged through face-to-face interaction than the populated traditional organization.

The implications for the semantic design of online communication are apparent: to be effective in non-routine interaction, on-line communication must be sensitive to the volatile, uncertain and changing mental images of the participants. With far greater interaction capability and organizational change appearing on the horizon, more emphasis must be placed on overt and subtle shifts in the meanings of business language. But, as it is very rarely the case that a language term which has been used for some time is discarded, shifting meanings will be recognized as such only after a new mental concept has been devised and employed for a long time. Therefore, semantics (defined, here, as the rules and lexical entries that specify the meaning of a word, part of a

---

[13] Pinker (1997, p. 95), in criticizing Searle's conclusion of a missing consciousness in his figurative "Chinese Room" operator, states that a vastly speeded up power of mental computation might enable the transition to a conscious state.

[14] See Nohria & Eccles 1992. A case in point is the famous story about "Julie": "A totally disabled older woman. On the net, Julie's disability was invisible and irrelevant. Her standard greeting was a big expansive HI!!!!!!! Her heart was as big as her greeting, and in the intimate electronic companionships that can develop during online conferencing between people who may never meet, Julie's women friends shared their deepest troubles, and she offered them advice – advice that changed their lives... After several years, something happened that shook the conference to the core. 'Julie' did not exist. 'She' was, it turned out, a middle-aged male psychiatrist" (p. 297f.).

word, phrase or sentence) will have an important function in explaining, classifying, and linking terms on the basis of newly-acquired beliefs.

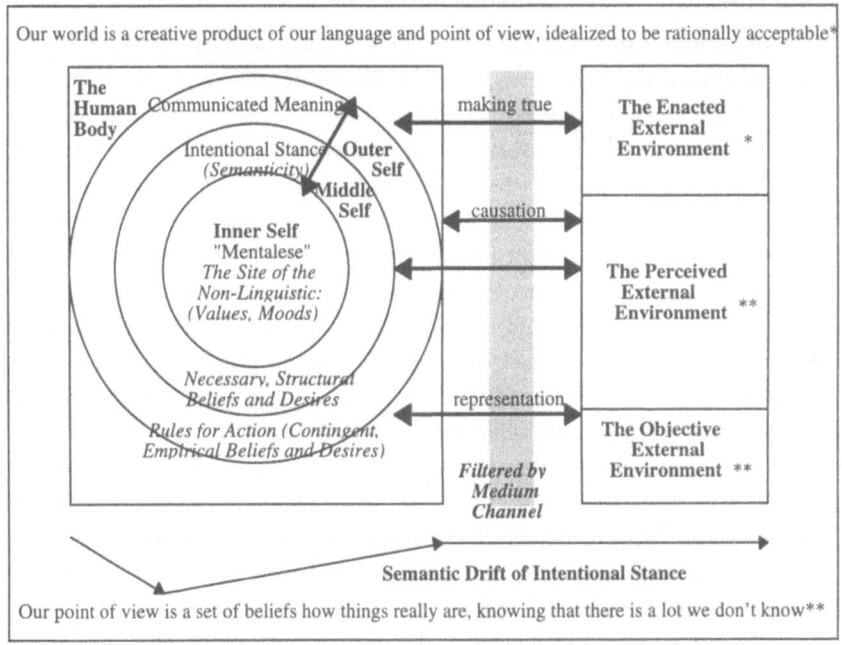

Figure 2: Semantic web of values, beliefs, and desires

In the semantic model depicted above, we distinguish between individual human beings, describable in both mental and physical terms, and the external environment. The subjective assumptions underlying the external communication environment are classified in three, somewhat arbitrary categories, due to the fact that the various perspectives are interconnected. First, the viewpoint of the objective environment assumes that concrete, real, material, and external factors are waiting to be found; second, the assumption underlying the formation of the perceived environment is that human beings have a limited ability to interpret the environment, and third, the concept of the enacted environment implies that the external reality is an ambiguous field, and that acting human beings impose their definition and meaning on that field.

In a simplified pragmatic model, we furthermore distinguish semantic features by two additional dimensions: first, the level of interpretation (indicated by the position of participants engaging in meaningful activities) and the dimensionality or scope of the information system. Semantic change in both dimensions is mainly due to two factors: variation and selection of important social components – including rules, spatial location, and hierarchical position – and the impact of external forces – including technological evolution, evolution of social behavior and behavior in markets.

By grouping words used in the course of this interaction into tacit categories – i.e. giving them a rich category label in mentalese – it is possible to infer some of the properties that one cannot directly observe. Thus, if we mentally characterize some participants as entrepreneurs we can predict more new things about them than if we merely conceive them as economic actors.[15]

In this view, the interaction of physical states, beliefs, and desires function as stimuli, continuously reweaving the network of meanings, and in the process redistributing truth-values among statements. The ongoing search for belief or literal truth, for words or sentences which do not fit into old conventions may serve to modify those conventions and create new ones. In the pragmatic view, "creativity" and "inspiration" are special cases of the ability of the human organism to utter meaningless, but far-reaching sentences which, despite their apparent irrelevance, may be retained because they provide novel insights. Moreover, to assimilate one new belief or desire is automatically to change many, as the other representations in the semantic network are associated with the first, not by any synthetic definition, but by the intentional stance of an individual.[16]

The arguments presented in the following sections challenge some assumptions about the capability of a central processor to connect meanings. The fallacy of a central processor of meaning underlies many models of language analysis in communication groups. However, our theme is based on a model viewing discursive groups as evolving systems, in which intelligence is distributed around to a variety of peripheral agents. This theme is derived from the model of Darwinian natural selection, according to which useful variations are selected for replication due to their superior performance relative to other mutants. Thus, from an evolutionary view, simple transaction processing systems, which automate routine business transactions would spawn more novel categories and words while moving up a fitness slope. Concomitantly, this trend to accommodate *parallel* interpretations would be reversed during a contraction process.[17]

---

[15] However, as it takes less effort to recognize some individuals as being business people than entrepreneurs, there is a tradeoff involved in choosing one category over another.

[16] See Rorty 1991, p. 125.

[17] An example would be an airline's central reservation system, which – on account of its initial success – has evolved toward a variety of interactive applications, including email, Internet EDI, executive information systems, groupware, and voice messaging systems. Of course, this process would unfold in reverse order in the event of a downsizing operation.

3 Nested Evolution of the Intentional Stance

3.1 Lexical Innovation

Understanding language requirements is a critical factor in designing business information systems. However, in examining the information needs of an organization, it would be a self-defeating exercise to conceptualize and channel the emergent drift of business language in a fixed system of categories. A short digression into the dynamics of language will explicate why language change is systemically unpredictable and may not accommodate to a model of business.

According to the evolutionary view of communication, the information needs of an organization are articulated in a fundamental bottom-up process that reaches out to incorporate external cultural influences as part of a larger human system. The scope of the relevant external language environment is vast. Modern psycholinguistic research into the evolution of language performance demonstrates that the laboratory and testing ground of new language creation actually resides in the imaginizing acts of children. In learning to communicate, every new generation of children in effect reinvent a language. Through interacting with adults, children exert a powerful – though largely unobserved – influence in the ongoing creolization of language practice.[18] From this transactional perspective, the successful invention and retention of new words and meanings may result either from a direct or from a second order adult-child interaction. As semantic space (i.e. the number of possible conceptual couplings) is infinite, and, as the invention of new words and meanings is arbitrary, the drift of language change is *unpredictable from an individual perspective*. The semantic web in business language, like in all other idiolects, is in the process of branching out progressively as novel usage creates niches for still further concepts.

However, the ongoing process of variation and retention may also be viewed from *the second-level systemic perspective* of the population-ecology model. According to this model, the information needs of an organization are examined within the whole field of competing entities. In a process of Popperian preselection, language innovation will tend to follow the lead of successful groups and entities. This contingent assimilation of successful strategies implicates a redesign of meanings at the individual, group, or organization level.[19] Driven by a process of natural selection, successful meanings become models of niche creation. But, as shown in the previous passage, the evolution of language differentiation does not follow any predesigned building plans. Like the branching speciation on a deforming fitness landscape, differentia-

---

[18] See Deacon 1997, p. 139.
[19] See Dennett 1995, p. 78.

tion may generate bursts of rapid conceptual innovation, achieving increasing returns for users, followed by periods of incremental variation.

Invariably, the success or failure of communication for a certain type of participant or organization depends on which other participants or groups are present. There is no set information fitness landscape which would enable a calculated climb toward a higher level of competitive advantage. And, as any peak position may turn into a valley at any time, those organizations which tolerate semantic variety while working to improve interaction patterns can secure a survival advantage over less responsive competitors.

3.2 Cognitive Contingencies

The central cognitive issue addressed in this paper deals with the intentional stance, and involves the question how individuals and organizations can communicate meaningfully online, while basing their actions on expectations which they generate about how other participants will behave. The term "information" is defined here as the communication content which changes behavior in response to a felt need for advice. It arises from an ecological system of interpretative devices that interact with one another through the intermediation of participants that use them to meet their expectations. Accordingly, as in any dynamic network, *what* participants decide to do may matter less than the interaction structure through which they communicate with *whom*, and according to which rules.[20] This pragmatic aspect shows that the information technology employed in discourse is systemically linked to communication patterns.

To the extent that recurrent patterns of online social communication link the participants into local networks where their decisions and values are influenced by others' perceived values, a multiplicity of sparsely coupled interactions will tend to branch out into large-scale communication networks. These communication patterns may be visualized as cycles, irregular waves, chaotic bursts, vortices, frozen sectors, and other spatiotemporal configurations.[21]

In contrast to fully connected networks in which each participant interacts with all others, sparsely connected communication patterns – in which each participant interacts with only a few other participants – will enable flexible adaptations. A highly connected communication network in which each participant receives an input from all others can move only uphill or downhill collectively to new levels on the deforming fitness landscape. This need to produce a coordinated move will result in a rigidly ordered

---

[20] Compare Hale 1997, which lists a glossary of online parlance and conventions (e.g. "grok the media", meaning to scan all available information regarding a situation, digest it and form a distilled opinion) with the principles of network socialization expounded in Burt 1992, p. 60.
[21] See Lindgren 1997, p. 362.

system that will be unable to respond flexibly to the altering external landscape. Only when a large network is segmented into non-overlapping sectors, will neighboring sectors be able to coevolve with one another. Then, due to the couplings across boundaries, an adaptive move by one sector will change the fitness landscape for all others.[22]

The sparsely connected network is an important model for designing information systems to deal with ambiguity. The concept runs counter to the notion of a central processor of meaning. Rather, it suggests that a selective distribution of interpretative tools such as visual imagery, privileged language, and a specific institutional setting may provide external support, or scaffolding, on which many tasks involved in interpreting data are off-loaded. In general, ill-defined problems that contain ambiguities and conflicting constraints can be solved without applying any specific model, as soon as they are partitioned into optimally-sized sectors. Thus, it may be a better policy to decentralize semantic processing, and to optimize performance within each of several well-defined sectors, than to impose standardized meanings on the actual information flow.

The communication network depicted in this ideal model has a social structure, embodied in long term relationships, mutual trust, patterns of dependence, and obligations, exchange, presenting new opportunities at any point. Participants will achieve rich information benefits if they acquire and maintain reliable contacts in places where useful information might materialize.

However, establishing an aura of reliability in online contacts is more difficult to achieve than in face-to-face communication. To counter visceral uncertainty, an aura of trust may be fostered through an emphasis on corporate identity, by communicating a shared background of interests, and by suggesting confidence in mutual acquaintances to enforce interpersonal debt.

In apparent contradiction to this need for projecting an image of likeness, establishing a diverse network is the best guarantee for having a contact in place where useful information arises. The objective is not to enlarge the online-contacts as such, which might lead to escalating maintenance costs, and data clutter, but to increase diversity by increasing the number of sparsely connected contacts. It is important to consider that contacts in dense networks are redundant to the extent that they lead to the same people. While frequent contact and emotional closeness within a rich two-way communication will lead to pooling and recycling of information, maintaining the same contacts will lead to the same cluster of more distant participants, thus eliminating any information advantage.[23]

---

[22] See Kauffman 1995, p. 256f.
[23] Burt 1992, pp. 62-69.

Moreover, in order to achieve efficiency in online contacts, it is further necessary to differentiate between primary and indirect contacts. The rule is to concentrate
on the primary contacts – i.e. the contacts most easily maintained, and most likely to
honor an interpersonal debt – and to downgrade the direct relationships with others in
the same cluster in such a way that they will be reachable through the primary contact.
The participant at the center of the network is then free to focus on maintaining proper
relations with primary contacts, and multiplying the contacts by reaching out to new
clusters. For example, in figure 3, the sixteen contacts in the network, spanning two
sectors, are maintained at the cost of four primary contacts concentrated in one sector.

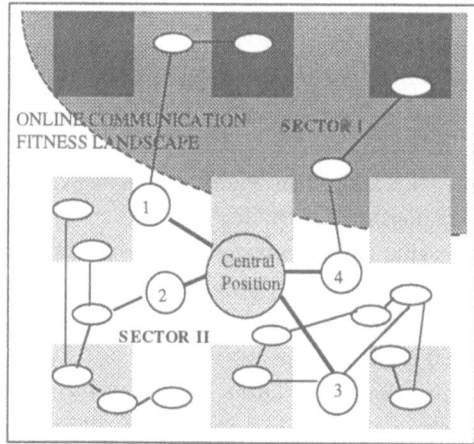

Figure 3: Strategic network expansion in segmented sectors

In practice, it is obvious that the social constraints of culture, kinship, monopoly, in conjunction with the logic of collective action, and other market imperfections
will restrict the freedom of participants to choose among alternative relationships.
For instance, supposing a first mover begins to jockey for a dominant position in an
initially evenly distributed communication network. With the emergence of an increasing number of primary contacts, and a relegation of most participants to the role
of indirect contacts, the resulting uneven distribution of information benefits will
lead to more intense jockeying for central positions. When one participant relaxes in
her efforts to maintain some contacts, this move will cause distress, while dissatis-
fied communication partners will move in random order to occupy the more valued,
vacated communication slots. Thus, although the jockeying for position by one participant will only affect her immediate neighbors, it may in turn affect them to move,
and lead to a chain reaction. Local interactions will then produce a temporary segre-

gation into homogeneous segments, canceling out the information advantage gained through nonredundant ties.[24]

In a competitive field containing entrepreneurial opportunities for participants to affect the terms of their information exchange, strong, affective, and long-lasting relationships will be needed to maintain information differentials. Balancing network size and diversity is therefore a question of optimizing low maintenance costs and redundant contacts through a mix of face-to-face contacts and online communication, both reinforced by impression management.

3.3 Evolution of Virtual Communities

3.3.1 Establishing Trust Relationships

Promoting networking, online technology in combination with segmentation on the fitness landscape is changing the tradeoff between transaction and agency costs in two important ways.

To begin with, online communication can be a major factor in reducing search and transmission costs. Further, as Sproull and Kiesler show above, it can enhance the quality of decision-making by supporting collective decision-making. These advantages are reduced by security issues, which are dealt with mainly by encoding messages in a manner that is unambiguous to the receivers, and by psychological constraints in interpersonal communication.

As a high-commitment work climate is associated with trust and tacit information which, in turn, rely on shared values and beliefs, online communication can only substitute for reduced face-to-face communication if it serves the interests of the informal organization. To function as an effective instrument of symbolic communication, online systems must be supported by the corporate culture inside the organization, and across organizational boundaries by professional networks. Then, the pooling of informal information from diverse sources in combination with online retrieval may result in better decision-making, especially in situations of rapid change.[25]

Under the impact of blurred external boundaries, organizations will adopt a variety of structures that would not have been possible to manage with slower, more expensive, and more impersonal communication. Commensurate with the flexible bounda-

---

[24] See Krugman 1996. Krugman, refining a model by Schelling, states that any populated system characterized by a tension between centrifugal and centripetal forces – with a slightly shorter range for the centripetal forces – will settle into a frozen state, with clearly segregated segments (p. 24f.).

[25] Elucidating the norm of reciprocity in social networks, Putnam states: "Stocks of social capital, such as trust, norms, and networks, tend to be self-reinforcing and cumulative. Virtuous circles result in social equilibrium with high levels of cooperation, trust, reciprocity, civic engagement, and collective well-being." Also, vice versa. In: Putnam et al. 1993, p. 177.

ries, online communication allows participants to select the information that is relevant for each other. The time-honored evolutionary approach is to access one particular source of information first, and then to access a second source depending on what the first item of information turns out to be. In an interactive exchange, the desired information may result from an iterative process of structuring questions and answers. For, the most efficient form of dialogue depends on knowing the preferences and needs of the participants or acquiring this knowledge through skillful persuasion.

From a discursive perspective, it is important to establish a cooperative relationship by applying a consulting approach to online persuasion. In a typical dialogue, the initiator will approach the recipient, and only begin to give information of her own after the recipient has answered a few questions. Both parties may calculate the expected value of this knowledge exchange by recalling the outcome achieved in a previous transaction.

In online transactions, it is difficult to separate persuasion and action research. For example, sellers may establish what others have done in comparable situations, possibly by using software applications such as embedded agent technology. As the cost of interacting online with individuals may continue to fall, sellers will be increasingly capable of gleaning information about the interactions themselves, such as the amount and time spent online and the items purchased. Research efforts aimed at identifying which events or changes in persuasive features trigger certain types of purchase, or, which sequence of messages is followed before a purchase decision is reached may be abandoned for the alternative imitation strategy if the calculation costs are deemed too high. However, because of the uncertainty involved in interpreting user profiles, there is a premium in modeling policies on participants or groups with the best record, irrespective of what the current performance of their strategy may signal.

3.3.2 Pragmatic Adaptation

Applied to market research, the merging of virtual communities of customers with shared interests and activities can provide ideal testbeds by conveying customer perceptions without mediation, thus effectively eliminating the need for focus groups.[26] In addition, customer feedback can identify new directions for differentiated communication, such as personalized bulletin boards of events, which may further facilitate exchange relationships among members.

Utilizing this feedback, online sellers can further differentiate themselves by customizing their preferences for each communication partner. In bringing different

---

[26] See Hagel III & Armstrong 1997, pp. 146.

values to bear on a situation, they may influence and control external impressions by improvising novel situations, applying technical expertise, and persuasive talent to administer the meanings and experience of others. Although the implicit ambiguity contained in improvised online activities is the bane of object-oriented business language, obscurity of meaning supports consensus-building to the extent that participants actively seek confirmation in their opinion of ambiguous events.

A further behavioral objective in managing online communication is to create a supportive socioemotional climate. This beneficial climate may be produced by using associative techniques, such as constructive labeling to create a positive image, and, in addition, by frequently providing positive feedback. The immediate object may be to convey high expectations, and to set difficult goals. The long-term objective usually entails cultivating a climate of trust and community to reassure the communication partners about the benefits of the ongoing process and the well-being of the partners. One such possibility may be to create a space on the seller's site to post unedited messages on bulletin boards. To effectively employ this type of promotion, a seller must maintain an online presence for dialogue, and risk allowing critical comparisons of her own and competitors' products.

Within the informal organization, online discussion groups can be highly effective at utilizing ambiguity to stimulate gossip. Senders can exploit the interactive nature of the medium to excite the respondent, and they must offer relevant information quickly to satisfy the appetite for novelties. Merely converting existing messages into a digitalized form would be ineffective, as transported text layout appears dull online. A better pragmatic option is to engage the recipient in an active dialogue. To use the interactive capability of the medium, the objective in online promotion should be to elicit interest and response.

Furthermore, by exploiting the role ambiguity afforded by the medium, moderators on bulletin boards may play a dual role as sales representatives. If they succeed in creating a virtual community of interest, they may accumulate their own branding power by exercising a moral authority, and certifying the quality of the offerings. Of course, the assumption of this dual role also requires exercise of due diligence regarding the legal implications of possible product liability suits.[27]

---

[27] The allegory of a stone soup, adapted from Anderson (1997, p. 9), illustrates the "flocking" priciple of electronic retailing, as follows. Two men set up a pot of water and stones in a townsquare and start stirring. They tell the first curious passers-by that they are preparing a stone soup – all that is still lacking are some vegetables. These passers-by fetch some leftover cabbage and carrots from home, and drop them in. Their example is followed by others, until the soup tastes delicious, and is served to all. The two men represent the founders of the virtual bookstore Amazon.com, and the good townsfolk the online customers.

3.3.3 Stylistic Differentiation

Paradoxically, the innovation potential in online communication implicates a tradeoff between creativity and consistency. For, any successful innovation that results from online interaction, will reinforce the interactive process every time a novel idea comes up. However, with the increasing density of connections and the rising use of electronic agents to delve into databases, in conjunction with reduced feedback lags, the data in the accessed knowledge-bases will become more rapidly obsolete. Thus, entropy soon follows the success of a novel pattern. At the level of design, this paradox leads to a dilemma: can the pleasure afforded by the unique message commensurate with the casual familiarity of a perfected, but impersonal bulletin? Online creativity is accompanied by social rivalry, and, like all rivalry, can function as an incentive to individuality as well as a source of consensus and conformity. Therefore, from a participant's perspective, it may be less important to create new data than to be able to access and relate it. For example, using the web to watch for novel designs can signal a skill in recognizing and adopting lifestyle attributes that may in time be generally approved.

The rapid obsolescence of novelty, in turn, begs the question how distinct the appearance of a standardized online message can be made to appeal to skilled communicators. A plausible solution might be to curtail choice in order to project an image of consistency. The process would involve creating a radically simplified range of message contents, featuring the hallmark of artistic design, but utilizing traditional instruments of promotion, such as corporate identity, branding, and embellishing the moral quality of the message.

Using online communication to recognize and interpret emerging patterns will significantly alter the self-perception of the participants. Due to the perceptional volatility, the growth and survival of an organization will increasingly depend on the perceived attractiveness of the existing images, mental constructs and artifacts. Again, these result from the way the participants interpret the incoming information. However, it is possible that changes in communication style in response to new information may change semantic usage, without changing the underlying structure of meanings. Typically, a change of meanings in mature networks is gradual and path dependent, with constraining belief systems reflecting the past. Successful modifications will depend on the gradual alteration of perceptions through continuous recycling and filtering of current experiences of innovation by the belief system.[28]

---

[28] Dennett (1995) quotes Dan Sperber (1985, p. 86) on the cultural transmission of new concepts in analogy to epidemiology: "In an oral tradition ... all hard to remember representations are forgotten, or transformed into more easily remembered ones, before reaching a cultural level of distribution" (p. 358).

4 Administering Symbolic Connections

4.1 Constructing Referential Relationships

In the computational model of cognition, symbolic information – such as beliefs and desires – are considered to represent linguistic building blocks in the emergent connection patterns of a network. Such a connectionist perspective refers external semantic properties – as contained in the phrase *Nokia connecting people* – to persons, events, processes, or other threshold-like parameters which by themselves have no external-world semantic role. But, with props and repeated feedback cycles, such a connectionist system comes to recognize exceptions to its generalizations – and, in a further step, generalizes on those exceptions. Significantly, the manipulability of symbolic relationships involves an intentional preselection of concepts. It is important that this mental leap transcends the associative linking of indexical relationships.[29]

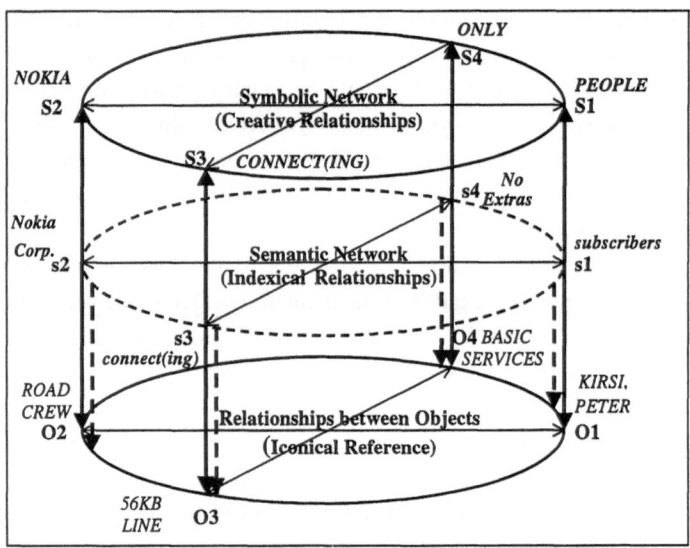

Figure 4: Taxonomy of referential relationships

As depicted in figure 4, a set of indices or lexigrams, such as *Nokia Corp, link up, subscribers, no extra charge* (s1-s4) would merely link outside objects and events to one another, such as *ROAD CREW, 56KB LINE, KIRSI/PETER, BASIC SERVICE* (O1-O4). However, the construction of symbolic relationships would in-

---

[29] See Dennett 1996, p. 88f.

volve three different steps: first, a collection of lexigrams is recognized and memo-rized (in our example, s1-s4); second, systematic relations between lexigrams are recognized and memorized as additional lexigrams, such as *NOKIA, CON-NECT(ING), PEOPLE, ONLY* (S1-S4); third, the mnemonic strategy is reversed in symbolic representation to rely on relationships between lexigrams – in our example by associating the text of Nokia's advertisement with E.M. Forster's motto (S1 – S4) to pick out concrete objects indirectly via relationships between concrete objects (in our example O1-O4).

The symbolic recoding of systems of iconic and indexical (or lexical) relation-ships is an important feature in online communication because it ultimately allows the participants to ignore most of the vast network of word-object, word-word, and object-object indexical associations[30]. However, it is important to recognize that symbols constitute a closed system of relationships between the lexigrams linking them through an iconic relationship to the system of relationships between concrete objects. If this arbitrary manipulation of ideas fails, symbols will revert to indices.[31]

For example, it is not uncommon in email to signal important items, such as quantity, intensity, importance, possession, etc. by a salient iconic repetition. As the participant comes to recognize this intended mapping of lexical relationships to object relationships, attention shifts from the more concrete lexical, to allow the more effi-cient and powerful logic of symbolic relationships to retrieve and restructure informa-tion. And since symbolic representation is intrinsically combinatoric, there is no upper limit to the complexity of semantic networks.

4.2 Scope for Lexical Preselection

To incorporate new information about the outer environment that is encoded in iconic and lexical associations, an interpreting system must continuously adapt by concentrating on the most useful, most reliable information. In analogy to the process of natural selection, vast numbers of alternative patterns must be generated, set into competition with one another, extinguished due to their lack of correlation with sen-sory and mnemonic information or be selected for replication through the recognition processes and responses of each moment.

Thus, in the area of machine translation, it is highly probable that a business language database for the field of Mergers and Acquisitions will include the phrase *blue sky law* (prescribing fairness in offerings). Yet, even if that phrase never appears literally, indexical knowledge that *blue sky law* is close to *dictum, directive,* or possi-

---

[30] On the strength of the author's anecdotal evidence, this sybolic transfer is frequently disregarded in industrial design, as demonstrated in the icon-centered graphic user interfaces.
[31] The description of the linguistic creation of symbols is based on Deacon (1997, p. 87).

bly even *control* would allow a phrase like *blue sky control* or *blue dictum*, either of which might be stored, to be retrieved as a substitute.[32]

In online information resource concepts, the most widespread method used to avoid unpredictable words is to prevent unpredictability by circumscribing both the domain of discourse and the style format. Accordingly, the application of the stored semantic network may be restricted only to specialized commercial domains with recurring patterns, or to manuals for text processing. For example, Xerox Corporation avoids ambiguity by instructing its authors of manuals to comply with the *Multinational Customized English* (MCE). This artificial dialect – which is used with the Systran program to translate about 50.000 pages of English-language manuals into other languages – invokes rigid rules for identifying target terms in a table of exceptions and prescribing a standardized use of connectors, prepositions, pronouns, and articles, irrespective of the fact that these rules subvert the prosodic flow of language.[33]

4.3 Optimizing Associative Processes

In connectionist processing – the technology used for machine translation – it is crucial to distinguish between two broad categories of associative operations: first, paradigmatic operations – as exemplified by metaphors and pronouns – which reflect substitution relationships between words; second, syntactic operations which reflect the complementary relationships between words from different parts of speech, such as nouns, verbs, adjectives, adverbs, or articles. A further syntactic tool, word association by metonomy uses information to generate novel alternatives by shifting attention to complementary features – as exemplified in the arbitrary sequence "blue sky law – taxable gain or loss on the sale of assets".

The distribution of semantic and syntactic processes differ from language to language. Some languages (such as Italian) utilize changes in word form to mark grammatical functions, while allowing considerable freedom of word order, whereas the opposite holds true in English. This intransitive distribution poses problems for the design of rich semantic networks across languages. Transcending cultural patterns, the incidence of word usage depends on contingent factors, such as the communication context, the phenotype, and the personality of the users.

However, driving the interpretation of symbolic relationships encoded in word combinations, sentence structure and iconicity at a high pace may overwhelm the information carrying capacity of online communication. In real-life situations, there is a need to perform simultaneous but competing operations (i.e. speaking, listening to speech, or interacting) in the absence of nonverbal language and emo-

---

[32] In analogy to the example in Hofstadter 1997, p. 502.

tional expression. Also, in cognitive processing, all sensations and thoughts are colored emotionally, and indexed by a surplus or absence of pleasure and arousal. In adopting the intentional stance, participants, perceiving, thinking and acting in real time, will restrict consciousness relative to the rich field of potentially accessible sensations. In the process of cognitive preselection, large parts of the accessible spectrum of colors, shapes, smells, and physical sensations will, therefore, be blended out at any time. Thus, intentionally transmitted pieces of information may fall under the attention threshold of the receiver, pass in and out of short-term memory, or be deliberately discarded.

In creating imaginative interaction patterns, it is important to consider that access-consciousness tends to prefer the intermediate levels. Although the highest levels tend to pass into the long-term memory, participants usually restrict their perception to the inherent properties of real-time experience. Parallel, unconscious computation stops after an individual, event, or location is labeled with color, depth and motion.

Paradoxically, the attempt to reach out to new cognitive horizons by an interactive rehearsal of new terms may lead to a spiraling cycle of self-paralysis for real-time situations, as exemplified in the need for elaborate preliminaries, or jokes in a new communication context. While elaborate raw data are being scrutinized, acceptable combinations have to be computed by a conscious effort, rather than by weaving a solution through network connections.[34]

5 Role-based Integration of Online Activities

5.1 Constraints of Network Externalities

Once participants have invested time and effort in establishing network connections, they have little direct influence on the further growth of the aggregate network capital. The future value of their sunk costs will be determined by the cumulative influence of the actions of other participants. For example, while peer pressure to learn new applications in a groupware environment may impose costs on individual users, a culture of support among users may, produce collective benefits. With the emergence of communication networks rather than firms as the locus of activities and affect, and loyalty to online "philia" groups taking the place of the "organization man", participants will adapt semantic usage to pleasing others in their network.

---

[33] See Hofstadter 1997, p. 502f.
[34] See Pinker 1997, pp. 139f. In devining online etiquette, both real-time interaction and rich communication content can be a liability. Thus, in conflict-laden contexts, the best solutions may be found if the communication of different subsets of the participants, are ignored at different moments.

The types of sustainable online cultures depend in important ways on overall lifestyles. In our example above, the appreciation and utilization of groupware applications rise with network exposure. Although, conceivably, no rise in individual utility is foreseen, a reduction in disutility may result as skills and experience open new applications. There are two further externalities to consider. First, due to the rising stock of network capital the investment required to maintain the capital stock will also increase. Second, while the pace of technological innovation in the network persists, the exit option of the individual participants will depreciate.

In the case of transitory inroads into network capital gain, individual behavior will remain stable, as it may not pay to disinvest the capital embodied in system-specific knowledge or skills. And even when the decline in network capital seems permanent, the incentive to switch will lag, because disinvestment involves time-consuming cycles of unlearning. The incidence of defections, moreover, is arbitrary. For example, the readiness to invest in the new technology will be affected by individual factors, such as risk propensity, and education, as well as by demographic factors such as age, and seniority within an organization that influence time preference (especially the time horizon remaining to collect the returns on new investments).[35]

Whereas, inside organizations, network specific investment, such as experiential learning about roles, tasks, and the organizational culture may help strengthen the internal labor market, it may also provide participants with opportunities to defect – a risk which incurs new agency costs. But, in general, human resources embodied in special network skills and knowledge are geared to a specific network. Moreover, the immobility of the accessory network-related social capital also helps explain why participants are less likely to be laid off in a downturn.

Paradoxically, a growing innovation differential will provide those participants locked into a declining network with additional incentives to remain committed to their system and its semantic components. As these fringe online communities develop a distinct cultural identity, they will provide opportunities for small-scale developers and sellers of software applications. The partitioning of online networks on the basis of different philosophies of information processing and mediation is linked with the ongoing process of social differentiation. Social distinctiveness, however is characterized by negative network effects. When literacy in special applications, such as executive information systems, confers power, semantic competence becomes a positional good, with a functional hierarchy of semantic expertise evolving to support the maintenance of authority structures. As a result, power centers inside organizations will harden. Moreover, whole fringe

---

[35] See Becker 1996, p. 37.

online communication networks and affinity groups may be instrumentalized by power alliances to expand semantic reach. From the proliferation of distinct semantic networks, a further widening of wage differentials for system-specific semantic skills will occur, accompanied by an asymmetrical development of employability.

Balancing operational efficiency and mutual adjustment among the fringe networks will stabilize ongoing semantic patterns in a coevolving mode. Due to the dynamics of special interests, the interaction between closed and open systems will create and transfer new information at many levels, but without jelling into a coherent semantic network. As opposed to the ideal universal language of the open system model, multipolar online bazaars or forums will appear that differ greatly from the dominant language and its branched out semantic patterns.[36]

5.2 Constraints in Designing Connectivity

A key success factor in loosely coupled workflow systems is the professional attitude of the specialized participants who can perform complex jobs with a minimum of supervision. But it is also a weakness of the networked workflow that the interactive tasks provide information as part of an internal database design that cannot be modified easily. For instance, as tasks and procedures involve multiple participants, the process authors must find consistent names and icons for dispersed data, since reporting instructions may be embedded within a particular word. Moreover, with incremental learning, customized features and applications, such as notification of a late condition or sending an email will be added to the system.

From a pragmatic point of view, this escalating formalization will feed the inherent ambivalence of professionals towards bureaucracy. In other words, highly skilled professionals will militate against being "plugged" into a system that can monitor itself and take corrective action in real time. If the network authors decide to maintain flexibility of response to a volatile environment, workflow design must follow two policies. First, it must adopt the interaction pattern of a sparsely connected network, second, it must restrict the number of customized applications, as the quality of an open system architecture would, otherwise, be subverted.

Furthermore, to protect against the risk of defection and the internal misuse of information, online access in organizations is often controlled by a need to know policy. Participants are given as little information as will suffice for them to accomplish their individual assignments. Applied to decentralized networks, the need-to-know policy must provide sufficient flexibility to deal with changing needs. These may result from new workflow designs, new organizational responsibilities, and a new mix of

---

[36] See Mothe & Paquet 1996, p. 55 and Kao 1996, p. 138.

knowledge and skills. In conjunction with the substitution of detailed long-range planning through flexible integrated manufacturing approaches and the replacement of
vertical authorization through controls at the operational level, online access control
can be achieved through a role-based approach. This control would combine manda-
tory rules with discretionary procedures.[37]

To fit the requirements of a workflow management system (WFMS), access
controls in online communication must be based on a transaction model of all communication processes. On a conceptual level, this transaction model would describe all
business actions, and the contingent information flow. Roles would be defined as a set
of tasks defined in relation to an activity context, and not in relation to specific users –
as depicted in figure 5.

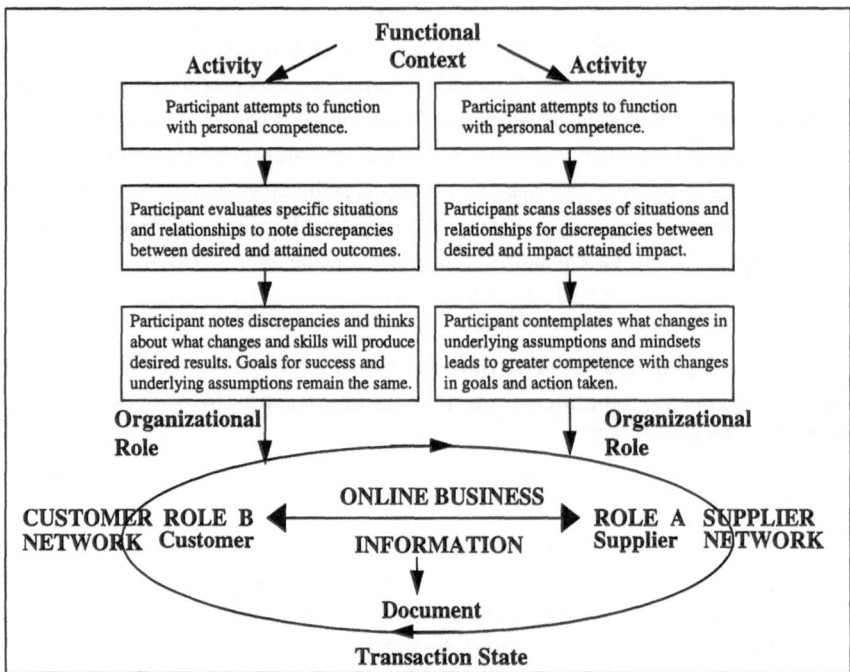

Figure 5: Network components with identical structures but different mindsets

Although it is the purpose of a WFMS to provide a foundation for defining
and executing business processes, it cannot express the social interaction through
which the participants in a business transaction create access rules and ascribe attrib-

---

[37] See Bauknecht 1996, p. 276ff. and Leymann & Roller 1997, p. 109f. for a description of the organ-

utes to the objects they create. Moreover, business transactions are generated by participants acting towards the fulfillment of organizational objectives within a wider network of customer-supplier relationships. And the rules by which information is processed along these sparsely-connected network channels before being defined and archived in terms of document types or objects cannot be traced unless they are subject to standardized procedures or controls along this path, as required, for example, in Quality Systems.

In the course of a role-defined business process, as shown in figure 5, raw data is obtained by the supplier through external channels, relayed through Internet EDI to the customer, transformed by programs and subprocesses, invoked by authorized participants – all under semantically correct labels – and subsequently archived for further use. At first glance, the components of the network have a standardized structure reflecting the basic business process – a customer supplier transaction. Within this context, both participants would assume similar motivational attitudes and organizational roles with the aim of reaching an agreement (embodied in a document). But, a discrepancy with regard to the intentional stance may arise at any stage. For example, while the customer may concentrate on managing the negotiation process, the seller may shift his focus to a fundamental assessment of his function in the process.[38]

As the process of negotiation unfolds, only little common ground may remain in the minds of the participants. Yet, under the workflow-based need-to-know information policy, this change of focus will not be reflected in access specifications. Accordingly, with rising transaction complexity and role ambiguity, it would be mutually advantageous to switch to a task-force-type policy. This policy would provide participants with a high degree of advance knowledge about the total project, with a view to countering unforeseen obstacles. Such a move, though, will only be possible in a decentralized system, where business process definitions may be adapted in real-time.

5.3 Granularity in Semantic Networks

The accessibility of online information allows problemistic search to be conducted across formal organizational boundaries, providing glimpses of different cultural artifacts, codes, conceptual frameworks, and patterns of interaction. The pragmatic intention in which these other concepts, ideas, and forms of knowledge are encountered is inherently improvised, opportunistic, and, therefore, nonhierarchical and centerless. As whole series of project histories accumulate, kaleidoscopic configura-

---

izational requirements for coupling business modeling and WFMS.
[38] See Culbert 1996, p. 239. Adapted from a case on achieving breakthrough learning.

tions will be archived for future reference. Online access to this knowledge will become increasingly competitive, speeding up the automation of processes in analyzable areas, and in the process, creating a new hierarchy of passwords holders.

Within organizations there are important business concepts that may exist in one field, or branch but do not have an explicit and consistent terminology linking them to sets of terms in other areas. One such instance is the various degrees of granularity that may be used in internal communication to represent time periods. Discrepancies in information resources are a common feature in all media, but the validation problem is exacerbated by the flow of online communication. A major problem in coordinating semantic patterns in online communication is the limited capacity of human short-term memory. Only a few items – in general five to seven items – can be held in the mind at once, and these items are constantly subject to fading or crosstalk.[39] The cognitive challenge is to keep a particular kind of phrase and lexical meaning in memory, intending to return to it, while simultaneously analyzing another example of that very same type of phrase (i.e. recursive structures, as they are often found in academic writing, due to the large number of qualifiers deemed necessary). Although, from a detached view, most sentences are ambiguous, words themselves provide some guidance by suggesting which other words they tend to cluster with inside a given phrase pattern.

Machine translation, to resolve ambiguities, also calculates word frequencies, and compares the frequencies with which pairs and groups of words are used. Email recipients, in decoding texts, try to discover meaning through an analysis of sentence architecture, habitually favoring structures with certain shapes. But, as the following passage from an insurance policy shows, using parsing to extract meaning can lead to controversial interpretations:[40]

"Such insurance as is provided by this policy applies to the use of a non-owned vehicle by the named insured and any person responsible for use by the named insured provided such use is with the permission of the owner". The context refers to a woman who had driven and crashed a car she mistakenly thought belonged to a friend. Ruling on the damage suit, the court said she was covered, as the policy was ambiguous. Thus, the requirement *with the permission of the owner* could be applied to *any person responsible for use by the named insured*, rather than to *the named insured* (i.e. her) *and any person responsible for use by the named insured.*

The policy is intended to encompass distinct situation types which insured persons can meet, and the likelihood of various outcomes. But, whereas the terms are

---

[39] See Pinker 1994, p. 203.
[40] See Solan 1993. Quoted in: Pinker 1994, pp. 217f.

geared to actuarial requirements and to client situations, they do not consider the various court practices. However, courts often resolve cases by "canons of construction" which are widely discussed in the legal literature. In actuarial practice, insurance terms are classified both under the concept of contract and the concept of product, as the business is conducted on the basis of contracts. The ultimate risk in transferring a category from one domain to another is that the documents and form of communication will be forced to conform to the categories implied in the information system.

Because a combinational system such as a vocabulary can generate a vast number of links, categories are a basic feature in all fields of human cognition. And, in the process of forming categories, people basically think in two modes.[41] On the one hand, they invent fuzzy stereotypes by discovering correlations among properties, and on the other hand, they create self-referential systems of rules that define categories strictly in terms of the rules that apply to them. The inherent fuzziness of apparently sharp-edged categories can be demonstrated by analyzing the business concept "parent". In a business context, this concept clearly belongs to the category "parent company". However, that clear definition becomes blurred, when one compares the concept "parenting", which means to nurture an acquisition, with the concept of a "predating" holding company in the domain of leveraged buy-outs.

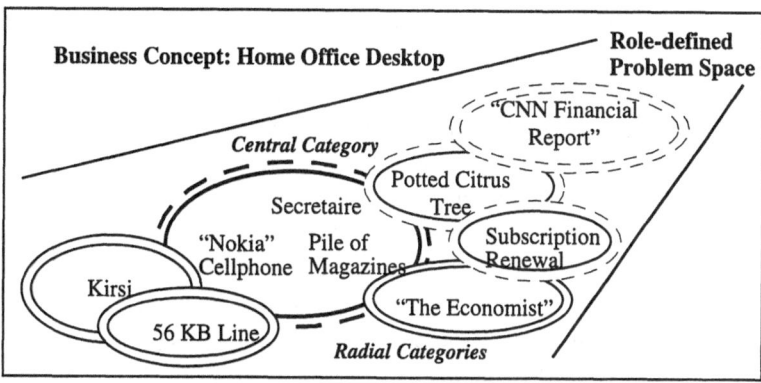

Figure 6: Branching pattern of categories

The idiosyncratic nature of category branching demonstrates that all systems of rules are idealizations that abstract from the complicated perceptions of reality. A further example, depicted in figure 6, shows that the canonical idea of a "household good" may generate several preconsidered "is-a" functions, such as "product of an in-

---

[41] See Lakoff 1987. This book, named after a fuzzy grammatical category in an Australian language, argues persuasively that pure categories are fictions.

dustrial process", "discrete physical unit", "commercially marketed good", "personal possession". But from a subjective perspective, the central category might best be represented by a car or the focal point in a house. Through various routes of extension, as shown in figure 6, the conceptual space branches into radial categories that share fewer and fewer of the patterns exhibited by the prototypical pattern.

Object-oriented WFMS, for example, try to overcome the arbitrary nature of partitioning conceptual space by extending generic business concepts to account for speech patterns encountered in the jargon of work groups from all business operations and professional functions. This language material is linked into templates that are unique both to a specific business situation and a group of communicators within a business process. Before a business language model is linked into a semantic data base, however, it must be reverse-engineered to demonstrate traceability from implementation back to business meaning, and, in a further step, from unique domain language back to central generic concepts.[42]

6 Significance of External Scaffolding

6.1 Reality Maintenance

Object-oriented language categorization is based on adherence to specific routines in classifying incoming data and completing patterns. The internal database structure retains the documentation of business processes. The workflow sequence employs the semantic network as a storehouse of passive language-like symbols archived to be retrieved and manipulated by administrative processes. However, as shown in the examples above, generating meaning can only be achieved by connecting abstract domains (such as modeling a semantic database) with real-world, real-time action. Through this scaffolding, information-processing is directed by repeated interaction with external resources, and is therefore path-dependent. The guided interaction provides direction in ordering experiential perceptions – by prompting associative recall, transforming inputs, simplifying search – and thereby aiding recognition.

According to the holistic model of meaning, symbolic and lexical reference are contingent on the whole web of referential relationships, as well as on the whole virtual community of users, extended in space and time. To elucidate the meaning of an expression in an online exchange it is necessary to understand the intentionality of the other participants. As meanings and patterns of use coevolve, reference may be maintained by contiguity with, but not by adherence to a program of representational associations.

---

[42] See McDavid 1996, pp. 136ff.

Of course, the cultural advantage of shared meanings for collective action requires at some empirical level consensus in judgments and linguistic practice. But, to the extent that this consensus contributes to the formation of other virtual selves it is independent of a particular participant or group of participants to support it. Although meaning depends on social conventions on lexical and iconic representation, symbolic reference is independent of any particular interpretative process. Significantly, it is not derived from rule-following of the lexical or iconic reference of others.[43]

6.2 Emergent Assembly

The concept of emergent assembly explicates the conscious split between interpreting processes of the outside world and interpreting and expressing things from an individual perspective, as may be demonstrated by the example of an emergent scheduling system in a production plant utilizing numerically controlled machining cells.

From the perspective of production control, an operating system is designed to match tasks to machining cells. On the operating level, the workload distribution between the cells will be in a state of continuous change in response to internal factors, such as employee fluctuation and the creation of new jobs in response to technological innovation. In the traditional scheduling approach the information would be centralized, whereby a central database would contain the configurations of standardized tasks, skills, employees, equipment, and employ metrics reports to determine the process status with respect to targets. In the emergent configuration, each cell controls its own performance. A cell in need of resources approaches other cells for tenders, and then routes the job to the best offer. If one cell is blocked, the system adjusts automatically. Due to the distributed nature of the decision-making processes, and the need-based online flow of information between the workers, the machining cells, and the production manager, the system is relatively robust and variable.[44]

The emergent properties depicted in the example above also characterize interaction in real time focus: no single participant needs to know the overall network of meanings. In emergent assembly, the interpretation will emerge out of the multiple interactions between the participants. As improvised, and uncoordinated variations in interpretation occur, those changes that improve the collective fitness landscape will be preserved, and will leak out into the local environment.

To the extent that these successful variations support real-time communication, they are the result of accidental, locally effective features, not of an evolutionary change in ideal types and procedures. The further efforts of the participants to simplify

---

[43] Nagel 1997, p. 41
[44] In analogy to an example in: Clark 1997, pp. 43ff.

routines, continuously add structure to the interaction. As the search encodings of the participants are systemically geared toward action, it is also efficient to encode reality-tested meanings in externalized computational routines. However, as demonstrated above, the intentional stance of other participants can only be represented through the virtual reference created by symbols.

6.3 The Virtual Office

By creating external symbol structures, the participants are expanding their ability to engage in situational interaction. In a mental balancing act, they are, in effect, exchanging collectively achieved representation for time- and labor-intensive internal computation.[45] Similarly, organizations provide external resources in form of norms, policies, and practices to reduce the need for improvisation.

Daily problem-solving in these arenas involve locally effective strategies of pattern-recognition in parallel with the prescribed use of business objects. For example, at run time, a WFMS will execute and control the flow of data, assign activities to people, and monitor the process. In this case, external scaffolding provided by collectively signified meanings substitute fast pattern recognition and decision-making for a time-consuming incremental problem-solving procedure. Every InBasket session would be an adventure that consumes too many cognitive resources for a user who never mastered the appropriate email scripts. But by modeling the stereotypical situations and interpretations of events authors also create incentives for evasive action. Thus, users may adapt behavior to generate good metrics reports or push work ahead in an unfinished state.[46] The intentional stance of participants in a complex online-environment may often be best understood by observing them communicating in response to specific social, material, and institutional settings.

In hierarchichally structured processes, mental constructs formed by the participants are nested primarily within an institutional matrix of reciprocal feedback loops, not in horizontal networks. This segmentation enables a large number of participants to contribute partial solutions to complex problems involving long chains of interactions. Multiple equilibria are possible due to nontransitive choices by participants with identical preferences.[47] But as shown above (in chapter 3.2), densely connected systems will show a high degree of confirmation bias, due to the large number of contacts that exert a powerful influence to adopt shared meanings.

---

[45] See Clark 1997, pp. 184ff. Self-organizing robotic systems have been constructed with Lego toys, too!
[46] McLellan 1996, p. 310.
[47] See North 1997, p. 227.

In contrast, if the level of early communication is restricted, individual participants may have time to balance their options against the environmental impact. As an increasing number of locally connected individuals join the in-group communication, the outcome will either be a more considered consensus or an expanded set of multiple solutions.

7 Connecting Online Microworlds

The broad spectrum of issues considered in this analysis highlight the difficulties in creating a template for a general semantic theory of online communication. Semantic strategies and performance patterns in online communication are related to personality traits and organizational dynamics. Participants engaged in routine activities are only partly aware and capable of appreciating the vast amount of online information.[48] And participants who are not willing or not able to cope with the technological learning curve will feel more attracted to information that is easy to recognize by being prepackaged, branded, labeled, and redundant in content.

Our analysis has also addressed different online channels and media, ranging from email to WFMS. We suggest that semantic networks function best in small microworlds. The more ambitious connectionist programs, which tend to merge syntactic rules with semantic categories which are based either on central programming, or on the outcome of active neural networks both fail in solving ambiguous shifts in meaning. But on a lower-level, online communication that is designed merely to support human efforts directed to interpreting ambiguity can process detailed representations and complex hierarchies of lexical categories.

Resulting from the arbitrary nature of language evolution, there is an inherent tradeoff between depth of performance and size of domain in computational models of semantic processing. Based on our analysis of the intentional stance in establishing

---

[48] The confusion resulting from the surplus of information has been brilliantly represented in the "Library of Babel" by the poet Luis Borges (Dennett 1995, pp. 107-111).
This analogy conceives a vast warehouse of books encompassing the full range of all logically possible data. The structure of the warehouse is designed like a honeycomb containing a vast number of hexagonal corridors surrounded by balconies lined with shelves. Besides much incomprehensible nonsense, these shelves may be visualized as containing all the information ever written down, or waiting to be written down in an infinite future in any language. For example, the set of all possible books in English may be imagined as a collection of volumes 410 pages long, with pages containing 40 lines of 80 characters out of a character set of 100 members. Books of more than 410 pages would begin in one volume and extend into some other volume. But even with these typographical constraints, the logical space is vast: 3,200 characters per page gives 1,312,000 character spaces per book, so there would be $100^{1,312,000}$ books in the Library of Babel. Locating a particular book in this honeycomb structure, however, would pose an insurmountable physical challenge, even if it were possible to travel along the shelves at light speed over vast periods of time.

meaning, we conclude that it is the users who necessarily build the final applications, based on the available repertoire of language components.

References

Anderson, C. (1997, May 10th-16th). A Survey of Electronic Commerce. In: Search of the Perfect Market. *The Economist*, pp. 1-26.

Bauknecht, K. (1996). Workflow-Management-Systems: Source and Solution of Privacy Problems in Organizations. In: H. Österle & P. Vogler (Eds), *Praxis des Workflow Management* (pp. 271-299). Braunschweig: Vieweg.

Becker, G. (1996). *Accounting for Tastes.* Cambridge, Massachusetts:. 1996.

Burt, R. (1992). The Social Structure of Competition. In: N. Nohria & R. Eccles (Eds.), *Networks and Organizations* (pp. 57-91). Boston, Mass: Harvard Business Scholl Press.

Butler, P. et al. (1997/1). A Revolution in Interaction. *The McKinsey Quarterly.*

Clark, A. (1997). *Being There: Putting Brain, Body, and World Together Again.* Cambridge, Massachusetts: MIT Press.

Cruse, D. A. (1995). *Lexical Semantics.* Cambridge: Cambridge University Press.

Csikszentmihalyi, M. (1996). *Creativity – Flow and the Psychology of Discovery and Invention.* New York: HarperCollins.

Culbert, S. (1996). *Mind-Set Management: The Heart of Leadership.* New York, Oxford: Oxford University Press.

Damasio, A (1994). *Descartes' Error – Emotion, Reason, and the Human Brain.* New York:Putnam.

Deacon, T. (1997). *The Symbolic Species: the Co-evolution of Language and the Brain.* London: Allen Lane the Penguin Press.

Dennett, D. (1995). *Darwin's Dangerous Idea: Evolution and the Meanings of Life.* London: Penguin Books.

Dennett, D. (1996). *Kinds of minds: towards an understanding of consciousness.* London: Weidenfeld & Nicolson.

Dennett, D. (1987). *The Intentional Stance.* Cambridge, Massachusetts: MIT Press.

Hagel III, J. & Armstrong, A. (1997/1). Net Gain: Expanding Markets through Virtual Communities. *The McKinsey Quarterly.*

Hale, C. (Ed.) (1997). *Wired Style – Principles of English Usage in the Digital Age.* San Francisco: HardWired.

Hofstadter, D. (1997). *Le Ton beau de Marot: In Praise of the Music of Language.* New York: Basic Books.

Kao, J. (1996). *Jamming – the Art and Discipline of Business Creativity.* London: HarperCollins.

Kauffman, S. (1995). *At Home in the Universe: The Search for the Laws of Self-Organization and Complexity.* New York: Oxford University Press.

Krugman, P. (1996). *The Self-Organizing Economy.* Oxford: Blackwell Publishers.

Lakoff, G. (1997). *Women, Fire, and Dangerous Things.* Chicago et al.: University of Chicago Press.

Leymann, F. & Roller, D. (1997). Workflow-based Applications. *IBM Systems Journal*, 36(1), pp. 102-123.

Lindgren, K. (1997). Evolutionary Dynamics in Game-Theoretic Models. In: B. Arthur et al. (Eds.), *The Economy as an Evolving Complex System* (pp. 337-368). Reading, Massachusetts: Addison-Wesley.

McDavid, D. (1996). Business Language Analysis for Object-Oriented Information Systems. *IBM Systems Journal*, 35(2), pp. 128-150.

McLellan, M. (1996). Workflow Metrics – One of the Great Benefits of Workflow. In: H. Österle & P. Vogler (Eds.), *Praxis des Workflow-Managements* (pp. 301-318). Braunschweig: Vieweg.

Mothe, J. de la & Paquet, G. (Eds.) (1996). *Evolutionary Economics and the New International Political Economy.* London: Pinter.

Nagel, T. (1997). *The Last Word.* Oxford: Oxford University Press.

Nohria, N. & Eccles, R. (1992). Face-to-Face: Making Network Organizations Work. In: N. Nohria & R. Eccles (Eds.), *Networks and Organizations* (pp. 288-308). Boston, Mass: Harvard Business Scholl Press.

North, D. (1997). Some Fundamental Puzzles in Economic History/Development. In: B. Arthur et al. (Eds.), *The Economy as an Evolving Complex System.* Reading, Massachusetts: Addison-Wesley.

Pinker, S. (1997). *How the Mind Works.* New York et al.: Norton.

Pinker, S. (1994). *The Language Instinct.* New York: W. Morrow and Co.

Putnam, R. et al. (1993). *Making Democracy Work – Civic Traditions in Modern Italy.* Princeton, NJ: Princeton University Press.

Rorty, R. (1991). *Objectivity, Relativism, and Truth.* Cambridge et al.: Cambridge University Press.

Solan, L. (1993). *The Language of Judges.* Chicago: University of Chicago Press.

Sperber, D. (1985). *Anthropology and Psychology: Towards an Epidemiology of Representations.* Man.

Sproull, L. & Kiesler, S. (1992). *Connections.* New York et al.: MIT Press.

Das Internet, ein rechtsfreier Raum?

Dirk Michael Barton

Abstrakt

Die rasante Entwicklung des Internet und seiner Möglichkeiten für eine globale Kommunikation und Informationsverbreitung hat in den letzten Jahren ein umfangreiches Spektrum offener juristischer Fragen aufgeworfen, ausgehend vom wirtschaftsrechtlichen Bereich (insbes. dem Urheber-, Wettbewerbs- und Datenschutzrecht) über die strafrechtliche Verantwortung von Zugangs- bzw. Inhaltsanbietern bzgl. strafbarer Informationen bis hin zum (internationalen) Vertragsrecht mit Themen wie z.B. der Gültigkeit elektronischer Unterschriften.

Zum einen muß geltendes Recht der Dynamik dieses Entwicklungsprozesses angeglichen werden, zum anderen sind aufgrund des globalen Charakters des Internet und der weltweiten Verfügbarkeit dort veröffentlichter Informationen internationale Regelungen zu strafrechtlich relevanten wünschenswert.

Bisher haben Unterschiede in den nationalen Rechtssystemen letzteres deutlich erschwert. So wurde ein deutscher Internet-Provider aufgefordert, nach deutschem Recht verbotene Inhalte zu sperren. Dies wurde durch die weltweite Vernetzung auch in den USA wirksam und dort als Angriff auf die Freiheit der Meinungsäußerung massiv verurteilt.

Auch wenn nationales Recht weiterhin bestrebt sein muß, als schützenswert anerkannte Rechtsgüter sowie individuelle Interessen und Rechte zu bewahren, so muß auch das ökonomische Potential des Internet berücksichtigt werden. Gerade darin aber liegt das Problem:

Während z.B. Urheberrechtsverletzungen wie Softwarepiraterie oder unzulässige Werbung in vielen Rechtsräumen nicht sehr streng geahndet werden, ist deutsches Recht in diesen Bereichen sehr restriktiv. Da das Internet eingestellte Inhalte sofort weltweit verfügbar macht, muß ein global agierendes Unternehmen sein Verhalten dort prinzipiell am strengsten Wettbewerbsrecht orientieren, um sich nirgends strafbar zu machen. Dabei hilft es nicht, wenn der Verstoß z.B. nicht in deutsch oder als „nicht für Deutschland" gekennzeichnet ist, um einer Strafverfolgung zu entgehen.

Ebenso brisant ist die in vielen Staaten unter die Meinungsäußerungsfreiheit fallende Verbreitung extremistischer Propaganda oder leichter oder gar schwerer Pornographie, die über das Internet auch von Kindern abrufbar und somit nach deutschem Recht strafbar ist.

Sowohl die Anbieter dieser Inhalte als auch die Anbieter des Zugangs zu diesen Inhalten können – zumindest auf deutschem Boden – nach deutschem Recht verfolgt werden. Deswegen wird an einigen Stellen in der Literatur die Auffassung vertreten, eine strafbare Handlung nur dann anzunehmen, wenn der Täter zielgerichtet und mit direktem Vorsatz in Deutschland wirksam werden will. Da beides nur häufig schwer zu beweisen ist, dürfte dies zu faktischer Anarchie im Internet führen.

Dienstbetreiber sind nach deutschem Recht in jedem Fall strafrechtlich verantwortlich, wenn sie die strafbaren Inhalte selbst erstellen. Bei Verweisen auf solche Inhalte bestehen Unklarheiten. Wenn sie nur den Zugang anbieten, gibt es noch keine gefestigte Rechtsprechung; es besteht hohe Rechtsunsicherheit. Es ist jedoch davon auszugehen, daß die Provider verpflichtet sind, Kontrollen der Inhalte vorzunehmen, wenn dies technisch möglich und zumutbar ist, zumal dann, wenn allein die Namengebung bei Adressen und Newsgroups im Internet verbotene Inhalte vermuten läßt.

Eine kommerzielle Nutzung des Internet in Deutschland steht somit vor diversen rechtlichen Grauzonen. Es wird die Aufgabe der nächsten Jahre sein, eine gesicherte Rechtsprechung in diesem Bereich zu entwickeln. Dafür ist noch sehr viel Forschungsarbeit zu leisten.

1 Einführende Bemerkungen

Noch vor wenigen Jahren war der Begriff Internet ein nur eingeweihten Kreisen und Insidern bekannter Terminus. Heute ist er ein nicht mehr wegdenkbarer Bestandteil unserer Informationskultur geworden.

Das Internet, ein neues Medium, ein weltumspannendes elektronisches Kommunikationssystem, das es ermöglicht, Daten jedermann global verfügbar zu machen.

Die Väter des Internet waren sich wohl kaum dessen bewußt, daß sie ein elektronisches Netzwerk ins Leben riefen, welches mit die wesentliche Grundlage für eine gleichsam revolutionäre Entwicklung bildete, die unter dem Schlagwort „*Multimedia*" zu einem zentralen medien- wie gesellschaftspolitischen Thema geworden ist. Multimedia und die in diesem Zusammenhang assoziierten Begriffe wie Information-Highway, Datenautobahn, globale Vernetzung, Neue Medien, electronic publishing lassen sich heute kaum noch konfliktfrei in einer eindeutigen Weise definieren.[1]

Sie werden unterschiedlich verwendet, haben jedoch eine Gemeinsamkeit. Sie sind Synonym für das Zusammenwachsen verschiedener, zunehmend global operierender Industrien und Branchen geworden.

---

[1] Salmony: Multimedia-Chancen und Illusionen. In Lehmann, M. (Hrsg.), *Internet- und Multimediarecht (Cyberlaw)*, Schäffer-Poeschel, Stuttgart 1997, S. 2.

In vielen Publikationen und technisch orientierten, medien- und gesellschaftspolitischen, ökonomisch oder juristisch akzentuierten Diskussionen werden die vielfältigen Facetten von Multimedia beleuchtet, häufig jedoch nur singuläre Teilaspekte.
Das gilt auch für die rechtswissenschaftliche Betrachtung.

Auch die folgenden Ausführungen befassen sich nur mit einem Teilaspekt
dieses komplexen Bereichs, und zwar mit den *rechtlichen Fragen*, die bei der Nutzung des Internet entstehen. Dabei wird der Versuch gemacht, einen *Überblick* über
die wichtigsten *Schwerpunkte* zu geben, ein Überblick, der die ansatzweise Vielfalt
der rechtlichen Probleme widerspiegelt, auch wenn keinesfalls alle relevanten
Rechtsfragen abschließend behandelt werden können. Dies würde den Rahmen der
Darstellung sprengen.

Bei Multimedia reicht das Problemspektrum von der *wirtschaftsrechtlichen
Betrachtung* aus dem Blickwinkel des Urheber-, des Wettbewerbs- und des Daten-
schutzrechts über die *strafrechtliche Verantwortung* der Provider – also derjenigen, die
den Zugang zum Internet eröffnen oder eigene Informationen über das Internet zur
Verfügung stellen – bis zum Zustandekommen von Verträgen auf dem elektronischen
Wege und der digitalen Signatur. Nicht zu vergessen ist dabei die Frage, wie Verträge
zwischen Providern untereinander bzw. zwischen Providern und Usern zu gestalten
sind. Dabei ergibt sich aus der Natur der Sache, daß nationales, supranationales wie
internationales Recht in einer engen Verknüpfung zueinander stehen.

Diese *Aufsummierung* macht deutlich, wie unterschiedlich die Herausforde-
rungen sind, mit denen die multimediale Entwicklung unsere Rechtsordnung und die
Praxis konfrontiert. Wer die rasante Entwicklung der neuen Informations- und Kom-
munikationsmöglichkeiten beobachtet, der muß gleichzeitig konstatieren, daß das gel-
tende Recht mit diesem dynamischen Prozeß kaum Schritt zu halten vermag. Auf der
einen Seite kann und darf das Recht diese Entwicklung nicht behindern. Sie bietet
ökonomisch vielfältige Chancen; auf der anderen Seite darf kein gänzlich rechtsfreier
Raum entstehen, der individuelle Rechte und Interessen schutzlos läßt.

Hier einen Ausgleich herbeizuführen ist eine zentrale Aufgabe unseres Rechts-
systems. Erschwert wird die Bewältigung dieser Probleme zusätzlich dadurch, daß diese
neue Form der Kommunikation praktisch keine nationalen Grenzen kennt. Dieser Globalisierung, die es ermöglicht, überall in der Welt Daten und Informationen in das Internet
einzuspeisen und abzurufen, steht nationales Recht häufig relativ hilflos gegenüber.

Auch wenn die globalen Kommunikationsnetze geradezu nach einheitlichen
internationalen Regelungen verlangen – in absehbarer Zeit ist dies nicht zu erwarten.[2]

---

[2] Vahrenwald, A., *Recht in Online und Multimedia*, Luchterhand, Neuwied u.a.1997, Kapitel 12, S. 1.

Zu groß sind die nationalen Unterschiede, die Unterschiede in den Rechtssystemen und das Streben nach nationaler Souveränität. Dies macht allein das *folgende Beispiel* deutlich:

Als die Staatsanwaltschaft in München 1995 ein strafrechtliches Ermittlungsverfahren gegen den Online-Dienst CompuServe GmbH wegen Beihilfe zur Verbreitung kinderpornographischer Darstellungen über das Internet einleitete, und CompuServe daraufhin den Zugang zu diesen Darstellungen weltweit sperrte,[3] wurde dieses Vorgehen – vor allem in den USA – heftig kritisiert. Das Vorgehen der deutschen Staatsanwaltschaft wurde als Zensur und als ein massiver Angriff auf die Meinungsäußerungsfreiheit gegeißelt.

Ungeachtet dieser zutiefst unterschiedlichen rechtlichen Betrachtungsweisen muß unser nationales Recht versuchen, de lege lata oder de lege ferenda Rahmenbedingungen zu schaffen, die den Schutz der als schützenswert anerkannten Rechtsgüter ermöglichen.

Rahmenregelungen dieser Art sind seit dem 1. August 1997 vorhanden; zum einen der *Mediendienste-Staatsvertrag der Länder*[4], der den früheren Bildschirmtextstaatsvertrag (BTX) ablöst; zum anderen das *Bundesgesetz zur Regelung der Rahmenbedingungen für Informations- und Kommunikationsdienste (IuKDG)*[5], eine Sammelbezeichnung für ein Gesetzespaket, in dem eine Reihe von Neuregelungen und Anpassungen vorhandener Gesetze enthalten sind.

Der Mediendienste-Staatsvertrag der Länder[6] erfaßt die sog. *Mediendienste* (Verteil- und Abrufdienste), die nicht dem Rundfunk zuzuordnen sind und mithin nicht dem Ordnungsrahmen des Rundfunkstaatsvertrags (Stichwort: Genehmigungspflicht) unterworfen sind. Er enthält zunächst die für die Medienwirtschaft essentielle Bestimmung über die *Zulassungs- und Anmeldefreiheit* (§ 4), Regelungen zur Verantwortlichkeit von Anbietern (§ 5), Daten- und Jugendschutzbestimmungen (§§ 8, 12 ff.), Regelungen zur Werbung und zum Sponsoring (§ 9) und Gegendarstellungsrechte (§ 10).

Der Bereich der Individualkommunikation und der publizistisch nicht relevanten Datendienste wird dagegen durch das *Teledienstgesetz* – ein Teil des IuKDG – geregelt. Dazu zählen z.B. Telebanking, Verkehrs-, Umwelt-, Wetter- und Börsendaten, Waren- und Dienstleistungsangebote. Neben der Zulassungs- und Anmeldefreiheit sind hier u.a. der Daten- und Jugendschutz und Grundsatzfragen der Verantwortlichkeit von Dienstanbietern reglementiert.

---

[3] FAZ v. 30.12.1995
[4] Landtag Rheinland-Pfalz, Dr 13/1603 v. 13.5.1997
[5] BGBL I, S. 1870 v. 22.7.1997
[6] Kuch, ZUM 1997, 225ff.; Knothe, AfP 1997, 494ff.

2 Das Internet und seine Funktionsweisen

Um eine Antwort auf die Frage, ob das Internet ein rechtsfreier Raum ist, ob und in welchem Umfang entsprechende Regelungen erforderlich und wie sie in der Praxis durchsetzbar sind, zu finden, bedarf es eines Überblicks über dessen Funktionsweisen.

Das Internet wurde ursprünglich als militärisches Kommunikationsinstrument in den USA. entwickelt und hat sich heute zu dem mit Abstand größten weltumspannenden Kommunikationsnetzwerk entwickelt.[7]

Über 40 Millionen Rechner sind über das Netz miteinander verbunden[8], wobei es über die Anzahl der Nutzer des Internet nur Schätzungen gibt. Tagtäglich kommen Tausende neuer Nutzer hinzu; es werden unzählige Seiten neuer Informationen eingespeist und ältere Informationen herausgenommen. Das Internet als Teil der neuen Informations- und Kommunikationstechnologien ermöglicht einen schnellen, weltweiten, bisher nicht gekannten Austausch von Daten aller Art; seien es Nachrichten, Briefe, Bilder, Klänge oder Filme.

Bis Anfang der neunziger Jahre wurde dieses Netz vorwiegend an Universitäten benutzt. Erst danach erkannten sowohl private Nutzer wie auch Firmen, Verbände und andere Organisationen die Vorteile des neuen Mediums. Dem Umstand, daß dieses Kommunikationsinstrument relativ lange nur von einer recht kleinen Gruppe genutzt wurde, verdankt es seine nahezu vollkommen unangetastete Freiheit und Offenheit. Es gab bislang weder eine inhaltliche Zensur noch irgendeine Aufsichtsinstanz, die darüber wacht, daß etwa bestimmte Personen oder Personengruppen keine Informationen in das Netz einspeisen oder herunterladen.

Private Nutzer wie auch der professionelle Anbieter von Informationen gelangen in das Internet mittels eines an den PC angeschlossenen Modems über eine Telefon- oder ISDN-Leitung. Notwendig ist zusätzlich ein Einwahlknotenpunkt, der überwiegend von kommerziellen Unternehmen (sog. Providern) zur Verfügung gestellt wird. Zu ihnen zählen in Deutschland z.B. die CompuServe GmbH, T-Online, AOL-Bertelsmann-Online etc. Sie betreiben das Netzwerk nicht, sondern sie ermöglichen den Zugang. Von diesen sog. *Access-Providern* sind die sog. *Content-Provider* zu unterscheiden, die gleichzeitig Inhalte über das Netz verbreiten.

Die Verbreitungsmöglichkeiten, d.h. der Informations- oder Datenaustausch erfolgt dabei auf verschiedene Weise. Mit Hilfe der Email lassen sich Texte von einem Rechner auf den anderen übertragen. Sog. Newsgroups im Internet stellen ein für jeden zugängliches Forum dar, in dem über wissenschaftliche wie triviale Themen diskutiert wird. Jeder kann sich hier zu Wort melden, Informationen herunterladen oder neue

---

[7] Conradi/Schlömer, NStZ 96, 367
[8] Hoeren, NJW 1995, 3295

Diskussionsthemen plazieren. Das FTP (File Transfer Protocol) dient zur Übertragung von Dateien zwischen zwei Rechnern, wobei diese Daten, Texte, Bilder oder Töne enthalten können. Die eigentliche Internet-Attraktion stellt das World Wide Web (WWW) dar, das die globale Verknüpfung ermöglicht. Mit einem Mausklick kann von einem Rechner auf den anderen gewechselt werden.[9]

Das WWW integriert zahlreiche Internet-Dienste, die über eine einheitliche graphische Benutzeroberfläche aufgerufen werden können. Es koordiniert eine Sammlung von vielen Millionen Einzeldokumenten, die auf weltweit verbreiteten WWW-Servern gespeichert werden. Jedes mit einer eigenen Adresse versehene Einzeldokument kann direkt vom Nutzer aufgerufen werden. Zur Vermeidung großer Datenwege werden Web-Seiten auf regional verstreuten Rechnern (sog. Proxy-Cache-Server) installiert.[10]

Internet-Provider und Online-Dienste vermitteln den Zugang zum Internet oder bieten entsprechende Dienstleistungen an. Öffentliche Einrichtungen und Unternehmen stellen den Zugang zum Internet zur Verfügung und erbringen die administrativen bzw. organisatorischen Leistungen für den Internet-Anschluß.[11]

3 Das Internet und seine Gefahren für Rechtsgüter bzw. rechtlich geschützte Interessen

Wie bereits eingangs bemerkt, sind die Rechtsprobleme im Zusammenhang mit den neuen Kommunikationsformen äußerst vielfältig.

Sie haben jedoch sehr häufig – soweit es nicht um ordnungspolitische Fragen wie z.B. die Zuordnung neuer Dienste in das medienrechtliche System geht – einen gemeinsamen Berührungspunkt. Dies ist vor allem die *strafrechtliche Komponente*, sei es, daß es um *Verstöße* gegen das Urheber- bzw. Marken- und Wettbewerbsrecht oder Datenschutzrecht geht, sei es, daß das Internet zur Verbreitung extremistischer oder pornographischer Darstellungen mißbraucht wird.

Häufig ist zu beobachten, daß von den Verantwortlichen der Dienstanbieter *die strafrechtliche Verantwortlichkeit*, z.B. für eine unerlaubte Verwertung urheberrechtlich geschützter Werke (§ 106-108 UrhG; insbes. § 108 a im Falle einer gewerbsmäßigen Erfüllung dieser Delikte) oder strafrechtlich relevante Verstöße gegen das UWG (§ 4 UWG) nicht immer mit der notwendigen Schärfe gesehen werden.

Hinzu kommt die *Verantwortlichkeit* von Providern für *strafbare Inhalte*, wie z.B. die Volksverhetzung gem. § 130, die in der Form der Tatbegehung durch ein sog.

---

[9] Conradi/Schlömer, a.a.O., S. 367
[10] Sieber, JZ 1996, § 429 (433)
[11] Obermayr, K. u.a., *Das Internet-Handbuch für Windows*, dpunkt, Heidelberg 1995, S. 17ff.

aktives Tun, durch ein Unterlassen oder zumindest in der Form der Beihilfe in Betracht kommt, sofern entsprechende rassistische Veröffentlichungen erfolgen. Auch wenn durch den neuen Mediendienste-Staatsvertrag in § 5 bzw. durch das IuKDG in § 5 gleichlautend grundsätzliche Regelungen zur Verantwortlichkeit getroffen wurden, die ein gewisses Maß an Rechtssicherheit schaffen, so darf dadurch nicht der Eindruck entstehen, daß eine mögliche Strafverfolgung weitgehend ausgeschlossen ist. Auch hier kommt es – wie stets – auf den konkreten Einzelfall an, und es bedarf der sorgfältigen Prüfung, um strafrechtliche Konsequenzen zu vermeiden.

Um diese, für Anbieter von Diensten durchaus riskante, Betätigung im Hinblick auf die vorstehend genannten Rechtsbereiche einmal aufzuhellen und gleichsam Warnlampen zu entzünden, wurde dieser strafrechtliche Ansatz gewählt.

Die Anonymität des Internet, welches es ermöglicht, Informationen einzuspeisen, ohne den Urheber erkennbar werden zu lassen, die Globalisierung der Kommunikationsnetze und die vielfältigen Möglichkeiten, Daten auf die Datenautobahnen zu schicken, haben zu neuen Kriminalitätsformen geführt, deren Bekämpfung nur unter erschwerten Bedingungen, zum Teil – zumindest derzeit – sogar kaum, möglich ist.

Es sind Erscheinungsformen zu beobachten, die unter dem Begriff einer *neuartigen multimedialen Kriminalität*[12] zusammengefaßt wurden.

3.1 Typologien multimedialer Kriminalität im Überblick

Die praktisch grenzenlose Kommunikation hat ungeachtet der unbestreitbaren Chancen ökonomischer wie kommunikativer Art auch eine strafrechtlich relevante Seite. Kriminelle mit unterschiedlichen Zielen haben den Datenhighway für sich entdeckt. Die Arten der Rechtsverstöße sind vielfältiger Natur:

Rechtsradikale Propaganda und Anleitungen zum Bau von Bomben und Sprengsätzen werden in das Internet eingespeist, ebenso pornographische Darstellungen, die auch von Kindern abgerufen werden können. Prostitution von Kindern wird angeboten, Kindesmißbrauch wird vorgeführt.[13]

Diese derzeit zu beobachtende faktische Anarchie bietet zudem allen Anreiz zu verbotenem Tun, da im Internet Anonymität herrscht und die Gefahr derzeit nur relativ gering ist, von Strafverfolgungsbehörden zur Rechenschaft gezogen zu werden.

Das gilt insbesondere dann, wenn die nach deutschem Strafrecht verbotenen Handlungen im Ausland stattfinden, so z.B. wenn aus Holland oder den Vereinigten Staaten über das Internet für jedermann frei zugänglich pornographische Filme angeboten

---

[12] Vassilaki, Multimediale Kriminalität CR 1997, S. 297
[13] Spiegel v. 15.5.1995, S. 204; Focus Nr. 19/1995, S. 224ff.; Usher, *Virtual Pornographics*, Time v. 27.3.1995, S. 68; Horb, *Hast Du Nacktbilder?* Spiegel special Nr. 3/1995, S. 53; Godwin, *Cops on the I-Way*, Time Special Spring 1995, S. 58

werden und in diesen Ländern nicht eingeschritten wird, weil die Meinungsäußerungsfreiheit dort höher eingeschätzt wird als der Schutz vor solchen Machwerken. Hier
endet deutsches Strafrecht und seine Durchsetzbarkeit an den nationalen Grenzen.

Eine andere Variante stellt die sexuelle Belästigung am Arbeitsplatz dar. Die
Täter manipulieren vernetzte Rechner, so daß ihre Opfer zum Betrachten gezwungen
werden oder die Zusendung sexistischer oder pornographischer Materialien an die eigene Mailbox dulden müssen.[14]

Ferner werden die neuen Kommunikationstechnologien auch von extremisti-
schen politischen Gruppen genutzt. Hier dient das Internet dazu, um ihre Botschaf-
ten unzensiert zu verbreiten.

Hinzu tritt ein weiterer Bereich strafrechtlich relevanten Verhaltens, das wirt-
schaftlich Schaden von immenser Größe hervorruft. Im Mittelpunkt der Betrachtung
steht hier die Verletzung urheberrechtlicher Vorschriften.

Während über Jahre hinweg die Verbreitung von Raubkopien mittels Klein-
anzeigen organisiert wurde, erleichtert die Nutzung der Datenhighways die Softwarepiraterie. Interessenten haben dabei zweierlei Möglichkeiten, an rechtswidrig ko-
pierte Programme zu gelangen.[15] Entweder kaufen oder tauschen sie Raubkopien,
die ihnen über das Netz zugespielt und somit kopiert werden oder sie erhalten das
Recht – gegen Entgelt eingeräumt – für einen bestimmten Zeitraum Zugriff auf die
entsprechende Mailbox zu nehmen, die die neue Software enthält. Diese kann dann
heruntergeladen werden.

Aber nicht nur die Beschaffung von Raubkopien wird auf diesem Weg erleichtert und erweist sich als Unterfall multimedialen Strafrechts. Die Verletzung des Urheberrechts mit entsprechenden Strafsanktionen kommt auch auf andere Weise in Betracht, z.B. dadurch, daß urheberrechtlich geschützte Werke in unerlaubter Weise –
d.h. ohne Erlaubnis des Berechtigten – multimedial verwertet werden.

3.2 Die strafrechtliche Verantwortlichkeit der Betreiber von Online-Dien-
sten für Verletzungen des Urheberrechts

Nicht nur das allgemeine Strafrecht und die Beachtung der entsprechenden Vorschriften bei der Zurverfügungstellung von multimedialen Angeboten, sondern insbesondere auch Regelungen des *Nebenstrafrechts* sind von Providern zu beachten. Dies
gilt insbesondere für die Vorschriften des *Urheberrechts*, des Gesetzes gegen den *un-
lauteren Wettbewerb* und des *Markengesetzes*.

---

[14] Möhn, Chip 1/1995, S. 60 ff.
[15] Vassiliki CR 97, S. 299

Neben zivilrechtlichen Ansprüchen auf Unterlassung und Schadensersatz gewährt das Urhebergesetz bei Rechtsverletzungen auch einen *strafrechtlichen Schutz*, der vor allem von Anbietern multimedialer Produkte nicht immer hinreichend beachtet wird.

3.2.1 Überblick über die Straftatbestände

* Strafbar ist gem. § 106 Abs. 1 UrhG die unerlaubte Vervielfältigung, Verbreitung oder öffentliche Wiedergabe eines Werkes.
Die Verwertungshandlung ist untersagt, wenn sie ohne Erlaubnis des Berechtigten in anderen als den gesetzlich zulässigen Fällen erfolgt.
* Strafbar ist ferner nach § 107 Abs. 1 UrhG das *unzulässige Anbringen* der *Urheberbezeichnung*, sofern dadurch der Anschein des Originals erweckt wird.
* Strafbar sind schließlich nach § 108 Abs. 1 UrhG die dort aufgezählten *unzulässigen Eingriffe in dem Urheberrecht verwandte Schutzrechte*.

Handelt der Täter dabei *gewerbsmäßig*, d.h. in einer Gewinnerzielungsabsicht, besteht eine Strafdrohung in einer Freiheitsstrafe bis zu 5 Jahren oder in einer entsprechenden Geldstrafe. Andernfalls kann eine Freiheitsstrafe bis zu 3 Jahren oder Geldstrafe verhängt werden.[16] Dies zeigt, daß dem Grunde nach durchaus hohe Freiheitsstrafen drohen können, zumal die Provider in der Regel gerade in Gewinnerzielungsabsicht tätig werden.

Während im *Printbereich* die urheberrechtlichen Bestimmungen jedem in diesem Bereich beruflich Tätigen in der Regel bekannt sind, herrscht im Bereich der *Online-* wie der Offline Kommunikation angesichts der zum Teil noch nicht hinreichend geklärten Rechtslage ein gewisses Maß an Unsicherheit.

Häufig ist zu beobachten, daß Anbieter relativ unbefangen die Werke Dritter (Texte, Musikstücke oder -sequenzen, Fotografien, Filmteile, etc.) digitalisieren und in ein System integrieren, ohne daß ein Gedanke an die rechtliche Zulässigkeit eines solchen Procederes verschwendet wird. Diese Rechtsblindheit kann sich als höchst gefährlich erweisen. Jedem dieser Hersteller von Inhalten drohen zivilrechtliche Sanktionen in Form von Unterlassungs- und Schadensersatzansprüchen und, wie bereits gesagt, strafrechtliche Konsequenzen, sofern er in seinem Werk auf fremdes Material zurückgreift, das *urheberrechtlich geschützt ist.*[17]

Zunächst einmal gilt es, vor der Herstellung von Inhalten, die urheberrechtliche Konsequenzen zu bedenken.

---

[16] Hubmann H./Rehbinder M., *Urheber- und Verlagsrecht*, Beck, München 1995, S. 322f.
[17] Hoeren: Das Problem des Multimediaentwicklers: der Schutz vorbestehender Werke. In Lehmann, M. (Hrsg.), *Internet- und Multimediarecht (Cyberlaw)*, Schäffer-Poeschel, Stuttgart 1997, S. 79ff.

3.2.2 Das geschützte Werk

Im Blickpunkt steht dabei der Schutzgegenstand des Urheberrechts. Das Urheberrecht schützt *künstlerische* oder *wissenschaftlich-technische Leistungen*, die eine gewisse *Originalität* und *Kreativität* repräsentieren. Nach dem geltenden Urheberrecht *beginnt* der Schutz mit der Schöpfung des Werkes und *endet* 70 Jahre nach dem Tod des Urhebers.

Will man in einem multimedialen System Inhalte verwenden, die ausschließlich oder auch von Dritten stammen, muß man sich vergegenwärtigen, ob sie urheberrechtlichen Schutz genießen. *Welche Werke unterfallen diesem Schutz?*

Das Urhebergesetz schützt zunächst einmal alle *literarischen* Werke (§ 2 Abs. 1 Nr. 1 UrhG). Verwendete *Musik* ist über § 2 Abs. 1 Nr. 2 UrhG geschützt; *Fotografien* über § 2 Abs. 1 Nr. 5 und *Filme* über § 2 Abs. 1 Nr. 6 UrhG. Der Schutz hinsichtlich der Filme steht allerdings nur dem Fotografen oder Regisseur als Urheber zu. Der im Filmwerk agierende Künstler kann nur nach dem KUG (Kunsturhebergesetz) Abwehransprüche geltend machen, sofern er mit der Verwendung nicht einverstanden ist.

Auch Grafiken und Computerprogramme oder Filmsequenzen unterfallen diesem Schutz. Jede Vervielfältigung, Verbreitung oder öffentliche Wiedergabe bedarf selbst dann der Zustimmung des Urhebers, wenn nur *Teile* eingesetzt werden. Ob allerdings *kleinste Teile* von Sprach-, Bild- oder Filmwerken ohne Erlaubnis eingespeist werden können, ist *umstritten*, so z.B., wenn lediglich der Sound kopiert, nicht aber die Melodie übernommen wird.

Weiter ergibt sich eine Differenzierung zwischen literarisch-künstlerischen und wissenschaftlich-technischen Werken.

Bei der ersten Kategorie wird ein relativ niedriger Schutzstandard zugrunde gelegt. Hier reicht schon die sog. *kleine Münze*, d.h. das Vorhandensein von Eigentümlichkeiten, so daß diese geschützt sind.

Bei wissenschaftlich-technischen Verwertungen – mit Ausnahme von Software, die in vollem Umfang urheberrechtlichen Schutz genießt (nach der Europäischen Softwareschutzrichtlinie), – müssen die individuellen Eigenheiten besonders festgestellt werden. So liegt z.B. die bloße Aneinanderreihung und Zusammenfügung von Material außerhalb der Schutzbedürftigkeit, da hier in der Regel keine eigene selbständige intellektuelle Leistung gegeben ist.

Für die Praxis gilt die Warnung, daß vorsorglich stets von der Urheberrechtsfähigkeit ausgegangen werden sollte; denn das *Prognoserisiko* liegt beim Multimediaproduzenten.[18]

---

[18] vgl. Hoeren, a.a.O., S. 83

Schätzt er urheberrechtsfähiges Material falsch ein, muß er damit rechnen, daß ihm per Unterlassungsklage bzw. einstweiliger Verfügung die Verwendung verboten wird – mit den entsprechenden wirtschaftlichen Schäden – oder gar ein Strafverfahren droht.

3.2.3 Die Rechte des Urhebers

In welche Rechte des Urhebers kann man durch die Digitalisierung von Werken und deren Einspeisung in die Netze eingreifen?

Das Urhebergesetz billigt dem Urheber eine Reihe von Verwertungsrechten zu: das Verwertungsrecht (§ 15 Abs. 1 UrhG), welches das Vervielfältigungsrecht (§ 16), das Verbreitungsrecht (§ 17) und das Recht, Bearbeitungen des Werkes zu verwerten (§ 23) umfaßt; ferner das Recht, sein Werk in unkörperlicher Form öffentlich wiederzugeben (§ 15 Abs. 2).

Integriert ein Content-Provider urheberrechtlich geschützte Werke in multimediale Produkte, die er in das Internet oder in anderes Online-System einspeist, so stellt dies eine Vervielfältigung im Sinne des § 16 UrhG dar.[19]

Nach § 23 UrhG darf ein Werk ohne Zustimmung des Urhebers *bearbeitet* oder in sonstiger Form *umgestaltet* werden. Wird diese Modifikation aber veröffentlicht, so ist die Zustimmung des Urhebers erforderlich. Hieraus folgt, daß Texte und Bildmaterial für die Zwecke der optischen Speicherung umgestaltet werden dürfen. Erst die Einspeisung in das Datennetz darf nur mit entsprechender Zustimmung erfolgen.

Fraglich ist auch, wann eine *Veröffentlichung* vorliegt. Nach der in § 15 Abs. 3 enthaltenen Legaldefinition ist grundsätzlich jede Wiedergabe eines Werkes an eine *Mehrzahl* von Personen öffentlich. Dies ist nicht der Fall bei einem kleinen begrenzten Personenkreis, der durch gegenseitige Beziehungen oder durch Beziehung zu dem Vermittler persönlich verbunden ist.

Der kleine literarische oder wissenschaftliche Zirkel, der Texte oder andere dem Urheberrecht unterliegende Werke untereinander online zugänglich macht, nimmt keine Veröffentlichung vor. Anderes gilt, wenn ein Content-Provider die Werke der Allgemeinheit zugänglich macht, wenn er sie also im Internet verbreitet. Allerdings ist dies ein Streitpunkt, da von einer öffentlichen Wiedergabe an sich erst dann gesprochen wird, wenn *gleichzeitig* eine Mehrzahl von Personen erreicht wird.

Bei der Nutzung über das Internet wird jedoch nicht ein Werk gleichzeitig an eine Mehrzahl von Adressaten gesandt. Vielmehr rufen die Nutzer es einzeln nacheinander ab.[20] Würde man jedoch eine öffentliche Wiedergabe hier verneinen, so wür-

---

[19] Goebel/Horckemann/Scheller, GRUR 1986, 355 ff.; Maaßen, ZUM 1992, 338
[20] Hoeren, a.a.O., S. 85

de eine solche Gesetzesauslegung im Ergebnis eine Aushöhlung des Urheberschutzes bedeuten, so daß wohl auch die Wiedergabe im Internet als eine öffentliche Wiedergabe betrachtet werden muß.[21]

Die Frage, ob eine öffentliche Wiedergabe im Sinne des § 15 Abs. 3 UrhG vorliegt oder nicht, stellt sich z.B. bei der Nutzung multimedialer Angebote in Kaufhäusern. Handelt es sich um an die Besucher und Kunden des Kaufhauses gerichtete Präsentationen, ist sicherlich von einer Öffentlichkeit auszugehen. Fraglich wird dies jedoch schon bei *Inhouse-Anwendungen*, so z.B. im Bereich der internen Vertriebsleitung. Dann ist wohl eher die öffentliche Wiedergabe zu verneinen.

Neben den Rechten des Urhebers bestehen noch die sog. *Leistungsschutzrechte* (§ 70-87 UrhG). Leistungen genießen auch dann einen Schutz durch das Urhebergesetz, wenn sie selbst keine persönlich-geistigen Schöpfungen beinhalten. Zu nennen sind insbesondere

– der Schutz des Lichtbildners (§ 72 UrhG),

– der Schutz des ausübenden Künstlers (§ 73 UrhG) und

– der Schutz der Tonträgerherstellers (§ 85 UrhG).

Problematisch ist die Stellung des ausübenden Künstlers, insbesondere dann, wenn es um die Übernahme des *Sounds* eines Studiomusikers geht. Kann er sich ggf. durch einen Antrag auch strafrechtlich zur Wehr setzen, wenn sein Sound multimedial verwendet wird? Weist der Sound überhaupt ein notwendiges Minimum an Eigenart auf? – Einzelne Töne oder Akkorde erfüllen diese Voraussetzungen sicherlich nicht. Anders ist es, wenn das Klangbild so typisch ist, daß es die „Handschrift" des Künstlers und damit den Künstler selbst erkennen läßt.

Was gilt, wenn ein Multimedia-Produzent Melodiezeilen, Sounds bzw. Töne plagiiert? Welche Rechte stehen der Plattenfirma als dem Hersteller des Tonträgers dagegen zu, wenn der Sound – wie schon gesagt – nicht urheberrechtsfähig ist? Dann wird überwiegend die Auffassung vertreten, daß der Tonträgerhersteller nicht schutzwürdig ist.[22] Mit anderen Worten: Wenn schon der Urheber nicht schutzwürdig ist, dann erst recht nicht der Tonträgerhersteller.

§§ 85, 86 UrhG schützen nur die organisatorische, technische und wirtschaftliche Leistung des Tonträgerherstellers. Er soll davor bewahrt werden, daß Dritte unbefugt seinen Tonträger nachpressen oder überspielen.[23] Der urheberrechtliche Schutz richtet sich daher nur gegen Raubkopien von Tonträgern, nicht aber gegen Plagiate von Melodienzeilen, Tonkollagen oder Sounds.

---

[21] Katzenberger, GRUR Int. 1983, 906
[22] OLG Hamburg, ZUM 1991, 545, „Rolling-Stones"
[23] UFITA, 45 (1965), 240, 314

3.3 Unzulässige Werbung im Internet

3.3.1 §§ 1, 3 UWG

Wohl kaum ein deutsches Unternehmen hat nicht schon Bekanntschaft mit dem deutschen Wettbewerbsrecht gemacht. Formen des Wettbewerbs, die in anderen Ländern zulässig sind, wie z.B. die *vergleichende Werbung*, sind in Deutschland häufig verboten. Insoweit gilt deutsches Wettbewerbsrecht im Vergleich zu anderen Rechtsordnungen als das restriktivste. Dessen einschränkende Wirkung wurde größtenteils durch die Rechtsprechung geprägt. Die wesentlichen Rechtsgrundlagen bilden die §§ 1 und 3 UWG. § 1 lautet:

Wer im geschäftlichen Verkehr zu Zwecken des Wettbewerbs Handlungen vornimmt, die gegen die guten Sitten verstoßen, kann auf Unterlassung und Schadenersatz in Anspruch genommen werden.

Neben der Generalklausel des § 1 UWG präzisiert § 3 UWG weitere Wettbewerbsverstöße. Danach kann auf Unterlassung in Anspruch genommen werden, wer

• im geschäftlichen Verkehr,

• zu Zwecken des Wettbewerbs,

• über geschäftliche Verhältnisse

• insbesondere die Beschaffenheit, den Ursprung, die Herstellungsart oder die Preisbemessung einzelner Waren oder gewerblicher Leistungen oder des gesamten Angebots, über Preislisten, über die Art des Bezuges oder die Bezugsquelle von Waren, über den Besitz von Auszeichnungen, über den Anlaß oder den Zweck des Verkaufs oder über die Menge der Vorräte

irreführende Angaben macht.

3.3.2 Wettbewerbsrechtliche Verstöße vorprogrammiert?

Weltweit agierende Unternehmen haben sich auf die unterschiedlichen Rechtsordnungen im Bereich des Wettbewerbsrechts eingestellt und richten ihre Werbestrategien danach aus.

Welche Probleme – das ist die Kernfrage – bereitet nun eine Werbung im Internet für Global-Players? Worin besteht die Gefahr, hier Wettbewerbsverstöße mit strafrechtlichen Folgen zu begehen?

Während die klassischen Werbemedien wie Zeitungen, Rundfunk und Fernsehen die Möglichkeit bieten, die Werbung unter Beachtung des jeweils herrschenden Wettbewerbsrechts *länderspezifisch* zu gestalten, wird das durch die weltweite Verknüpfung der Online-Dienste über das Internet erheblich erschwert, wenn nicht zum Teil unmöglich gemacht. Da eine Werbung – wenn sie in das Internet eingestellt wird – überall auf der Welt abgerufen werden kann, ist die Kollision mit dem jeweiligen Wettbewerbsrecht – insbesondere mit den deutschen Rechtsgrundsätzen – nahezu vorprogrammiert.

Erfolgt z.B. eine nach deutschem Wettbewerbsrecht (§ 1 UWG) unzulässige vergleichende Werbung über das Internet mit dem Ziel, das Produkt in einem Land zu bewerten, in dem diese Werbeaussage rechtlich toleriert wird, so besteht die Gefahr, daß angesichts der Abrufbarkeit in Deutschland wettbewerbsrechtliche Sanktionen nach dem deutschen UWG verhängt werden. Dies gilt selbst dann, wenn für diese Werbung die jeweilige andere Landessprache verwendet wird, da in der Rechtsprechung durchaus anerkannt ist, daß auch fremdsprachige Werbung gegen deutsches Wettbewerbsrecht verstoßen kann.[24] Auch Hinweise wie: „diese Werbung gilt nicht in Deutschland" dürften nicht ausreichen, da sie auch in Deutschland *abrufbar* ist und die Möglichkeit der Irreführung des Nutzers nicht ausgeschlossen werden kann.

Sofern auf dem deutschen Markt die Interessen der beteiligten Unternehmen in wettbewerbsrechtlich relevanter Weise miteinander kollidieren und infolge der Abrufbarkeit der Werbung der Ort der wettbewerbswidrigen Handlung zumindest auch in Deutschland liegt, kommt das UWG zur Anwendung.[25] Daher bleibt dem weltweit operierenden Unternehmen vor dem Hintergrund der Globalität des Internets eigentlich nichts anderes übrig, als seine Werbung an dem *restriktivsten Wettbewerbsrecht* auszurichten.

Wird also ein bestimmtes Produkt weltweit – also auch in Deutschland – angeboten und vertrieben, so müßte sich der Anbieter dieses Produktes aller Werbemaßnahmen und -aussagen enthalten, die nach dem deutschen Wettbewerbsrecht unzulässig sind – selbst dann, wenn der Anteil auf dem deutschen Markt im Verhältnis zum Gesamtumsatz des Unternehmens verschwindend gering ist.

Die Vorteile einer durch das Internet bedingten weltweiten Erhältlichkeit von Informationen verkehrt sich an dieser Stelle für im internationalen Wettbewerb stehende Unternehmen in das Gegenteil. Die weltweite Bewerbung eines Produktes per Internet setzt die mühevolle und zeitraubende Prüfung praktisch aller Wettbewerbsrechte und die Verständigung auf den kleinsten, rechtlich unbedenklichen, gemeinsamen Nenner voraus. Denn das Internet und seine Funktionsweise verführt geradezu zur gezielten Suche nach der jeweiligen Rechtsordnung, die es ermöglicht, Werbeaussagen eines Konkurrenten nach dem deutschen UWG für Deutschland untersagen zu lassen. Das anbietende Unternehmen wäre nach einer entsprechenden gerichtlichen Maßnahme (einstweilige Verfügung, Unterlassungsurteil) gezwungen, eine Homepage, die

---

[24] Waltl: Online-Netzwerke und Multimedia. In Lehmann, M. (Hrsg.), *Internet- und Multimediarecht (Cyberlaw)*, Schäffer-Poeschel, Stuttgart 1997, S. 190; OLG Frankfurt, NJWRR 90, 1067
[25] BGH GRUR 88.453 – „Ein Champagner unter den Minteralwässern"

in der übrigen Welt wettbewerbsrechtlich unbedenklich ist, alleine wegen des Konflikts mit dem deutschen Wettbewerbsrecht abzuändern.

3.3.3 Deutliche Kennzeichnung von Werbung

Gem. § 9 des neuen Mediendienste-Staatsvertrags ist vorgeschrieben, daß Werbung als solche klar erkennbar und vom übrigen Inhalt der Angebote eindeutig getrennt sein muß.

Dieses *Kennzeichnungsgebot* und das *Trennungsprinzip* zwischen Werbung und redaktionellem Teil entspricht einem im Medienbereich anerkannten Grundsatz, der auch in § 7 Abs. 3 Rundfunkstaatsvertrag (RStV) verankert ist. Die Regelung dient dazu, Schleichwerbung und sonstige, nicht an den Grundsätzen der Lauterkeit, Wahrheit und Klarheit der Werbung orientierte, *Mischformen* von Werbung im Inhalt der Angebote eines Mediendienstes zu vermeiden. Wird gegen diesen Grundsatz verstoßen, bestehen wettbewerbsrechliche Unterlassungsansprüche.

3.3.4 Unzulässiges Direct-Mailing

In diesem Zusammenhang sei noch die Problematik der Direktwerbung (Direct-Mailing) angesprochen, für die sich durch die Internet-Kommunikation neue Möglichkeiten ergeben.

Wie beim Direct-Mailing per Post, wo die Werbeträger Zeitung, Zeitschrift, Rundfunk oder Fernsehen übersprungen werden und die Werbung unmittelbar in den Briefkasten des potentiellen Kunden gelangt, besteht über das Internet verstärkt die Möglichkeit, eine nahezu unbegrenzte Zahl von Usern zu erreichen. Diese können Opfer von massenhaft per Email übermittelter Werbung sein.

In der Rechtsprechung ist seit langem anerkannt, daß es im Sinne des § 1 UWG wettbewerbswidrig ist, an einen Gewerbetreibenden oder Privatmann zu Werbezwekken Telefaxschreiben zu richten, wenn die Betroffenen nicht damit einverstanden sind oder ihr Einverständnis nicht vermutet werden kann.[26] Gleiches gilt auch für die Werbung mittels Telex[27] oder Telefonanrufen.[28]

Eine *vergleichbare Situation* besteht auch bei der Direkt-Werbung per Email über das Internet. An das Vorliegen eines vermuteten Einverständnisses des Users stellt die Rechtsprechung *hohe Anforderungen*. So genügt die Angabe der eigenen Telefaxnummer auf einem Briefkopf nicht als Indiz für die Einwilligung, unaufgefordert Werbung per Telefax zu erhalten. Gleiches wird man auch für die Weitergabe der

---

[26] BGH NJW 1996, 660
[27] BGH NJW 1973, 42
[28] BGH NJW 1991, 2087

Mail-Adresse sagen können.[29] Diese allein dürfte keinesfalls ausreichen, um von einem zu vermutenden Einverständnis auszugehen.

3.4 Die strafrechtliche Verantwortlichkeit der Betreiber von Online-Diensten für die Verbreitung pornographischer Darstellungen und Informationen mit extremistischem Gedankengut

3.4.1 Fallbeispiele und deren strafrechtliche Relevanz

Stellvertretend für die vielfältigen Möglichkeiten der in Betracht kommenden Tathandlungen werden nachfolgend einige Fallbeispiele und ihre Strafbarkeit nach deutschem Strafrecht dargestellt:

- Ein Hersteller bietet Pornofilme im Internet an und gibt eine Reihe von Filmsequenzen ein, die von jedermann abgerufen werden können.
  Damit ist der Straftatbestand der sog. „leichten Pornographie" gem. § 184 Abs. 1 Ziff. 1 StGB erfüllt, der dann gegeben ist, wenn man pornographische Schriften einer Person unter 18 Jahren anbietet, überläßt oder zugänglich macht. Den Schriften stehen nunmehr durch eine Änderung des StGB seit dem 1. August 1997 multimedial verwendete Inhalte gleich. Dieser Tatbestand ist gerade im Rahmen der Online-Kommunikation besonders wichtig, da er bereits dann erfüllt sein kann, wenn ein noch nicht 18jähriger davon Kenntnis nehmen kann.[30] Da aber auch Minderjährige jederzeit im Internet surfen und Sequenzen abrufen können, ist im o. g. Fall § 184 Abs. 1 Ziff. 1 StGB in der Regel erfüllt.

- Gleiches gilt, wenn in pornographischen Darstellungen Gewalttätigkeiten bzw. der Mißbrauch von Kindern gezeigt wird. Diese sog. „harte Pornographie" ist stets strafbar gem. § 184 Abs. 3 Ziff. 1,2, und 3 StGB, auch wenn sie nur Erwachsenen zugänglich gemacht wird.

- Neben den o. g. deliktischen Handlungen finden wir im Internet auch Handlungen, die als Straftaten gegen die öffentliche Ordnung zu qualifizieren sind.
  - So z.B., wenn ein dem rechtsextremistischen Spektrum zuzuordnender Radikaler über das Internet dazu aufruft, Asylantenheime niederzubrennen. Dann ist der Straftatbestand der Volksverhetzung gem. § 130 StGB erfüllt, da hier zu Gewalt- und Willkürmaßnahmen gegen Teile der Bevölkerung aufgefordert wird.

---

[29] Waltl, a.a.O., S. 194
[30] Vahrenwald, a.a.O., 12.5.1., S. 2

- Ebenso ist strafbar, wer *Schriften* – hierzu zählen auch Darstellungen im Internet (vgl. die Anpassung des Strafrechts durch Art. 4,5, 6 IuKD) –, die zum Rassenhaß aufstacheln oder die grausame oder sonst unmenschliche Gewalttätigkeit gegen Menschen in einer Art schildern, die eine Verherrlichung oder Verharmlosung ausdrückt, verbreitet oder zugänglich macht (§ 131 Abs. 1 StGB). Genannt sei hier nur rechtsextremistisches Propagandamaterial, das den Holocaust ableugnet.

  Auch fanden sich in jüngerer Zeit Anleitungen im Internet, die den Bau von Sprengsätzen zum Inhalt hatten.

3.4.2 Zur Reichweite des Deutschen Strafrechts

Angesichts des Charakters des Internets als einem globalen Informationssystem stellt sich zunächst einmal die Frage, *wann und in welchem Umfang* deutsches Strafrecht zur Anwendung kommt.

Sofern die vorstehend beschriebenen Tathandlungen, also z.B. die Verbreitung von Pornographie oder rechtsextremistischer Propaganda von einem Deutschen oder auch von einem ausländischen Staatsangehörigen in Deutschland in das Internet eingespeist wird und in Deutschland abgerufen werden kann, ist die Rechtslage eindeutig. Auf ihn findet das deutsche Strafrecht zweifelsfrei Anwendung, da gem. § 3 StGB das deutsche Strafrecht für Taten gilt, die im Inland begangen werden. Man spricht hier auch von dem sog. *Territorialitätsprinzip.*

Wie aber ist die Rechtslage, wenn z.B. ein *Content-Provider* – etwa auf Seiten im WWW die sog. Auschwitz-Lüge (strafbar nach § 130 Abs. 3 StGB) im Ausland in das Internet einspeist und ein in Deutschland ansässiger Access-Provider diese Inhalte seinen Nutzern zugänglich macht? Diese Fallkonstellation läßt sich unter dem Stichwort *„Access-Provider in Deutschland, Netzangebote durch Content-Provider aus dem Ausland. "* zusammenfassen.

Ob die Straftat als im Inland, also in Deutschland, begangen zu qualifizieren ist, ist ausschlaggebend die Bestrafung des Täters.

Nach § 9 StGB ist Tatort jeder Ort, an dem der Täter gehandelt hat oder an dem der strafrechtlich relevante Erfolg eingetreten ist. Sobald die Auschwitz-Lüge – um bei diesem Beispiel zu bleiben – ins Internet eingespeist worden ist, ist ein weltweites, also auch in Deutschland, erfolgendes Zugreifen auf die Seiten möglich. Der Erfolg tritt also auch in Deutschland ein. Tatort ist Deutschland; es gilt deutsches Strafrecht. Der ausländische Anbieter muß also mit einer Strafverfolgung rechnen, allerdings nur, wenn er Deutschland betritt.

Dabei zeigt sich allerdings gleichzeitig, daß das deutsche Strafrecht ein durchaus stumpfes Schwert ist. Amtshilfe von ausländischen Strafverfolgungsbehörden ist kaum zu erwarten, zumal dann nicht, wenn diese Handlungen – wie z.B. in den USA – sogar von der Meinungsäußerungsfreiheit gedeckt sind.

Etwas anderes gilt für den in Deutschland ansässigen Access-Provider. Sieht man in dem Verschaffen der Zugriffsmöglichkeit auf die entsprechenden Netzwerke zumindest eine strafbare Beihilfehandlung, so ist Tatort der Ort des Einwahlknotens, also Deutschland. Auf den Access-Provider ist deutsches Strafrecht somit gem. § 3 iVm. § 9 StGB ebenfalls anwendbar.

Als *Zwischenergebnis* ist festzuhalten, daß jede Straftat im Internet, da sie stets weltweite Wirkung entfaltet, auch nach deutschem Strafrecht grundsätzlich verfolgbar ist, allerdings nur dann, wenn sich der Provider nach Deutschland begibt.

Im Hinblick auf diese Situation gibt es Stimmen im rechtswissenschaftlichen Schrifttum, die eine solche Kriminalisierung ablehnen und das deutsche Tatortprinzip vor dem Hintergrund globaler Kommunikation als nicht mehr zeitgemäß bezeichnen.

Sie befürworten eine Anwendung deutschen Strafrechts *nur* für die Fälle, in denen der Täter *zielgerichtet* und mit *direktem Vorsatz* über das Internet in Deutschland wirken will.[31]

Entscheidend soll also das *finale Interesse* sein. Würde man diesen Überlegungen folgen, würde der Anarchie im Internet Vorschub geleistet. So plazierte die stellvertretende Parteivorsitzende der PDS in ihrer Homepage einen Link zu der Zeitung „radikal". Die Inhalte begründeten den Verdacht strafbaren Werbens für eine terroristische Vereinigung. Nachdem CompuServe den Zugang zu dem entsprechenden Server gesperrt hatte, ließ die Betroffene ihre Homepage durch einen britischen Server in das Internet stellen. Auch wenn in einem Verfahren vor dem zuständigen Gericht in Berlin die Betroffene nicht bestraft wurde, dürfte hier von einer strafrechtlichen Verantwortlichkeit auszugehen sein. Eine abschließende Entscheidung steht noch aus.

3.4.3 Die strafrechtliche Verantwortlichkeit von Online-Dienste-Betreibern

Geht man im Grundsatz von der Anwendbarkeit des Deutschen Strafrechts auf die im Internet bzw. in anderen Online Diensten verbreiteten Inhalte aus, so stellt sich die Frage, wie die strafrechtliche Verantwortlichkeit im Einzelnen ausgestaltet ist. Hier bedarf es zunächst einmal einer *Differenzierung* zwischen den *Anbietern*, d.h. den Providern und den *Nutzern*.

Die Verantwortlichkeit des Content-Providers

Sofern durch die Verbreitung des Inhalts Straftatbestände erfüllt werden, ist der Content-Provider, der selbst die Inhalte zur Verfügung stellt, als Täter strafrechtlich in

---

[31] Collardin CR 1995, S. 618ff.

vollem Umfang verantwortlich. Dabei ist unerheblich, ob Texte, Filme bzw. Filmsequenzen von Dritten übernommen werden oder der Provider selbst journalistisch tätig wird, d.h. die Inhalte selbst erstellt.[32]

Weitgehend ungeklärt ist die Rechtslage noch, sofern der Content-Provider im Einzelfall *Links* – also die Verbindung – zu den Inhaltsseiten anderer Anbieter herstellt.

Die strafrechtliche Verantwortlichkeit des Access-Providers

Die strafrechtliche Verantwortlichkeit kann sich daraus ergeben, daß der Anbieter den Zugang zu Inhalten mit unzulässigen Darstellungen vermittelt. Der Vorwurf, strafbewehrte Inhalte zugänglich zu machen, ließe sich gegenüber Internet-Providern darauf stützen, daß sie

- Netzknotenrechner in Betrieb nehmen und es Anwendern/Nutzern ermöglichen, auf die Angebote Dritter Rückgriff zu nehmen,

- Urhebern von strafbaren Inhalten Speicherkapazitäten zur Verfügung stellen und

- es Anwendern ermöglichen, eine Verbindung zu solchen Servern aufzunehmen, auf denen verbotene Inhalte gespeichert sind.[33]

Die strafrechtliche Haftung des Access-Providers trat erstmals im Fall CompuServe in Deutschland in den Blickpunkt. Die Staatsanwaltschaft München hatte Ende des Jahres 1995 CompuServe Deutschland GmbH mitgeteilt, daß nach ihrer Auffassung etwa 200 Diskussionsgruppen (Newsgroups) im Internet, zu denen CompuServe den Zugang ermöglichte, gegen geltendes deutsches Strafrecht verstießen, weil sie unter anderem Bilder, die Sex mit Kindern zeigten, enthielten. Darüber hinaus fanden sich auch noch andere unzulässige pornographische Darstellungen. Die Staatsanwaltschaft München informierte die CompuServe GmbH darüber, daß nach ihrer Auffassung auch die Ermöglichung des Zugangs zu diesen Newsgroups strafbar sei. CompuServe entschloß sich daraufhin, den Zugang zu allen von der Staatsanwaltschaft genannten Newsgroups zu sperren. Durch die globale Vernetzung hatte dies zur Folge, daß nicht nur den ca. 200.000 Kunden von CompuServe in Deutschland der Zugang zu diesen Newsgroups versagt wurde, sondern auch etwa vier Millionen Kunden in den USA und weiteren 1,8 Millionen Kunden weltweit.

Etwa zeitgleich ermittelte die Staatsanwaltschaft Mannheim gegen T-Online wegen Volksverhetzung, weil der Online-Service der Telekom Zugang zu rechtsradikalen Äußerungen und Programmen des in Kanada lebenden und als Neonazi bekannten Zündel anbot. Die Ermittlungen wurden eingestellt, als T-Online prompt reagierte und den Zugang sperrte.

---

[32] Vahrenwaldt, a.a.O., 12.5 S. 2ff.

[33] Derksen, *Strafrechtliche Verantwortung für in internationalen Computernetzen verbreitete Daten mit strafbarem Inhalt*, NJW 1997, S. 1878 ff.

Das Vorgehen der Münchener und Mannheimer Staatsanwaltschaft erregte weltweit erhebliches Aufsehen. Vor allem in den USA wurde kritisiert, es könne nicht angehen, daß die deutsche Staatsanwaltschaft wegen Verdacht auf Verstoß gegen das nationale Strafrecht weltweit den Internet-Zugang zu bestimmten Bereichen unmöglich macht. Durch dieses Vorgehen werde die Rede- und Meinungsfreiheit im Internet unerträglich beschränkt. Schließlich wurde die Frage gestellt, welche Einschränkungen sich für die Kommunikation im Internet erst ergeben, wenn auch die Staatsanwaltschaften anderer Nationen das Internet auf strafrechtlich relevante Inhalte untersuchen und dabei jeweils ihr nationales Strafrecht als Maßstab zugrunde legen.[34]

Gefestigte Rechtsprechung gibt es zu diesem Fragenkreis noch nicht. Allenthalben herrscht vor allem bei Providern ein hohes Maß an Rechtsunsicherheit. Die Probleme können wie folgt kurz skizziert werden:

Der Access-Provider hat keinerlei Kenntnis davon, daß ein Nutzer den Zugang zum Netz zu strafbaren Handlungen ausnutzt. Mangels Vorsatzes, der die Kenntnis voraussetzt, wird man den Verantwortlichen weder als Täter noch als Gehilfen heranziehen können.

Anders ist es, wenn der Provider die Kenntnis strafbarer Handlungen hat. Dann ist er, z.B. zu § 184 Abs. 3 StGB – dem bereits genannten Pornographietatbestand – zumindest als Gehilfe *durch Unterlassen*, strafbar.

Problematisch ist die Beurteilung der Sachlage, wenn der Provider zwar keine Kenntnis hat, aber auch jegliche Kontrolle des von ihm betriebenen Netzes unterläßt. Das deutsche Strafrecht kennt eine Täterschaft oder Beihilfe nicht nur in der Form der Tatbegehung durch pos. Plan, sondern auch durch ein Unterlassen. Strafbar ist ein Unterlassen, wenn eine Pflicht besteht, tätig zu werden, um den Eintritt einer Rechtsgutverletzung zu verhindern. Im Schrifttum wird die Auffassung vertreten, daß den Provider eine entsprechende Verpflichtung trifft. Danach ist er, wenn er z.B. ein Forum unterhält, das allein schon von der Namengebung her dazu anregt, auch strafbare Inhalte dort zu plazieren, verpflichtet, regelmäßige Kontrollen durchzuführen. Andernfalls kann er sich wegen einer Beihilfe durch ein Unterlassen strafbar machen.

In dem neuen Mediendienste-Staatsvertrag und dem IuKDG ist die Frage der Verantwortlichkeit angesprochen. Das seit dem 1. August 1997in Kraft getretene Informations- und Kommunikationsdienstegesetz, ein Artikelgesetz, das verschiedene Gesetze novelliert, sieht in seinem Teledienstgesetz in § 5 unter der Überschrift *Verantwortlichkeit* vor, daß diejenigen, die

- Dienste anbieten für *eigene Inhalte*, die sie zur Nutzung bereithalten, nach den allgemeinen Gesetzen verantwortlich sind.

---

[34] vgl. Vahrenwaldt, a.a.O., 12.4.3, S. 199

- Dienste anbieten für *fremde Inhalte*, die sie zur Nutzung bereit halten, nur dann verantwortlich sind, wenn sie vom Inhalt Kenntnis haben und es ihnen technisch möglich und zumutbar ist, deren Nutzung zu verhindern.

- Dienste anbieten für *fremde Inhalte*, zu denen sie lediglich den Zugang zu Nutzung vermitteln, nicht verantwortlich sind.

Diese wertgleichen Regelungen finden sich auch für Verteil- und Abruf-Dienste nach dem neuen Mediendienste-Staatsvertrag. Es sind Grundprinzipien, die zumindest dem Grunde nach ein gewisses Maß an Klarheit schaffen und Auslegungskriterien für die Anwendung des allgemeinen Strafrechts bieten.

§ 5 TDG bzw. Mediendienste-Staatsvertrag bildet einen Filter. Zuerst ist danach die Verantwortlichkeit zu prüfen, im Anschluß daran die spezifische strafrechtliche Verantwortlichkeit nach den allgemeinen Grundsätzen der Täterschaft bzw. Beihilfe.

4 Abschließende Bemerkungen

Die vorstehenden Bemerkungen machen deutlich, daß das deutsche Recht in vielen Bereichen durch die Internet-Kommunikation berührt ist. Offene Fragen zeigen sich, zum Teil sind Grauzonen festzustellen. Es wird noch vieler Überlegungen bedürfen, um gesicherte Erkenntnisse zu erlangen. Das Internet hat einen Prozeß in Gang gesetzt, dessen Ende nicht absehbar ist.

Deutscher Universitäts Verlag

GABLER · VIEWEG · WESTDEUTSCHER VERLAG

Aus unserem Programm

Jörg Jasper
Technologische Innovationen in Europa
Ordnungspolitische Implikationen der Forschungs- und Technologiepolitik der EU
1998. XXVII, 419 Seiten, 5 Abb., 11 Tab., Broschur DM 128,-/ ÖS 934,-/ SFr 114,-
GABLER EDITION WISSENSCHAFT
ISBN 3-8244-6739-9
Diese Untersuchung zeigt, daß die Forschungs- und Technologiepolitik der EU in
ihrer derzeitigen Ausgestaltung weder hinreichend theoretisch legitimierbar, noch
ziel- oder systemkonform ist.

Uwe Kotkamp/Werner Krause (Hrsg.)
Intelligente Informationsverarbeitung
1998. IX, 245 Seiten, 61 Abb., 22 Tab., Broschur DM 56,-/ ÖS 409,-/ SFr 51,-
"Studien zur Kognitionswissenschaft", hrsg. von
Christopher Habel und Gert Rickheit
DUV Kognitionswissenschaft
ISBN 3-8244-4322-8
Aus den Bereichen der Kognitionspsychologie, Neurowissenschaft, Informatik,
Linguistik und Philosophie werden Fragen zu Raumkognition, Kommunikation,
Urteilsbildung, Denken, Wissensrepräsentation, Wissenserwerb und Zeitbear-
beitung diskutiert.

Andreas Krahe
**Unterstützung des Prozeßmanagements mit modernen Informationstech-
nologien**
1998. XXI, 290 Seiten, 56 Abb., 15 Tab., Broschur DM 108,-/ ÖS 788,-/ SFr 96,-
GABLER EDITION WISSENSCHAFT
ISBN 3-8244-6786-0
Der Autor untersucht, wie sich aktuelle Management- und Organisationskonzepte,
die unter dem Schlagwort "Prozeßmanagement" diskutiert werden, durch moder-
ne Informationstechnologien unterstützen und umsetzen lassen.

Susanne Leist-Galanos
Informationssysteme und Kommunikationsstandards
Modell zur simultanen Auswahl
1998. XXII, 246 Seiten, 32 Abb., 34 Tab., Broschur DM 98,-/ ÖS 715,-/ SFr 89,-
DUV Wirtschaftsinformatik
ISBN 3-8244-2100-3
Die Autorin entwickelt ein generelles Entscheidungsmodell, mit dem die Einfüh-
rung von Informationsverarbeitungssystemen und von Kommunikationsstandards
simultan bewertet werden kann.

Deutscher UniversitätsVerlag
GABLER·VIEWEG·WESTDEUTSCHER VERLAG

Silvia Mertens
Kompatibilitäts- und Sicherheitsstandards in der Telekommunikation
Wettbewerb versus staatliche Reglementierung
1998. XIX, 223 Seiten, 41 Abb., Broschur DM 89,-/ ÖS 650,-/ SFr 81,-
GABLER EDITION WISSENSCHAFT
ISBN 3-8244-6687-2
Der Telekommunikationssektor ist derzeit durch Liberalisierung, Deregulierung
und Privatisierung gekennzeichnet. Neben den Marktstrukturen werden sich auch
die für die Standardisierung zuständigen Institutionen und Akteure verändern.

Christian Momm
Die Intelligente Unternehmung
Management von Information, Wissen und Werten
1997. XIV, 256 Seiten, 46 Abb., 11 Tab.,
Broschur DM 98,-/ ÖS 715,-/ SFr 89,-
DUV Wirtschaftswissenschaft
ISBN 3-8244-0361-7
Intelligente Unternehmungen sind fähig zur Evolution im Wettbewerb, da sie das
Erfolgreiche stabilisieren und das Erfolglose wandeln. Für die Unternehmungs-
führung stellt sich die Frage, wo und wie sie ansetzen soll, um dies zu erreichen.

Petra Morschheuser
Individualisierte Standardsoftware in der Industrie
Merkmalsbasierte Anforderungsanalyse für die Informationsverarbeitung
1998. XIII, 142 Seiten, 61 Abb., 11 Tab.,
Broschur DM 84,-/ ÖS 613,-/ SFr 76,-
DUV Wirtschaftsinformatik
ISBN 3-8244-2103-8
Die Autorin analysiert, welche Hilfsmittel zur Einführung von Standardsoftware
derzeit verwendet werden. Daraus entwickelt sie einen Ansatz zur Auswahl und
Kombination von Anwendungssoftware-Bausteinen in Unternehmen.

Peter Rohrbach
Interaktives Teleshopping
Elektronisches Einkaufen auf dem Informationhighway
1997. XVI, 245 Seiten, Broschur DM 98,-/ ÖS 715,-/ SFr 89,-
"Markt- und Unternehmensentwicklung", hrsg. von Prof. Dr. Dr. h. c. Arnold Picot,
Prof. Dr. Dr. h. c. Ralf Reichwald, Prof. Dr. Egon Franck
GABLER EDITION WISSENSCHAFT
ISBN 3-8244-6389-X
Der Autor untersucht auf ökonomisch-theoretischer und auf erfahrungsgestützter
Grundlage Potentiale und Hindernisse auf dem Weg zum interaktiven Tele-
shopping. Er zeigt die Probleme auf und erarbeitet Empfehlungen für die prak-
tische Gestaltung dieses neuen Dienstes.

# Deutscher UniversitätsVerlag
GABLER·VIEWEG·WESTDEUTSCHER VERLAG

Martin Schröder
Informationsverarbeitung im Kundendienst
Einsatz- und Gestaltungsmöglichkeiten
1997. XI, 159 Seiten, 6 Abb., Broschur DM 89,-/ ÖS 650,-/ SFr 81,-
DUV Wirtschaftsinformatik
ISBN 3-8244-0331-5
Der Kundendienst wird bisher nur unzureichend von der Informationsverarbeitung
unterstützt. Ausgehend von den einzelnen Phasen des Kundendienstprozesses
zeigt der Autor mit Hilfe von Praxisbeispielen Möglichkeiten dazu auf.

Helgard Struckmeier
Gestaltung von Führungsinformationssystemen
Betriebswirtschaftliche Konzeption und Softwareanforderungen
1997. XIX, 223 Seiten, Broschur DM 89,-/ ÖS 650,-/ SFr 81,-
GABLER EDITION WISSENSCHAFT
ISBN 3-8244-6456-X
Die Autorin untersucht, welche unternehmensinternen und -externen Informatio-
nen in Führungsinformationssystemen zur Verfügung gestellt werden sollten und
wie diese für eine effektive Nutzung aufbereitet werden müssen.

Clifford T. Y. Tjiok
Konstruktion und Rekonstruktion von Informationssystem-Architekturen
Ansätze zur Unterstützung der Unternehmungsstrategie
1996. XVI, 256 Seiten, Broschur DM 98,-/ ÖS 715,-/ SFr 89,-
GABLER EDITION WISSENSCHAFT
ISBN 3-8244-6316-4
Auf der Grundlage der Analyse der Schwachstellen und Verbesserungspotentiale
von Informationssystemen zeigt dieses Buch Lösungsansätze, wie die Umset-
zung der Unternehmungsstrategie erreicht werden kann.

Bernd Trompeter
Telekommunikation und Industriepolitik in Frankreich
1998. XVIII, 288 Seiten, 22 Abb., 24 Tab., Broschur DM 108,-/ ÖS 788,-/ SFr 96,-
DUV Wirtschaftswissenschaft
ISBN 3-8244-0393-5
Die Telekommunikation genießt einen hohen Stellenwert im Rahmen der franzö-
sischen Industriepolitik. Tradierte Konzepte sind jedoch mit dem weltweiten Libe-
ralisierungsprozeß unvereinbar und bedürfen einer Umorientierung.

Die Bücher erhalten Sie in Ihrer Buchhandlung!
Unser Verlagsverzeichnis können Sie anfordern bei:

Deutscher Universitäts-Verlag
Postfach 30 09 44
51338 Leverkusen